Remembering Genocides in Central Africa

Scene of one of the biggest genocides of the last century Rwanda has become a household word, yet bitter disagreements persist as to its causes and consequences. Through a blend of personal memories and historical analysis, and informed by a lifelong experience of research in Central Africa, the author challenges conventional wisdom and suggests a new perspective for making sense of the appalling brutality that has accompanied the region's post-independence trajectories.

All four states adjacent to Rwanda are inhabited by Hutu and Tutsi and thus contained in germ the potential for ethnic conflict, but only in Burundi did this potential reach genocidal proportions when, in 1972, in response to a local insurrection, at least 200,000 Hutu civilians were killed by a predominantly Tutsi army. By widening his analytic lens, the author shows the critical importance of the Burundi bloodshed to an understanding of the roots of the Rwanda genocide, and in later years the significance of the mass murder of Hutu civilians by Kagame's Tutsi army, not just in Rwanda but also in the Congo.

The regional dimension of ethnic conflict, traceable to the Belgian-engineered Hutu revolution in Rwanda in 1959, three years before its independence, is the principal missing piece in the genocidal puzzle of the Great Lakes region of central Africa. But this is by no means the only one. Reassembling the missing pieces within and outside Rwanda is not the least of the merits of this highly readable reassessment of a widely misunderstood human tragedy.

René Lemarchand is Emeritus Professor of Political Science at the University of Florida, USA. He is the author of *The Dynamics of Violence in Central Africa* and *African Kingships in Perspective*.

Mass Violence in Modern History
Edited by Alexander Korb (University of Leicester, United Kingdom) and Uğur Ümit Üngor (Utrecht University, the Netherlands)

Despite the horrors of nineteenth-century conflicts including the US Civil War and the Napoleonic Wars, it was not until the twentieth century that mass killing was conducted on an industrialized scale. While the trenches of Flanders and the atomic bomb were major manifestations of this, mass violence often occurred outside the context of conventional war or away from the traditional battlefield. Research has understandably tended to focus on major events and often within a binary superpower narrative. In fact, instances of mass violence are often hard to pin down as well as being little known, and involving civilians and citizens of a wider range of territories than is publicized. The books in this series shed light on mass violence in the modern era, from Armenia to Rwanda; from Belarus to Bosnia-Herzegovina and many points in between.

1. Knowledge and Acknowledgement in the Politics of Memory of the Armenian Genocide
   Vahagn Avedian

2. Local Dimensions of the Second World War in Southeastern Europe
   Edited by Xavier Bougarel, Hannes Grandits and Marija Vulesica

3. The White Terror: Antisemitic and Political Violence in Hungary, 1919–1921
   Béla Bodó

4. The Holocaust in the Romanian Borderlands: The Arc of Civilian Complicity
   Mihai I. Poliec

5. The Construction of National Socialist Europe During the Second World War
   Raimund Bauer

6. Cultural Violence and the Destruction of Human Communities: New theoretical perspectives
   Edited by Fiona Greenland and Fatma Müge Göçek

7. Remembering Genocides in Central Africa
   René Lemarchand

Remembering Genocides in Central Africa

René Lemarchand

Routledge
Taylor & Francis Group

LONDON AND NEW YORK

First published 2021
by Routledge
2 Park Square, Milton Park, Abingdon, Oxon OX14 4RN

and by Routledge
52 Vanderbilt Avenue, New York, NY 10017

Routledge is an imprint of the Taylor & Francis Group, an Informa business

British Library Cataloguing-in-Publication Data
A catalogue record for this book is available from the British Library

Library of Congress Cataloging-in-Publication Data
A catalog record has been requested for this book

ISBN: 978-0-367-65415-3 (hbk)
ISBN: 978-1-003-12933-2 (ebk)

Typeset in Sabon
by SPi Global, India

For Georgie

Contents

Acknowledgements		viii
List of Abbreviations		x
Glossary		xii
Preface		xiii
Maps		xvii
1	A region awash in violence	1
2	Rwanda 1959–1962: Where it all began	34
3	Burundi 1972: A genocide too far?	51
4	The view from Uganda: Refugee warriors at the gates	79
5	Mass murders in Rwanda: Unhealable wounds	95
6	Concluding thoughts: Lessons learned (and unlearned)	126
	References	142
	Index	145

Acknowledgements

This slim volume owes a big debt to the many friends and colleagues who helped me find my way across the Great Lakes, a safari that began in 1960 and lasted for more years than I can remember. The group of scholars gravitating around the Institute of Development Policy and Management at the University of Antwerp has been particularly helpful and generous. Filip Reyntjens, Stef Vandeginste and Bert Ingelaere were always willing to extend a helping hand; I am particularly grateful to Filip, my long-time friend, ever ready to extend both when I needed them. I've learned more about the complexities of North and South Kivu from Koen Vlassenroot, my colleague at the University of Ghent, than from anyone else; I am equally grateful to Tomas Van Acker, also from Ghent, for improving my grasp of the recent convulsions of Burundi politics. My heartfelt thanks also to Bernard Leloup for providing me (and a few other colleagues) with the logistics indispensable to discover the barren landscape of the high plateau area of South Kivu that is home to the historic Banyamulenge. No one has done more to alert me to the importance of looking at politics from the bottom up than Severine Auteserre, and for this I owe her a huge debt. Marie-Eve Desrosiers took time out of her busy schedule to read and comment on an early draft of the manuscript, for which she deserves my warmest thanks. I owe a similar debt of gratitude to Stephen Weissman for sharing with me his critical comments and suggestions about the role of the CIA in DRC.

André Guichaoua and Roland Tissot are among the few friends I have in France who were especially patient and generous of their time. Anne-Claire Courtois was kind enough to let me have access to her excellent set of papers on contemporary Burundi. Devon Curtis, whose expertise on the history and politics of Burundi is unmatched, has been a major source of inspiration in my academic travails. David and Catherine Newbury have given me countless opportunities to benefit from their first-hand knowledge and fine-grained grasp of the Great Lakes. I also wish to record my thanks to Judi Rever for sharing with me a wealth of important insights into the massive human rights abuses of the Kagame regime, long before making them accessible to a wider public. Ambassador James Yellin was kind enough to share with me his comments and criticisms, not all of which were heeded.

Among my many African friends special thanks are owed to Eugene Nindorera, the leading light for some thirty years of the human rights advocacy organization, IBUKA (dignity) for his help, to Joseph Sebarenzi, who was kind enough to draw my attention to a number of inaccuracies in an earlier version of this text, and also to Pierre Nzokizwanimana, Gervais Rufyikiri and Jean-Marie Ngendahayo, for sharing with me their intimate knowledge of the region; their help proved invaluable.

Two of my colleagues at the University of Florida offered their much-appreciated assistance: Daniel Reboussin, our African librarian, went beyond the call of duty by reading the entire manuscript before anyone else, and making suggestions about publication outlets; I am also grateful to Leo Villalon, formerly Head of the African Studies Center and now of International Studies, for his encouragement, and for harpooning his tech-savvy graduate student assistant, Luke Whittingham, to help reformatting and cleaning up the typescript. Sincere thanks are owed to all three.

Finally, I wish to mention the names of two of my long-time mentors at the University of California at Los Angeles, from whom I learned much of what I know about the continent: James S. Coleman and Leo Kuper. This book is meant as a posthumous homage to their memory.

Permission to quote has been obtained from the following sources:

Rever, Judi. *In Praise of Blood: The Crimes of the Rwandan Patriotic Front*. New York: Random House, 2011, pp. 130, 158, 161, 165.

Lemarchand, René. *The Dynamics of Violence in Central Africa*. Philadelphia: The University of Pennsylvania Press, 2009.

Gleijeses. Piero. *Conflicting Missions: Havana, Washington, and Africa, 1959–1976* Copyright ©2002 by the University of North Carolina Press. Used by permission of the publisher. http://www.uncpress.unc.edu

Abbreviations

AFDL	Alliance pour la libération du Congo-Zaire
ANC	Armée Nationale Congolaise
APL	Armée Populaire de Libération
APRA	Arusha Peace and Reconciliation Agreement
APRODEBA	Association des progressistes et démocrates du Burundi
APROSOMA	Association pour la promotion sociale de la masse (Rwanda)
BBTG	Broadly Based Transitional Government (Rwanda)
CDR	Coalition pour la Défense de la République (Rwanda)
CIA	Central Intelligence Agency
CND	Conseil National de Dévéloppement (Rwanda)
CNDD/FDD	Conseil national pour la défense de la démocratie/Forces pour la défense de la démocratie (Burundi)
CNDP	Congrès national pour la défense du peuple (Congo)
CNL	Congrès National pour la Libération (Burundi)
DAMI	Détachement d'assistance militaire (Rwanda)
DMI	Directorate of Military Intelligence (Rwanda)
FAR	Forces Armées Rwandaises
FARDC	Forces Armées de la République Démocratique du Congo
FDLR	Forces démocratiques pour la libération du Rwanda
FNL	Forces nationales de libération (Burundi)
FRODEBU	Front pour la démocratie au Burundi
FRONASA	Front for National Salvation (Uganda)
ICTR	International Criminal Tribunal for Rwanda
IFO	International Francophone Organization
IMF	International Monetary Fund
IRC	International Rescue Committee
IRSAC	Institut pour la recherche scientifique en Afrique Centrale (Congo)
ISDR	Institut Supérieur de Développement Rural (Congo)
JNR	Jeunesses Nationalistes Rwagasore (Burundi)
JRR	Jeunesses Révolutionnaires rwagasore (Burundi)
MDR	Mouvement démocratique républicain (Rwanda)
MNC	Mouvement National Congolais

MPLA	Popular Movement for the Liberation of Angola
MPR	Mouvement Populaire de la Révolution (Congo)
MRND	Mouvement révolutionnaire national pour le développement (Rwanda)
MSH	Mouvement social Hutu (Rwanda)
NRA	National Resistance Army (Uganda)
NSC	National Security Council (US)
OTP	Office of the Prosecutor (Rwanda)
OVAPAM	Office de Valorisation Agro-Pastoral du Mutara (Rwanda)
PALIPEHUTU	Parti pour la libération du peuple Hutu (Burundi)
PARMEHUTU	Parti du mouvement de l'émancipation Hutu (Rwanda)
PDC	Parti Démocrate Chrétien (Rwanda)
PL	Parti Libéral (Rwanda)
PSD	Parti Social Démocratique (Rwanda)
RADER	Rassemblement démocratique Rwandais
RANU	Rwanda Alliance for National Unity
RCD	Rassemblement congolais pour la démocratie
RNC	Rwanda National Congress
RPA	Rwanda Patriotic Army
RPF	Rwanda Patriotic Front
RRWA	Rwanda Refugee Welfare Association
SNR	Service National de Renseignements (Burundi)
UNAMIR	United Nations Mission in Rwanda
UNAR	Union nationale rwandaise
UNHCR	United Nations High Commission for Refugees
UNITA	Uniao Nacional para a Independencia Total de Angola
UPC	Union des patriotes congolais (Congo)
UPRONA	Union pour le progrès national (Burundi)
USAID	US Agency for International Development

Glossary

Given the close similarity between the languages of Rwanda [Kinyarwanda] and Burundi [Kirundi], the linguistic labels have been omitted.

abacurabwenge	those who forge intelligence
abagumyabanga	those who can keep a secret
abakombozi	liberators
agufuni	a short-handed hoe
akazu	a little hut, metaphor for Habyarimana's presidential entourage
bajeri (sing. *mujeri*)	wild dogs
banyamulenge	the people from Mulenge
bazungu (sing. *muzungu*)	white people
bula matari	crusher of rocks (Lingala)
dawa	medicine or magic (Swahili)
ganwa	princely or noble status group
ibyitso	accomplices or spies
ihandagi	pits (intended for torturing prisoners)
imbonerakure	those who see from afar
impuruza	Watch out!
impuzamugambi	those who share the same goal
interahamwe	those who work together
inyenzi	cockroach
karinga	royal drum
kubohoza	to liberate
kwihutura	identity change from Hutu to Tutsi
mugaragu (pl. *bagaragu*)	client, as in a patron–client relation
ndongozi	guide
nyakuri	true, genuine, authentic
rubiyikuro wihebye	hopeless youth
rugo	hut
shebuja	patron (as in patron–client relations)
simba	lion
uburetwa	corvée labor
ubwenge	intelligence (in the sense of street smart)
umuhamagaro	a God-ordained calling

Preface

I have been teaching, writing and ruminating on issues of ethnic violence in the Great Lakes region of Central Africa for most of my professional life. With what benefits to my students and colleagues is not for me to say. But as I look back to what I have learned in nearly half a century of meanderings across the region it occurs to me that the time has come to share my thoughts with the reader on the complicated sequence of events that has accompanied the blood-stained trajectory of some of the most beautiful, and attaching, countries in the continent. What follows is a somewhat hybrid mix of personal memories and historical slices, stitched together under thematic and chronological vignettes, starting with my first encounter with the three states of ex-Belgian Africa sixty years ago. It is impossible today to recapture the sense of excitement most of us, budding Africanists, felt as we watched the birth of new states, a rare experience in anyone's life. This moment of exhilaration, brief as it was, is one I shall never forget.

If 1960 was a turning point in the march of African states to self-government, for me, a French-born graduate student working on a PhD at UCLA, it turned into a memorable rite of passage. It was in 1960, while enjoying the mixed blessings of a teaching assistantship at Lovanium University in Leopoldville (now Kinshasa) that I had the opportunity to come in contact for the first time with the three states that were still part of Belgian Africa – the Congo, Rwanda and Burundi. The first crossed the threshold of independence on June 30, 1960 only to dissolve into armed mutinies, urban rioting and separatist movements; the other two, former German colonies, by then forming a single entity, the Trusteeship Territory of Ruanda-Urundi, became independent on July 1, 1962, one as an ethnically cleansed Hutu-dominated republic, the other an ethnically mixed constitutional monarchy.

Naively oblivious of the turmoil roiling across much of the Congo I took advantage of the sacrosanct academic summer holiday to travel through the provinces, arriving in Bukavu, capital of the Kivu province, in early September. It was my good fortune to spend a few weeks at the *Institut pour la Recherche Scientifique en Afrique Centrale* (IRSAC), in Lwiro, a magnificently located, efficiently run research center a few miles away from the border with Rwanda. This is where I met a couple of Belgian colleagues who kindly offered to take me along on a three-day visit to Rwanda and Burundi. What none of us had anticipated as we crossed the Ruzizi river into Rwanda is that we would inadvertently run smack into the early phase of what became known as the Hutu revolution. The mayhem was hard to miss: huts set aflame, Tutsi children speared to the ground, scores of Belgian paratroopers trying to contain long lines of Hutu peasants armed with machetes, such was the unsettling tableau unfolding across one of Africa's most beautiful landscapes. Few events have left a deeper imprint on my consciousness than this brutal encounter with the legacy of Belgian colonial rule.

As I try to make sense of the mind-numbing violence that has ravaged the states of former Belgian Africa, a flurry of images crosses my mind. Some are painful reminders of the friends and colleagues I have lost, others bring back to life wonderful moments spent in their company, others still are evocative of the breathtaking landscapes discovered in the course of countless visits to all three countries. Some of these images have turned into an obsession: what are the words to explain to readers unfamiliar with their history how, through unforeseen circumstances, events in one state impact on the other, how violence spills across boundaries, and as it gathers momentum becomes almost unstoppable.

My initial failure to grasp this dimension turned out to be a serious hurdle, confounding my expectations. What I found most striking from my visit was the contrast between the surge of revolutionary mayhem in Rwanda and Burundi's apparent tranquility. It didn't take me long to figure out why. Briefly stated, Burundi, while sharing much the same ethnic map as Rwanda, the same institutions and colonial background, had as its distinctive feature a more complicated social structure, which made it more flexible, more accommodating to the challenge of modernity. Rwanda, by contrast, was the epitome of the politics of inequality, containing in germ as it were the explosion of violence I had witnessed. My reading of this oddly bifurcated path seemed to hold up reasonably well, at least until 1972, when things changed utterly. Long before Rwanda, Burundi is where took place, virtually unnoticed by the outside world, the first genocide in independent Africa. In Rwanda in April 1994 the victims were overwhelmingly Tutsi and the *génocidaires* Hutu; in Burundi, the roles were precisely the reverse. What I had failed to appreciate was the contagiousness of the Rwandan template, or, put differently, Burundi's vulnerability to the ethnic enmities imported from Rwanda.

This effort to revisit familiar grounds is not a replay of what I have tried to explain at greater length elsewhere. Nor is it an attempt to pick up where others left off. My aim, in a nutshell, is to sketch out in broad strokes the tangle of interconnections behind the human dramas that have played out in the Great Lakes, with pride of place to the two states that have attracted much of my attention over the years, Rwanda and Burundi, the legendary "false twins". Readers familiar with the history of the Great Lakes are unlikely to learn much from this discussion; if it has any merit it lies in its comparative bent; only by turning the spotlight on the violent interactions among the crises in each state can one begin to make sense of this tale of woe.

The argument I set forth in this book is straightforward: if we are to grasp the roots of the 1994 genocide of Tutsi in Rwanda we need to take into account the cascading effect of repeated killings on Hutu *outside* Rwanda, most notably in Burundi in 1972 and 1993, often at the hands or with the assistance of Tutsi refugees from Rwanda, most of them pushed out of their homeland by the Belgian-assisted Hutu revolution of 1959–1960. Failure to give appropriate attention to this critical dimension helps explain the limitations of the exclusively Rwanda-focused tunnel vision that has characterized most efforts at making sense of the senselessness of the genocide.

Whether, in trying to shed a glimmer of light on the history of the region, I have been reasonably unprejudiced is for the reader to decide; but I take comfort from the fact that I am equally reviled by the regimes of Paul Kagame in Rwanda, and Pierre Nkurunziza in Burundi, neither known for their neutral stance on ethnic issues.

Despite the outpouring of media attention generated by the Rwanda bloodbath, explanations as to why it happened are remarkably scarce. Even among competent observers of the Rwanda scene the critical significance of regional interactions rarely receives the scrutiny it merits. Nor is the mix of humbug and prejudice surrounding the why and how of the Rwanda tragedy likely to shed light on individual and collective responsibilities. These are among the more challenging paradoxes I try to resolve.

Missing from this discussion are the unseen wounds of war, the unrecorded agonies of millions of innocent victims. Those lucky enough to survive are living testimonies of the sufferings inflicted by such large-scale butchery. But there are many more whose voices will never be heard. To all of them, whose lives were cut short because they were who they were, this essay is dedicated.

The book is constructed around five overlapping themes, each consisting of a mix of historical narratives and personal memories, some trivial, others tragic. The first chapter (A Region Awash in Violence) is an overview of the convulsions experienced by the Congo during the Mobutist era and successor regimes, laying stress on the murderous game-changer introduced by Kagame's entry on the regional stage. The next chapter (Rwanda 1959–1962: Where it All Began) is an effort to underscore the pivotal significance of Hutu revolution (1959–1962), by far the most critical and to this day widely misunderstood event in the background of the Great Lakes upheavals. Chapters 3 (Burundi 1972: A Genocide Too Far?) and 4 (The View from Uganda: The Refugee Warriors at the Gate) deal respectively with the sequence of events leading to the 1972 mass murder of Hutu in Burundi, and the invasion of Rwanda by Tutsi refugees from Uganda, the triggering factor behind the country's long civil war, culminating with the carnage of 1994. Both are among the most searing episodes in the history of the continent: while occurring at different intervals they are linked to each other through the legacy of the 1959 Hutu revolution. The last chapter (Mass Murders in Rwanda: Unhealable Wounds) is a reconsideration of one of the biggest bloodletting of the last century (the title's plural is intentional). We conclude with an effort to pin down the few lessons I have learned while trying to rethink the history of the Great Lakes.

I have, on a few occasions, drawn freely from some of my previous works, but made no attempt to "cut and paste" or to rehash what has already been explored at length by other scholars. Nor do I claim to be exhaustive in my effort to recapitulate some critical episodes; there is no dearth of scholarly works to help connect the missing dots. I have tried to use footnotes sparingly, only where needed to clarify a point or challenge previous interpretations.

A note on terminology. Before it became the Democratic Republic of Congo (DRC) in 1987 the country was officially known as the Republic of the Congo, only to be renamed Zaire in 1965. We have used the Congo or RDC interchangeably throughout the text. I have occasionally used the terms Banyarwanda and Barundi to describe the inhabitants of Rwanda and Burundi, as they are known in their respective countries, rather than Rwandans and Burundians. The term Banyamulenge, meaning "the people of Mulenge," refers to a culturally distinct group of Tutsi who migrated into the Congo from Rwanda in pre-colonial times, and settled in what is now South Kivu. For the sake of clarity it may help to stress at the outset that the term has been used by self-styled "authentic" Congolese to stigmatize as foreigners all Tutsi elements residing in the Congo. Many died because they were not what others thought they were.

Which brings me to one last note of caution: when dealing with the ethnic underpinnings of mass murder it is all too easy to hold one ethnic community or another globally responsible for such atrocities. Ethnic categorization must not be allowed to define interpretation. Even though Tutsi elements in Burundi were indeed responsible for the death of tens of thousands of Hutu in 1972, and Hutu *génocidaires* in Rwanda for the extermination of nearly half a million Tutsi in 1994, in neither case are entire ethnic communities to be held accountable. Indeed, in both countries many were those, Hutu and Tutsi, who took great risks to save the lives of their friends and neighbors, irrespective of their ethnic identities; all too few, they heeded the voice of their common humanity, the voice of Baudelaire's Other, "*mon semblable, mon frère.*"

Maps

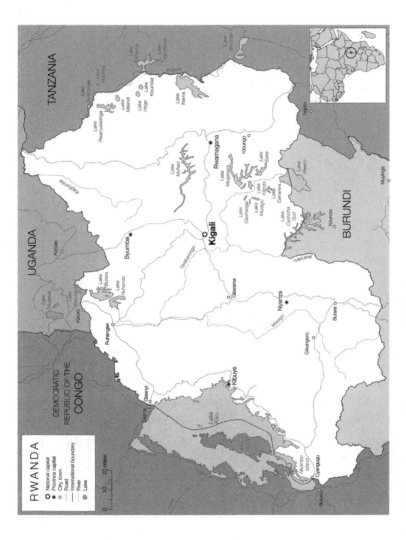

Map 1 Rwanda. (Supplied by Olivier Walther, University of Florida)

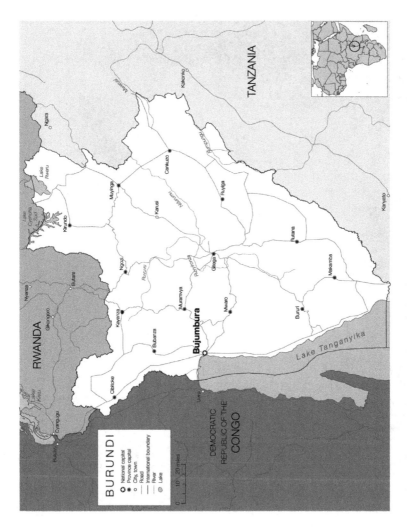

Map 2 Burundi. (Supplied by Olivier Walther, University of Florida)

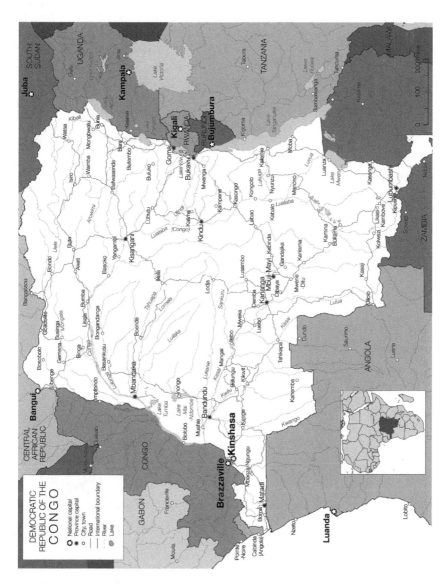

Map 3 Democratic Republic of Congo. (Supplied by Olivier Walther, University of Florida)

1   A region awash in violence

Few other countries have experienced a pre-capitalist exploitation so harsh, predatory, socially disorganizing and unrestrained; a colonial system of bureaucratic authoritarianism so massive, so deeply penetrative, paternalistic, and insulated from external monitoring; a democratic experiment before independence of such fleeting brevity and politicized ethnicity; an indigenous leadership so denied of experience and unprepared for independence; an imperial evacuation so precipitate and ill-planned; an initial post-colonial period of such Hobbesian chaos, secessionism and external manipulation; and the subsequent post-colonial agony of a protracted and seemingly interminable personalistic and patrimonial autocracy by one of Africa's most durable presidential monarchs.

– James Coleman and Ndolamb Ngokwey
on Mobutu's Congo

Mobutu Sese Seko: He was the Guide, the Messiah, the Helmsman, the Leopard, the Sun-President, the Cock who jumps on anything that moves, and – it was Ronald Reagan who said it – A voice of good sense and good will.

– Bill Berkeley, *The Graves Are Not Yet Full*, p. 109

The Congo leapt to independence, on June 30, 1960, ushering a brief moment of hope, soon followed by a nightmarish plunge into the unknown. As one who lived in Kinshasa at the time I am still astonished by the abrupt, dramatic disconnect between the buoyant expectations of the African populace as it stood on the cusp of a long-awaited epiphany and the ensuing sense of shock when the mutiny of the *Force Publique* (the Belgian-led Congolese army) suddenly erupted. Soon after the joyful atmosphere of the early days – nicely captured in the syncopations of the Afro-Cuban rhythms resonating through Kinshasa, most memorably in Joseph Kabasele's runaway hit "Independence Cha-Cha" – came a far more somber sequence of events. It comes through with singularly evocative force in the urban paintings assembled by Bogumil Jewsiewicki in his lavishly illustrated *Mami-Wata: La Peinture Urbaine au Congo*.[1] Better than any other source, the book

---

[1] Bogumil Jewsiewicki, *Mami Wata: La Peinture Urbaine au Congo* (Paris, 2003).

brings into focus the popular representations of the more tragic episodes of the Congo's colonial history. Unsurprisingly, Lumumba's assassination in January 1961 stands out as a central leitmotiv. Resurrected through multiple reincarnations – from a Christ-like figure (*Lumumba christique*) to an ethnic (Tetela), regional (Kasaian) and national hero – he is remembered as the symbol of hopes thwarted, promises betrayed, rebirth aborted.

The element of continuity between the grisly images of *la colonie belge* and the avatars that followed independence is unmistakable. Large-scale violence as a phenomenon inseparable from the Congo's colonial experience is a theme that has received considerable attention from journalists, historians and anthropologists, but nowhere has it been more brilliantly explored than by Adam Hochschild in his widely acclaimed *King Leopold's Ghosts*.[2] In it the author lays bare the hidden threads leading to the appropriation of the biggest and richest piece of real estate in the continent by one of Europe' most villainous monarchs. Only in Belgium did the book receive mixed reviews, prompted by the suggestion that the human losses caused by the ravages of the Leopoldian Free State – aptly described in Conrad's memorable phrase, as "the vilest scramble for loot that ever disfigured the history of human conscience" – could have reached as many as ten million. Despite corroborating evidence from noted historians many in Belgium reacted with skepticism if not outrage to such an earth-shaking conclusion. Its accusatory sub-text did not go unnoticed. Hochschild's bombshell sent ripple effects far and wide. Efforts to refute the scale of his assessment did not prevent the Congolese historian Ndaywel e Nziem to up the ante to 13 million.

Today, in the wake of George Floyd's murder at the hand of a white policeman (appropriately named Chauvin), the mood in Belgium is shifting dramatically. At no other time in the country's history has the Leopoldian myth been so reviled. No longer is the architect of the Congo Free State whitewashed for what he really was, a self-seeking despot responsible for the death of millions. The smearing of his graffiti-tagged equestrian statue in Brussels on June 10, 2020, bears testimony to the global impact of the Black Lives Matter movement. Of course, the Congolese did not wait 60 years to confront their colonial past; as a long-awaited symbolic gesture, Leopold's statue in Kinshasa was finally brought down in 1966, six years after independence. And yet, unanimity on that score is still a long shot. There is indeed a strange paradox in the suggestion recently made by Princess Esmeralda, Leopold's great granddaughter, that the sixtieth anniversary of the Congo's independence be the occasion to present official excuses for the atrocities committed by her ancestor, and the message played out in Lumbubashi, capital of the rich Katanga province, where stands the statue erected to Leopold's memory in 2018, one of several resurrected

---

[2] Adam Hochschild, *King Leopold's Ghosts* (New York, 1998).

historic figures, along with Lumumba, standing side by side with his nemesis, Mobutu Sese Seko.[3] The somber prankishness of historical memories is hard to miss.

Nor is there much of a consensus about the number of deaths traceable to the Leopoldian scramble for loot. As is the case for most of the estimates of human losses in the region precise figures are nowhere to be found. Even when dealing with orders of magnitude extreme caution is in order. Rather than engage in what Jan Vansina called the "numbers game" about the appalling atrocities exacted by the Leopoldian state, the more important point is to underscore the enduring, long-term effects of the devastating social dislocations forced upon the Congolese people in the name of the Leopoldian "civilizing mission." In response to the consensus of opinion by Belgian historians that there is no discernible trace of recollection of the Free State abominations among Congolese – and hence no adverse legacy – Michela Wrong reminds us that "it is possible to be traumatized without knowing why; that indeed, amnesia – whether individual or collective – could sometimes be the only way of dealing with horror, that human behavior could be altered forever without the cause being openly acknowledged."[4]

Despite occasional spurts of stability, the Mobutist interlude (1965–1997) opened a Pandora's box of violent confrontations – armed mutinies, provincial secessions, large-scale rural rebellions, ethnic uprisings, political assassinations and arbitrary repressions. Much of this now sounds like ancient history, or as mere preliminaries before the immensely more costly civil wars touched off by the Rwandan intervention in 1996.

By then Mobutu had ceased to be Uncle Sam's closest ally against the clear and present danger of communist expansion. The contrast is illustrative of the drastic refashioning of the geopolitical map following the end of the Cold War.

In the next few pages we try to sketch out the main features of the Mobutist state, and show how the clientelistic strategies that helped consolidate the dictator's grip on society also led to his demise once the imperatives of the Cold War had evaporated, opening new opportunities for a major reshuffling of regional alliances. The appalling bloodshed that has accompanied the replacement of one dictatorship by another is impossible to ignore.

---

[3] See Pierre Englebert and Lisa Jené, "Aujourd'hui comme sous Léopold II, le Congo reste la façade institutionnelle d'un voleur érigé en Etat," *Le Monde*, June 24, 2020. Note the authors' comment:

> Presenting excuses is undoubtedly well-intentioned, but it ignores the heart of the problem which is the continuous reproduction of the Leopoldian project through the colonial and postcolonial periods. If the Belgians were seriously concerned about the fate of the Congolese they would rather stop facilitating this reproduction by their assistance to the Congolese state, their episodic military interventions, their diplomacy, and even their recognition.

[4] Michela Wrong, *In the Footsteps of Mr. Kurtz* (New York, 2000), p. 58.

The Mobutist state: Bula Matari ascendant

The "crusher of rocks" (Bula Matari in Lingala) – a metaphor inherited from the Free State to designate the crushing impact of the colonial juggernaut – serves as a convenient label to sum up the oppressiveness of the Mobutu dictatorship. No one has used it more effectively than Crawford Young, a leading authority on Congo politics, in his compelling anatomy of *The African Colonial State*.[5]

The reconstruction of something resembling a state did not happen overnight, nor without considerable bloodshed. What I witnessed in the months that followed the independence festivities was the collapse of the post-colonial architecture, symbolized by the now risible motto *Congo uni, Congo fort!* The intrusion of a US covert influence, on a scale few had anticipated, did little to stem the rise ethnic conflicts so intense and widespread as to threaten to undo what little had been accomplished to lay the foundation of a stable polity.

In the days that followed Lumumba's overthrow the country was effectively divided into three rival regimes. In Leopoldville (now Kinshasa), Mobutu's army stood watch over the "legitimate" government as the day-to-day tasks of administration were entrusted to a College of Commissioners; in the Katanga the break-away government of Moise Tshombe, backed financially by Belgian interests and militarily by French and Belgian mercenaries, held its ground against the twin menace of Lumumbist sympathizers and UN forces. In Stanleyville (now Kisangani) pro-Lumumba supporters tried in vain to consolidate their hold over the city while awaiting the return of their nationalist hero. His tragic fate at the hands of his captors, acting with the blessings of US and Belgian advisors, would soon turn him into a near-Messiah.

Once lambasted on the floor of the US Senate as "a cheap embezzler, a schizoid agitator, half witch-doctor, half Marxist, an opportunist ready to sell out to the highest bidder,"[6] his death opened the way for a far more consequential "sell out" of the Congo resources to Western bidders

Despite claims by some analysts that the Cold War created the context for a stability of sorts, its disastrous consequences cannot be overemphasized. Besides driving a deep wedge between rival factions backed by warring ideological patrons, it ensured that the support gained by aspiring politicians would hinge on their degree of sympathy for the West (or antipathy for the East), never mind their ability to promote economic development or democracy. Seen through such binary lens one can better understand some Cold War paradoxes: why, for example, as will be explained in another chapter, the Belgian government's bête noire, the Tutsi-led *Union Nationale Rwandaise* (Unar), representing the interests of a defeated Rwandan monarchy,

---

[5] Crawford Young, *The African Colonial State in Comparative Perspective* (New Haven and London, 1994).

[6] Senator Olin Johnston, quoted in Kevin Dunn, *Imagining the Congo* (London, 2003), p. 93.

was consistently viewed in the West as a vehicle of Marxist venom, working in cahoots with Lumumba (only to morph years later as the closest friend of Washington and London in its post-Cold War Rwanda Patriotic Front [RPF] incarnation); or why the Burundi monarchy, drawing its left-leaning inspiration from radical Tutsi courtiers, was seen in much the same way, a dangerous funnel of communist infiltration, in thrall to Communist China and North Korea.

Again, consider the now-familiar story of how as Washington's closest ally in Africa Mobutu rose to power, and held a tight grip over his people for some 30 years as one of the most corrupt pro-Western dictators in the continent. The unrelenting economic, financial, military and diplomatic support enjoyed by "our man" in Leopoldville is, of course, inextricably tied up with the involvement of the CIA. In his 2007 memoir Larry Devlin, the CIA chief of station in Kinshasa, sums up the "many unfortunate things" facing Lumumba as he tried to assert his authority: "Patrice Lumumba, who as the head of the government was the central political figure of the moment, found himself having to deal with many unfortunate things: an army mutiny for which he was partly responsible; the secession of the country's wealthiest province; a government paralyzed by personal and tribal rivalries, including his own with President Kasavubu."[7] Missing from this list, however, is the most serious of all the unfortunate things faced by Lumumba: the sustained efforts of the CIA to bring down his government and ultimately to send him to his grave.

Even today, with the benefit of hindsight, I find it hard to imagine the extent to which Cold War issues shaped US perceptions of Lumumba as the thin edge of the wedge that would enable Moscow not only to gain control over the Congo but ultimately to extend its tentacles over a huge chunk of East and Central Africa.

This is how Devlin impressed his views on the CIA top boss at the time, Allen Dulles: "I outlined to the director my belief that if the Soviets achieved their objective of influencing and eventually controlling Lumumba, they would use the Congo as a base to infiltrate and extend their influence over the nine countries or colonies surrounding the Congo – Congo-Brazzaville, the Central African Republic, Sudan, Uganda, Rwanda, Burundi, Tanganyika, Rhodesia and Angola. Had the Soviets gained a position of control or influence in the nine countries or colonies that would have an extraordinary power base in Africa. In addition to gaining control or influence over the minerals, raw materials and oil produced in Africa, it would also have greatly increased their influence in the Third World, as well as extending their influence in the UN." Persuading his boss of the dangers posed by this Manichean scenario required little effort. "I suspect," he added, "that I was preaching to the choir because he had probably already reached the same

---

[7] Larry Devlin, *Chief of Station, Congo: A Memoir of 1960–67* (New York, 2007), pp. 24–25.

conclusion."[8] That the dynamics of what came to be known as "the Congo disaster" stemmed from factors unrelated to East–West rivalries and more directly connected to ethno-regional issues apparently never entered the mind of the real movers and shakers of US policies. However remote from reality, the CIA fantasies became something of a self-fulfilling prophecy.

A careful inquest by Stephen Weissman, who worked as staff director of the US House of Representatives Subcommittee on Africa from 1986 to 1991, lays bare what some already suspected: "US government documents including a chronology of covert actions approved by the National Security Council (NSC) subgroup reveal US involvement in, and significant responsibility for, the death of Lumumba, who was mistakenly seen by the Eisenhower administration as an African Fidel Castro. The documents show that the key Congolese leaders who brought about Lumumba's downfall were players in Project Wizard, a CIA covert action program responsible for channeling hundreds of thousands of dollars and military equipment to these officials who informed their CIA paymasters three days in advance of their plan to send Lumumba into the clutches of his worst enemies... The US authorized payments to the then-President Joseph Kasavubu four days before he ousted Lumumba, furnished Army strongman Mobutu with money and arms to fight pro-Lumumba forces, helped select and finance anti-Lumumba government, and barely three weeks after his death authorized new funds for the people who arranged Lumumba's murder."[9]

Only now, thanks to Weissman's exemplary scrutiny of newly available materials, do we have the full picture of just how extensive the role of the CIA has been in shaping the Congo's destiny: "The CIA engaged in pervasive political meddling and military action between 1960 and 1968 to ensure that the country retained a pro-Western government and to help its pathetic military on the battlefield." The price tag was in proportion to the magnitude of the enterprise, "ranked as the largest covert operation in the agency's history, costing an estimated \$90–\$150,000 in current dollars, not counting the aircraft, weapons, and transportation and maintenance provided by the Defense Department."[10]

Covert US support did wonders. A reasonably coherent state system came into existence, albeit a starkly authoritarian one, bolstered by large infusions of economic aid, and military assistance whenever threatened from within or without.

Only years later did the sordid truth emerge from the files of the CIA. What came out of my own files – which I was able to consult in 1975 under the Freedom of Information Act – was neither true nor sordid but more

[8] Devlin, *Chief of Station, Congo*, p. 48.
[9] Stephen R. Weissman, "Opening Secret Files on Lumumba's Murder," *The Washington Post*, July 21, 2002.
[10] Stephen R. Weissman, "What Really Happened in the Congo," *Foreign Affairs*, vol. 93, no. 4 (July–August 2014), p. 15.

like a comedy of errors worthy of *Black Mischief*, Evelyn Waugh's comical masterpiece.

Sidebar – a draft dodger up against the CIA and Catholic clerics

The incident that triggered a steady flow of back-and-forth communications between the CIA and the FBI over my role in the Congo occurred in early 1961, when the Most Reverend Bishop Fulton Sheen of New York denounced the presence of "two young men at Lovanium University where they have been removed because of their pro-communist and revolutionary activity." The alarming revelation appeared in *The Tablet*, a well-known Catholic weekly newspaper. The information was immediately picked up by Senator Frank J. Lausche, an Ohio Democrat, and communicated to the FBI, and then to the CIA. As I ploughed my way through reams of redacted documents, I eventually noticed a reference to Bishop Sheen's contact, a Lovanium-based African cleric named Barnabas Leyka, and then proceeded to read what was described by the FBI as "the portion of the letter that would appear to be of most interest to the Bureau": "It is perhaps useful to communicate to you what I learned from a colleague, a professor at Lovanium University: the advisers on Congo at the department of African Affairs in Washington are two young men who were last year at Lovanium where they have been removed because of their pro-communist and revolutionary activity. This is a very serious affair; I think it will be useful that the authority examines this question, because of the bad reputation the US and especially the Kennedy administration are acquiring unwillingly by the mistakes that will inevitably follow from such defective officers."[11]

Fifteen years went by before I read these lines; and then something clicked in my mind. Returning from my tour of the Congo provinces in October 1960 I was summoned by the formidable Monseigneur Gillon, the rector of Lovanium, and was told in no uncertain terms that the time had come for me to pack my bags and go home.

Going home, for me, was not as simple as it sounds. Returning to France was out of the question, going to the US was not immediately feasible. Vehemently opposed to France's neocolonial war in Algeria, I was able to evade conscription into the French army through a student deferment. The image of myself as a *tiermondiste engagé* was impossible to reconcile with that of a colonial army recruit fighting off Algerian rebels in defense of *Algérie française*.[12] By 1960, however, my deferment had run out. A six-month prison sentence had been issued by a Paris-based military tribunal for

---

[11] "Unknown Subjects: Two Former Students of Lovanium University," *The Congo*, May 29, 1961 (Author's files). I would assume that the other suspect, whose name was redacted, was Herbert Weiss, an American graduate student who also worked in the Congo in 1960.

[12] Although I was not among the signatories I could not but endorse wholeheartedly the content of the so-called Manifesto of the 121, a petition of leading French intellectuals calling for military disobedience, including draft dodging, by Algerian war draftees.

failing to show up. Though unwilling to end up in a French jail, I was just as reluctant to enter the US without a visa. With an expired student visa and a prison sentence over my head, the prelate's pronouncement left me wondering what to do next, other than get on the first flight to Brussels.

He declined to tell me the reason for his decision, but the news was not entirely surprising. In the palpably clannish, gossipy, often stifling academic milieu of the Kimuenza campus, aka the *colline inspirée*, my Danish wife and I simply didn't fit. We never attended mass, a fact that didn't go unnoticed. My overt sympathy for Lumumba ruffled not a few feathers. As I was asked during my travels about the prevailing mood at Lovanium I made no effort to conceal the fact that my closest colleague at Lovanium, Professor Jean Buchman, told me before boarding his plane for Brussels that he had no intention to come back, a statement later held against me as *inadmissible*. How could I possibly misrepresent the sacrosanct *vacances académiques*? Only later did I become aware of the more serious concern behind the rector's attitude.

I am still at a loss to figure out how a totally off-the wall accusation of Communist sympathies by an unknown African cleric could have found its way into Bishop Sheen's "God Love You" column *in The Tablet*, and, via a senator's letter, end up in the bowels of security agencies. For all my disappointment to have to leave the Congo at such a critical time, a more promising turn of events was about to materialize, for which I owe the monseigneur a heavy debt of gratitude.

My stroke of luck can only be appreciated if one recalls the arm's-length relation between right and left in the Belgian metropolitan context. No sooner was I back in Brussels than I set out to reach out to the *Institut de Sociologie Solvay*, located in the lovely Leopold Park, which at the time was home to a number of distinguished left-leaning Africanists. Invited to meet with the head of the Institute, Professor Arthur Doucy, I briefly explained the unfortunate circumstances that led me to leave the Congo a few months before the end of my assignment. Much to my surprise his reaction was one of immediate sympathy. Arrangements were promptly made to bring me on board. In addition to being offered a much-needed research assistantship at Solvay, I was able to link up with a very friendly and well-informed group of scholars. The extremely pleasant and productive year and a half spent at the Solvay Institute would never have happened without the less-than-cordial farewell from the Catholic prelate.

It was during my stay at the Institute that I came to realize the depth of the disagreements that drew the Belgian-based Africanist community into separate camps. To the persistent allegations of CIA involvement voiced by a number of well-informed Belgian observers, most US-connected academics (myself included) responded with mockery-tinged skepticism. The ripple effects of the polemics over the role of the CIA were felt also in the US. The issue took center stage in the debate on US campuses about the sources of funding of academic research in Africa. All this would only be of anecdotic interest were it not for the fact that it focused public attention on a critical dimension of US policies in the Congo: the reliance of a fair amount of academic research on CIA-sponsored military and financial assistance to the Mobutist regime – one "pattern variable," to use the social science jargon in fashion at the time, that was unlikely to figure in some of the more improbable schemes of structural-functional analysis applied to the Congo.

A few years later in an effort to take a critical look at the shenanigans of the agency I dipped my pen in vinegar and wrote a hard-hitting piece under the subversive title of "The CIA in Africa: How Central, How Intelligent?" which appeared in *The Journal of Modern African Studies*, in 1975. The piece – marred by what some readers told me were several inaccuracies – caused a bit of a stir among the Africanist community, particularly in France, where some of my *chers collègues* gleefully dropped heavy hints that I was an academic mole authoring a deliberately critical article to allay suspicions.

As events in eastern Congo made dramatically clear, the CIA remained deeply involved in the violent restoration of "peace and stability."

Simbas, Mercs and the CIA

The biggest threat to US interests came in 1964–1965 with the so-called Simba ("lion" in Swahili) rebellion, when in, the wake of a violent rural insurgency, half the country came under the sway of so-called Mulelistes (after the rebel leader Pierre Mulele, who instigated a Maoist-type rebellion in the Kwilu region in 1965), causing untold casualties.[13] Rooted in part in the sense of social deprivation experienced by a large segment of the rural population, in part in the illusory promise of a quick victory, nurtured by the insurgent's use of magic (*dawa*), believed to turn bullets into water, administered by sorcerers and witch doctors, the rebellion broke out along the Congo's eastern border like a bolt out of the blue. Paul Masson, a Belgian journalist with years of experience in the Kivu region, described the velocity of the phenomenon: "Like a brush fire in the dry season, the rebellion spread along the route followed by the Arabs, Kabambare fell on July 1st, Kabalo the 10th, Kongolo the 13th, Kasongo the 15th, Kindu 24th, and Stanleyville (now Kisangani) August 5th." The "psychotic fear of the Simbas," he added, along with the incompetence of the commanding officers, helps explain the routing of the of the *Armée Nationale Congolaise* (ANC) units. Few had anticipated such rapid collapse. Precisely when the army showed unmistakable signs of imminent disintegration, Crawford

[13] For an outstanding effort to revisit the role of the CIA in recruiting proxy forces to quell the rebellion, see Jeffrey Michaels, "Breaking the Rules: The CIA and Counterinsurgency in the Congo, 1964–1965," *International Journal of Intelligence and Counterintelligence*, vol. 25, no. 1 (2012), pp. 130–159. Contrary to the previous CIA modus operandi, where the aim was to support US military involvement, in the Simba rebellion the main objective was to make sure the US military would not get involved, thus "breaking the rules." I am grateful to Stephen Weissman for drawing my attention to this important contribution.

Young, in a surprisingly upbeat assessment, paid tribute the "undisputable headway made by the ANC since the dark days of 1960."[14]

The Simba's revolt is associated in my memory with the horrific *sauve-qui-peut* stories told by survivors and the brutal cleansing operations conducted by CIA-funded mercenaries (mercs). Traveling through Bukavu and Goma in the summer of 1965 I remember meeting European and Congolese nuns and priests still under the shock of what they saw and endured at the hands of their tormenters. Only years later did I come across eyewitness testimonies of how the Mike Hoares and Bob Denards, two of the best-known and more flamboyant mercenaries, were able to quell the revolt, and how, ultimately, trying to make political capital out the insurgency, Che Guevara and his Cuban *compañeros* vainly attempted to create an insurrectionary *foco* in eastern Congo.

Although there are excellent scholarly accounts of the roots of the revolt,[15] there has been a tendency to overstress the internal fissures of the movement at the expense of the external blows delivered through mercenaries and anti-Castro Cuban pilots flying bombing missions against rebel positions. Again, little is said of Che Guevara's astonishing misadventure into the wilds of eastern Congo as he tried to re-enact the Sierra Maestra scenario. What follows is an effort to add a few footnotes to the story.

The Simba's atrocities and the Mercs' often-indiscriminate repression intersect in disturbing ways. In the estimation of knowledgeable observers, the total number of victims killed by both sides could have reached as many as 100,000. Much has been made in the Western media of the serious menace posed to US and Belgian interests by the sudden eruption of a rebellion that swept across a huge swath of territory, with only minimal attention to the brutality of the methods used by some 500 mercenaries drawn primarily from South African and Rhodesian soldiers of fortune.

Under the command of the legendary Mike Hoare (aka "Mad Mike") they met the challenge of the Simbas with ruthless efficiency, scoring one victory after another in each of the town under rebel control.[16] From Albertville in southeastern Katanga and heading north towards Stanleyville (now

---

[14] Crawford Young, "Hopeful Interlude," *Africa Report*, October 1963, reproduced in Helen Kitchen ed., *Footnotes to the Congo Story* (New York, 1964), p. 55. The quote from Paul Masson is from his *Dix Ans de Malheur (Kivu 1957–1967)* (Bruxelles, 1968), p. 129.

[15] Notably Crawford Young, "Rebellion in the Congo," in Robert Rotberg and Ali Mazrui eds., *Protest and Power in Black Africa* (New York, 1970), pp. 969–1011, and Jeffrey Michaels, "Breaking the Rules."

[16] For a gripping *"je ne regrette rien"* sort of account of the mercs's saga in eastern Congo, see the candid, day to day, chronicle of their bloody encounters with the Simbas by the central actor, Michael Hoare, *Congo Mercenary* (London, 1967). "I make no apologies for being a mercenary soldier," he writes

Quite the reverse. I am proud to have led 5 Commando, I am proud to have fought shoulder to shoulder with the toughest and bravest band of men it has ever been my honor to command. I am proud that they stood when all else failed. I have no regrets.

(pp. 14–15)

The Calcutta-born author died in Durban in 2020, aged 100.

Kisangani), the capital of Orientale province, they fought their way to Kongolo, Kibomba, Kindu, Bunia and Lubutu, inflicting heavy losses on the witch-crazed Simbas, many in their teens, until they were able to establish contact with the Belgian paratroopers airdropped over Stanleyville, both engaged in a race against time to liberate the hundreds of Europeans and the handful of US consular personnel, including the consul, Michael Hoyt, held captive by the Armée Populaire de Libération (APL), commanded by the rebel leader Gaston Soumialot. Hoare describes the APL second in command, "Major Bubu... a gross monster of a man, a deaf and dumb mongoloid, who stood gesticulating in front of the prisoners, dressed in a monkey skin robe. Kill, kill! He grunted in pantomime acting out his orders in an inarticulate frenzy – until someone fired a shot. It was the signal for the massacre to begin. Machine guns blazed out at point blank range, the Simbas carefully selecting women and children for their first targets." Once the guns fell silent, 22 hostages lay dead. "It was an act of unparalleled savagery," he concluded. "Stanleyville bore witness on 24th of November 1964 to one of the most hideous and barbaric crimes of the century."[17] One wonders how the author would have described the vastly more horrific mass murders perpetrated in the region some 30 years later. Nonetheless it is to his credit to record, sometimes with a touch of gallows humor, some of the more ignominious crimes committed by his soldiers. Consider what happened in "liberated Stanleyville" when one of his men in a house to house search ran into a panic-stricken young Congolese girl hiding in a shower room. "He stripped off her clothes till she was naked. He liked what he saw. 'Shower' he ordered her, 'then lie on that bed.' Without a word she obeyed. He raped her. Then he ordered her downstairs with the other prisoners and marched her to the river's edge... She knew she was going to die. With the impulse of revenge, tinged with a spark of genius, she turned and screamed at the sadist words which would last him the rest of his life. "You don't' know how to make love... you're too small!'"[18]

It is difficult to avoid the impression that many of the more gruesome scenes witnessed by the author were intentionally left out. Some of the accounts offered by Western journalists make the mind reel. Writing in the *Cape Times* one South African mercenary wrote of the "senseless, cold-blooded killings, of their rule of never taking prisoners (except for the odd one for questioning after which they were executed) after torturing them." The British weekly *The Observer* declined to show picture of mercenaries at work but described how "(they) not only shoot and hang their prisoners after torturing them, but use them for target practice and gamble over the number of shots needed to kill them." Colin Legum, in an off-the-record conversation with Mike Hoare, described his men as "appalling thugs." In Boende in Orientale province, one Italian journalist described their performance: "Occupying the town meant blowing out the doors with rounds of

---

[17] Hoare, *Congo Mercenary*, pp. 122–123.
[18] Hoare, *Congo Mercenary*, pp. 127–128.

bazooka fire, going into the shops and taking anything, they wanted that was movable... After the looting came the killing. The shouting lasted for three days. Three days of executions, of lynchings, of tortures, of screams and of terror."

The recruiting, training, transport, and planning of marching orders for hundreds of mercenaries did not happen overnight. Only after weeks and months of tough negotiations with Congolese actors, and between them, complicated by occasional discords between US diplomats and their European counterparts, was agreement was finally reached on the intervention of "operational technicians," to use the official euphemism, with the understanding that the CIA would foot the bill (average monthly pay estimated at $300,000 per mercenary) and make all necessary arrangement for the use of C-130s for the transport of mercenaries and their equipment. What could not be assuaged through cash payments was the sense of anger shared by large segments of the Congolese population. With the appointment of the widely reviled Moise Tshombe to the premiership of the country in June 1964, followed by the "collateral damage" of the US–Belgian raid on Stanleyville and the extremely brutal mercs-led mopping up operations in neighboring cities – Boende, Bafwasende, Paulis, Banalia, Watsa, Bunia – anti-Western feelings in eastern Congo hardened into ill-contained fury. This situation played directly into the hands of the Che's strategy to export the Cuban revolutionary model.

Enter Che Guevara

Havana's interest in gaining a foothold in Congo increased in proportion to the gathering momentum of the Simba insurrection during the second half of 1964. By January 1965 the Congo ranked at the top of Che's revolutionary agenda: "Zaire (Congo) is not just an African problem... but a problem that concerned all of mankind."[19] This was the central theme of his discourse each time he met with African leaders during his trip to Dar es Salaam in 1995, when he met for the first time a 26-year-old Simba leader named Kabila. During the seven months that he stayed in the Congo Che had ample occasions to measure the multiplicity of problems he faced as he tried to get his Sierra Maestra-like foco off the ground.

What becomes clear from Che's writings it is his sense of exasperation as he waited for days and weeks for a virtually unknown Congolese rebel politician named Laurent Kabila to show up for planned meetings at one location or another (Kibamba, Baraka, Fizi) on the western shores of Lake Tanganyika. Practicing his French and Swahili while waiting for Kabila did little to calm his nerves. Unpredictable, distrustful, addicted to liquor and

---

[19] All the quotes in this paragraph are from Piero Gleijeses's invaluable contribution, *Conflicting Missions: Havana, Washington and Africa, 1959–1976* (Chapel Hill, 2002), pp. 72–73, and from Che's diary, *Pasajes de la Guerra Revolucionaria: Congo*, parts of which are reproduced in William Galvez, *Le reve africain du Che* (Brussels, 1998).

women, this, in brief, is how the future president of the Congo struck his Cuban mentor.[20] Meanwhile, the Cuban trainers were at a loss to find trainees. "There were now thirty-two Cubans and no rebels to train," lamented Gleijeses. "Che fell ill with malaria, complicated by a violent flare-up of his asthma." Then on June 7 tragedy struck when the boat carrying Mitoudidi, the Cubans' best ally, capsized on Lake Tanganyika.[21]

Not the least of the problems facing the Cubans stemmed from internal quarrels between Congolese and Rwandans. Following the military setback suffered by a group of Rwandans of Tutsi origins and Congolese assailants at Katenga, the Rwandans, under the command of an officer named Mudendi, were reported on the brink of a mutiny. "The Rwandans categorically refuse to fight on, and some are deserting... Those remaining at the camp say they will take part in other combats only if the Congolese agree to join them... Deserters were held largely responsible for the Katenga disaster: out of one hundred and sixty assailants sixty deserted before they even fired a shot."[22] Doubts among Congolese about the inefficiency of *dawa* (the medication expected to make one invulnerable to bullets), or incompetent witch doctors, did little to smooth out ethnic tensions.

Of all the elements that help explain the ultimate fiasco of Che's attempted revolutionary uprising one of the most decisive was the decision of a Kivu-based Tutsi sub-group known as Banyamulenge (of which more later) to pull out of the coalition.[23] They did so not because of basic discords over tactics or strategy but because of their sense of shock at the sight of their proverbially venerated cattle being slaughtered to feed the combatants.

If the Cubans "had definitely not expected the eerie calm they found in Fizi-Baraka,"[24] neither did they anticipate the use of magic by *docteurs-féticheurs* as a revolutionary weapon, or for that matter the slaughtering of Rwandan cattle as a motive for triggering a major defection from the ranks of the rebel army. Unfamiliarity of the Cubans with the social context of their revolutionary enterprise also comes through with painful honesty from Gleijeses's observation that "Che's sense of insecurity was heightened by the feeling that he did not belong: he was Latin American, not African. He was white, they were black. He was in a world he did not know – not

---

[20] Interestingly, in a 2002 interview by Francois Soudan Kagame retrospectively admitted to have "misjudged Kabila." "We should have read what Che Guevara had written about him." Francois Soudan, "Paul Kagame: La guerre est finie," *Jeune Afrique/L'Intelligent*, no. 2179, October 14–20, 2002, p. 32.

[21] Gleijeses, *Conflicting Missions*, pp. 113–114.

[22] Galvez, *Le reve africain du Che.*, pp. 142–143.

[23] Arguably, the sympathy felt by some Tutsi elements towards the Cubans stemmed from their early exposure to radical, neo-Marxist ideas; this ideological streak is traceable, according to one observer, to their experience in refugee camps, where "they absorbed the ideology of anti-imperialism inspired by the revolutionary examples of Fidel Castro, Che Guevara, and the Vietnamese leaders Ho Chi Minh and Vo Nguyen Giap." Stephen Kinzer, *A Thousand Hills: Rwanda's Rebirth and the Man Who Dreamed It* (New York, 2008), p. 48.

[24] Gleijeses, *Conflicting Missions*, p. 111.

the language, not the customs, and not the way of thinking. He was utterly dependent on Kabila's goodwill."[25] That last remark alone seems sufficient to explain the Che's undoing.

From the standpoint of the Rwandans of South Kivu their defection turned out to be a windfall. By turning against the Simba, they earned the gratitude of Mobutu. No longer relegated to a marginal position in relation to other communities, they now had access to the privileges they had long been denied, like access to education, to urban housing and admission into the police and armed forces. But this unexpected windfall, as will be seen, did not prevent them from joining in droves the ranks of the Rwanda-backed Banyamulenge insurgency when the time came to turn against Mobutu.

The Katanga Tigers: Shaba I (1977) and Shaba II (1978)

While the Simba episode brings into view groups and personalities that will reappear in a new guise at a later stage, so also with Shaba I and Shaba II, when the Katanga gendarmes aka the Tigers – once the main prop of Moise Tshombe's secessionist regime in Katanga (1960–1963) – twice attempted to invade Katanga from their bases in Angola before reappearing on the Congo stage as Kabila's ally in1996. By then, however, a new generation of rebels had taken the place of the aging gendarme-veterans, no longer as supporters of a break-away state but as the enemies of Mobutu's dictatorship.

Out this somewhat confusing picture, several things are reasonably clear: in view of their early incarnation as the Katanga gendarmes their loyalty to the secessionist regime also meant a strong aversion to anything even remotely reminiscent of the centralizing Mobutist state. Although their tactical opportunism was evident in the course of their shifting alliances, their detestation of the Mobutu regime was a constant. Contrary to what has been claimed, their decision to invade Katanga (then known as Shaba) in 1977 and 1978, after years of exile in Angola, was by no means dictated and militarily assisted by Cuban or Soviet advisors, but stemmed from the determination of their leaders, most notably the tough-minded Nathanael Mbumba, to overthrow the Mobutu regime as the necessary first step before returning to their homeland.

By projecting the image of the Shaba crisis through a Cold War prism Mobutu gained immediate support from the West. What made the Angola-based rebellion so ominous was the threat posed to the mineral-rich areas of the Katanga. Officially, of course, the villains were Marxist rebels manipulated by the Angolan faction known as the *Popular Movement for the Liberation of Angola* (MPLA) – which after their coming to power in Angola in 1975 became the main ally of the Katanga Tigers in exile – but the evidence is sketchy. After vehemently denouncing the responsibility of Fidel Castro

---

[25] Gleijeses, *Conflicting Missions.*

and his Angolan minions Mobutu's call for help did not go unheeded. His Western allies promptly sent in reinforcements – Moroccan troops airborne by French aircraft (at Uncle Sam's expense) in 1977, and 420 French foreign legion soldiers and Belgian paratroopers in 1978. There is no question that the capture of the mining town of Kolwezi during Shaba II was seen with considerable concern in the West, in part because of the menace faced by its substantial European resident population, but it is doubtful that the invaders were involved in the death of 37 of them, as claimed by Mobutu. Both during Shaba I and Shaba II every effort was made to distract public attention from the crimes against civilians committed by the Congolese army, and instead point the finger at the invading Afro-Marxists. The image of Mobutu holding at bay Communist hordes with a little bit of help from his friends went a long way towards burnishing his anti-Marxist credentials but did nothing to clean up his reputation as a hugely corrupt autocrat.

Just how far corruption penetrated into the sinews of the state came to full light in 1978, shortly after Shaba II, when the International Monetary Fund (IMF) charged Erwin Blumenthal, a long-time German civil servant associated with the Bundesbank, to investigate the National Bank of Zaire's mounting irregularities. In pointing to the presidency as the crux of the problem Blumenthal did not mince words: "Who is going to shout 'Stop the thief!'? It is an impossible task to monitor the transactions within the president's office. Within that office no distinction is drawn between personal needs and state expenditures. How can it be that international organizations and Western governments blindly trust President Mobutu?" Reflecting on Blumenthal disclosures, Van Reybrouck denounced "the systematic embezzlement of government funds, the discovery of a whole slew of secret bank accounts in Europe, the bald-faced systematic greed of Mobutu and his clique."[26] What went unmentioned was the intimate causal connection between the US-assisted rise to power of the Mobutist state and the depth of its corrupt practices.

No matter how crucial in consolidating Mobutu's hold on the state, external ties of dependency can only reveal part of the story. Just as important was the political machine built around the single party state. In its patrimonial dimension Bula Matari emerges as a vast patronage operation built on personal favors and privileges; material rewards are the flipside of political loyalty, and punishment the inevitable sanction of trust betrayed. Only through an adroit combination of carrot and sticks can the machine resist the threats of shifting loyalties and internal dissent. A standard practice to lessen the risks of subversion from within is to seek potential clients among ethnic groups that are too weak in terms of numbers and political clout to pose a threat to the reigning autocrat.

This is where the courting of some key political refugees from Rwanda could serve as a cautionary tale about the fickleness of patron-client ties.

---

[26] David Van Reybrouck, *Congo: The Epic History of a People* (New York, 2014), p. 375.

Rwanda: the wild card

Long before its accession to independence in 1962 Rwanda had experienced an extremely violent upheaval (see Chapter 2). While the departing Belgian authorities deliberately chose to ignore the warnings of the UN Trusteeship in order to install a "friendly" Hutu government by way of a Belgian-engineered revolution, tens of thousands of Tutsi refugees whose lives were in danger had no option but to seek asylum abroad. Many went to Uganda and Burundi, others to the Congo. Forcefully expelled from their homes, they came to be known as "the fifty niners." Many were Tutsi chiefs or sub-chiefs, or held high positions in the colonial bureaucracy. Compared to other refugee communities, they were relatively well off, better educated and determined to cope as best they could with the blows of circumstantial adversity.[27]

The Congo offered a congenial environment. In the Kivu province, across the border, where most settled, they found echoes of their homeland. Not only was the physical landscape much the same, but so were the customs, attitudes and language of some of neighboring communities. Only if we remember the irrelevance – indeed the non-existence – of fixed boundaries in pre-colonial Africa can we begin to understand the presence in eastern Congo of multiple Kinyarwanda-speaking enclaves. "Seeing like a state," to use the title of James C. Scott's seminal contribution,[28] meant tracing fixed boundaries where none existed before; it meant the bureaucratic imposition of national identities where only linguistic and cultural affinities held sway; it meant a blurring of distinctions among clans, status groups, family ties. In this context where social ties cut across geographical boundaries the "fifty niners" were able to interact with long-established kin groups who also identified as Congolese citizens.

Some, like the so-called Banyamulenge ("the people from Mulenge"), had settled in the high-lying plateau of the Itombwe region in South Kivu since time immemorial; the same is true of other Kinyarwanda-speaking communities, Tutsi and Hutu, of Bwisha in North Kivu; others came during the colonial period to meet the demand of white settlers for labor on coffee and tea plantations. Far from being a culturally undifferentiated lump of Kinyarwanda-speaking humanity, each group had their own peculiarities and historicities, and the Banyamulenge perhaps more so than any other.[29] For all their efforts to identify the Congo as their home, they would eventually end up facing the same stigma as "enemy aliens."

---

[27] For a seminal contribution to our understanding of the distinctive historicities of refugee flows, see David Newbury, "Returning Refugees: Four Historical Patterns of 'Coming Home' to Rwanda," *Comparative Studies in Society and History*, vol. 47, no. 2 (2005), pp. 252–285.

[28] James C. Scott, *Seeing Like a State: How Certain Schemes to Improve the Human Condition Have Failed* (New Haven, 1998).

[29] The best source on the history and politics of the Banyamulenge is Muller Ruhimbika, *Les Banyamulenge (Congo-Zaire)* (Paris, 2001).

Years went by before this change of fortunes morphed into open hostility. A potential source of conflict stemmed from the ability of the fifty niners to acquire large tracts of land, in part through Mobutu's policy of "Zairianisation" (1973), ostensibly aimed at transferring foreign-owned property to Congolese hands. The unexpected rise to prominence of a shrewdly manipulative Tutsi refugee from Rwanda, Barthélemy Rwema Bisengimana, proved immensely valuable. Until his fall from grace in 1977 he served as the privileged intermediary between Mobutu and the "fifty niners." As Mobutu's *chef de cabinet* no one was better positioned to facilitate the transfer of huge chunks of real estate into Tutsi hands. He himself stood first on the receiving end of the line, claiming as his property the Osso ranch, one of the largest in the region; according to one testimony he also owned tea or coffee plantations on Ijwi island, on Lake Kivu; other beneficiaries included such personalities as Kasugu and Ndakola with holdings of 100,000 hectares each, Ngizayo with 2,000 hectares, and so forth. Some of this land, in one of the richest and most densely populated parts of Kivu province (Masisi), had once been the property of Belgian settlers, but in many instances the previous owners belonged to indigenous, non-Tutsi communities (Hunde, Nande and Nyanga). At the stroke of a pen they found themselves evicted from their holdings, expellees from their own and.[30]

Access to land implied citizenship. In helping redefine citizenship rights to the advantage of the refugee population Bisengimana's influence proved invaluable. Even though most of the time citizenship requirements were simply ignored, the 1972 legislation – for which Bisengimana, by now director of the *Bureau Politique* of the ruling party, *Mouvement Populaire de la Révolution* (MPR), deserves full credit – granted citizenship rights to anyone living in the Congo at the time of independence, a significantly more permissive threshold than the one previous set by law.

How, from a privileged refugee minority they found themselves targeted as an undesirable foreign presence is a complicated story, traceable, first and foremost, to Kagame's invasion of Rwanda in October 1990.

The ground is shifting

In a matter of weeks much of Rwanda was turned into a war zone. With thousands of "refugee warriors" from Uganda – now reincarnated as Rwanda Patriotic Front (RPF) soldiers – fighting their way back into the

---

[30] I am grateful to Joseph Sebarenzi and David Newbury for sharing their information on Bisengimana's real estate holdings. To quote from Newbury's email:

> Bisengimana's real targeted areas were multiple cattle farms in the Masisi region, a favored settler area for the resettlement of some 40,000 Rwandan laborers from the late 1940s through the mid-1950s: the infamous MIB (Mission Immigration Banyarwanda) aimed to provide adequate labor resources to attract Belgian settlers to this gorgeous pasturage. Bisengimana seized several of these domains.

His plantations on Idjwi, he adds, never covered more than 20–25 percent of the island's surface.

country, huge flows of Hutu refugees moved into eastern DRC, where they eventually coalesced into networks of resistance. After taking control of Rwanda in 1994 the RPF's immediate priority was to clean out every nest of resistance from the eastern DRC, which, as is now painfully clear, in effect meant killing thousands of Hutu civilians in the process.[31] Caught between the two-pronged menace of incoming RPF soldiers and Hutu civilians trying to do all they could to stop the invasion of their turf, many Banyamulenge found it impossible to stay neutral. Some acted as a "fifth column" for the RPF. Violent settlings of accounts followed. How to tell a long-time Tutsi resident from an invading refugee warrior was not self-evident. Nor was the fault line between civilians and soldiers clearly drawn. The impression one gets from eyewitness reports is one of appalling cruelty. RPF unirs were not known for shilly-shallying: as they expanded westward in DRC every Hutu was fair game, civilian or not. To this critical episode we shall return in a moment.

Long before push came to shove the DRC was the scene of mounting ethnic enmities. As competition over land grew steadily in the early 1990s the ethnic temperature between "native Congolese" and Rwandan "immigrants" rose in proportion. In early 1993 large-scale violence erupted in parts of North Kivu, notably in Walikale and Masisi, each claiming a high concentration of indigenous Tutsi elements, killing thousands (one reliable source mentions 14,000).

This violent outburst marked the culmination of tensions that had been building up over the years. One telltale sign was Mobutu's decision to abrogate the 1972 citizenship law by a 1981 ordinance making it virtually impossible for those designated as "migrants" to claim citizenship. Then came the decision by the organizers of the much-touted National Sovereign Conference (1991) to systematically exclude all Tutsi from participating in the debates on the grounds of their "dubious nationality." By then every effort was made by local officials to heap scorn on anyone whose nationality was presumed doubtful, which in effect meant virtually all Tutsi elements, irrespective of the date of their arrival.

Ratcheting up inter-group hatreds were two dramatic, game-changing events in Burundi, the first in 1972, the other and 1993. Each drove an ever-deeper wedge between Hutu and Tutsi throughout the region. In spite of a 21-year interval between them, and different underlying circumstances, they brought into relief the depth of antagonisms between the two communities. Nineteen seventy-two is when Burundi experienced a collective trauma from which it has never really recovered. As many as 200,000 Hutu civilians are believed to have been murdered at the hands of a predominantly Tutsi army, in response to a local Hutu-led insurgency that may

---

[31] See Howard W. French, *A Continent for the Taking: The Tragedy and Hope of Africa* (New York, 2004); and Filip Reyntjens and René Lemarchand, "Mass Murder in Eastern Congo, 1996–1997," in René Lemarchand, ed., *Forgotten Genocides: Oblivion, Denial and Memory* (Philadelphia, 2011), pp. 20–36.

have caused thousands of deaths among Tutsi. The spinoff was immediately felt in Rwanda, then under Hutu rule: by way of revenge dozens of Tutsi students were attacked by their Hutu neighbors, setting off bitter internal quarrels which in July of the following year led to a northern-inspired army coup by Juvenal Habyarimana.

The 1972 Burundi bloodbath was followed by a long period of Tutsi rule that only came to an end with the election of Melchior Ndadaye in July 1993, the first popularly elected Hutu president. The news of his assassination at the hands of the Tutsi dominated army on October 21 unleashed ethnic hatreds far beyond the borders of Burundi.

A sea change would soon reconfigure the geopolitics of the region. In July 1994, less than a year after Ndadaye's death, Kagame's FPR was in full control of Rwanda's capital city, but the raids mounted from the Congo by Hutu extremists – most of them ex-*Forces Armées Rwandaises* (FAR) and *interahamwe* – caused considerable chronic insecurity along the border. In Rwanda the genocide of Tutsi had come to an end, but with over a million Hutu civilians fleeing en masse into eastern Congo, accompanied by scores of former officials of the Habyarimana government,[32] many eager to take revenge, the prospects for peace were dim.

As the vortex of conflict shifted to the Congo in 1996, the stage was set for the deadliest war since WWII, also known as the Great Congo War. The aim for Kagame was not just to eliminate deadly refugee-led cross-border raids from the Kivu region, or for that matter to simply bring down the Mobutist state. The broader strategic objective was to put in place a Rwanda-friendly, obedient client state in Kinshasa.[33] No other event in the history of the Great Lakes is more deserving of being called a game changer. Its aftereffects will impact on the Congo's destinies for years to come.

The Banyamulenge rebellion

What is often referred to as the Banyamulenge rebellion is a semantic oversimplification. It included not just pre-colonial migrants from South Kivu, but "fifty-niners" from North Kivu as well as anti-Mobutist elements

---

[32] For an chilling sample of the attitude of some hard-line Hutu extremists, consider the statement by Francois Karera, former prefect of Kigali, as reported by Jane Perlez: "The Tutsi are originally bad. They are murderers. They are physically weak, look at their arms and their legs. They just command. The others work... They deserved to die." Jane Perlez, "A Hutu Justifies Genocide," *International Herald Tribune*, August 16, 1994.

[33] This episode, like many others elsewhere in the continent, gives the lie to Jeffrey Gettleman's singularly off-the-beam interpretation of what he calls "Africa's Forever War." "There is a very simple reason," he writes,

> why some of Africa's bloodiest, most brutal wars never seem to end. They are not really wars. Not in the traditional sense at least. The combatants don't have much of an ideology; they don't have clear goals. They couldn't care less about taking over capitals or major cities.

(Jeffrey Gettleman, "Africa's Forever Wars,"
Foreign Policy, March–April 2010, pp. 1–2)

indigenous to eastern Congo, and, crucially, a solid cadre of RPF crack troops along with some Ugandan army men. Its significance as a pivoting event cannot be overestimated. It signaled Rwanda's military entry into the Congo and the point of no return for the collapsing Mobutist state.

To reduce the story to its essentials, it began in eastern Congo as an externally assisted anti-Mobutist insurgency before expanding into a full-scale war, and ultimately into a genocidal bloodbath, causing the deaths of tens of thousands of Hutu refugees, combatants and civilians.

The last chapter of the anti-Mobutist crusade is also the first in the story of the Second Congo War. By mid-1998 tensions between the Congolese client and his Rwandan patron had almost reached the boiling point, soon splitting the anti-Mobutist insurgents into warring factions. On August 2, 1998 Laurent Desire Kabila – the hand-picked nominal leader of the rebellion and former ornery co-conspirator of the Che during his ill-fated expedition – turned the tables on his Rwandan godfather and his Banyamulenge allies. Thus, began a reversal of alliances that paved the way for one of the most costly conflict since WWII.

But, before going any further, who, exactly, are the Banyamulenge? Merely to raise the question is to stir controversy. For many self-described authentic Congolese, they are foreigners, recently immigrated from Rwanda. As such, they simply do not qualify as citizens, a view vigorously contested by most Banyamulenge, who argue with justice that they came from Rwanda generations ago, long before the advent of colonial rule. Their turf is in the high plateau area of South Kivu, in the area known as Itombwe, where they found an ideal climate for cattle grazing. Unlike the "fifty niners" they were not political refugees but pre-colonial migrants, whose metamorphosis from Banyarwanda to Banyamulenge can best be thought of a case of ethno-genesis. By adopting the collective label of Banyamulenge they affirmed their identity as another Congolese "tribe," and made clear their intention *not* to be identified as Banyarwanda. Furthermore, in asserting themselves as a Congolese community they were now able to press their claims for political rights, including the legal recognition of their collective identity as a separate local government entity, or *collectivité*.[34] Even after their self-interest pushed them into an alliance with the RPF they never turned away from their Congolese roots.

I remember traveling to Itombwe's principal commune, Minembwe, in 2009, with four other Belgian colleagues. A mutual friend of ours, Bernard Leloup, working for the UN, had kindly offered to take us by helicopter from Uvira, capital of South Kivu, to Minembwe. What struck me most forcefully, besides the very cool temperature and the immensity of the grasslands stretching across the horizon, was the distinctive aloofness of the handful of notables we met. Friendly, but distant, as if inhabiting a universe

---

[34] For a useful contribution to the history and politics of the Banyamulenge, see Koen Vlassenroot, "Citizenship, Identity Formation and Conflict in South Kivu: The Case of the Banyamulenge," *Review of African Political Economy*, vol. 29 (2002), pp. 499–516.

of their own, too subtle to be shared with the *bazungu*. Few understood French. I am reminded of Lieve Joris's phrasing in her arresting travel narrative: "Their tall and thin silhouettes, their archaic pride and their majestic cattle enabled them to eclipse each of the communities they came in contact with on the high plateaus."[35] Despite strenuous efforts by Kagame to integrate them into Rwanda by a transfer of populations, they consistently declined the offer. And when units of the RPF used force as a substitute for persuasion, some extremely bloody encounters followed.

If the historic Banyamulenge are indeed a group apart, among "native" Congolese the term soon became a convenient catch-all label to cast aspersions on all Kinyarwanda-speaking communities. The stage was set for a dramatic confrontation between "natives" and "foreigners." To this day Kinyarwanda-speakers are seen by many Congolese as the collective bogeyman responsible for their misfortunes.

My first face-to-face contact with the Banyamulenge happened by chance. During a trip to Goma in the summer of 1991 I came across a Rwandan historian I had met in Kinshasa on a previous occasion. We talked about the prospects of a FPR victory in the ongoing war unfolding in north Rwanda. As I expressed misgivings about the likelihood of a victorious outcome he picked up his mobile phone and invited two young Tutsi recruits to join our conversation. The impression that sticks to my mind from this chance encounter was their extraordinary self-confidence – and their farewell high-five: "We shall win!" And win they did. Three years later the RPF had won one battle; they were about to engage in another, their sights set on the capture of Kinshasa.

By July 1994 Kagame had emerged triumphant from a four-year civil war against the Habyarimana regime. What did not come to an end was the appalling revenge killings of Hutu civilians – the latter conveniently lumped together as génocidaires – perpetrated by Kagame's security forces in the months following their victory. The mass slaughter of Hutu civilians by the FPR in the camps where hundreds of thousands had sought refuge in eastern Congo is inseparable from the rebellion that brought the Mobutist regime to its knees.

The rebellion, spearheaded by what came to be known as the *Alliance des Forces Démocratiques pour la Libération du Congo* (AFDL), was jointly planned by Kagame and Museveni months in advance, in consultation with US officials. It unfolded in different stages. The first phase aimed at "cleaning out" the refugee camps"; the next one, more ambitious, had as its objective to capture the major towns, including Mbuji-Mai the capital of the diamond-rich Kasai Oriental, and Kisangani, which in effect would made it possible for the war to be self-financing; the ultimate goal was to take Kinshasa and bring down the Mobutist state. As it turned out, the plan proved a stunning success. The AFDL successfully fought its way across hundreds

---

[35] Lieve Joris, *Les Hauts Plateaux* (Paris, 2009), p. 11.

of miles before capturing Kinshasa on July 17, 1997, at which point the Mobutist house of cards was a pushover.

The Banyamulenge played a major role at each step of the way. Their courage and motivation are easy to understand when we recall the scurrilous accusations repeatedly hurled at them by Congolese politicians from the Kivu, collectively described as Rwandans in disguise "sharing the morphology and ideology of Paul Kagame"[36] pretending to pass as Congolese. The tale of woe, familiar to many, bears repeating.

Threats followed, in the form of a resolution adopted on April 28, 1995 by the Congolese parliament calling for the expulsion of all Banyamulenge from the Congo by December 31. Further fueling this surge of xenophobic abuse, a huge number of Hutu fleeing the avenging arm of the RPF – including a substantial segment of the defeated Rwandan Armed Forces (FAR), and *interahamwe* militia – were now regrouping in North Kivu near the Rwanda border, hoping to snatch victory from the jaws of their recent defeat. As many as 1.3 million Hutu were now huddling in refugee camps.

In early October the vice-governor of South Kivu publicly stated his intention to expel the Banyamulenge. Threats soon turned into killings, causing a major exodus of Congolese Tutsi to Rwanda. Others were not so lucky. In Uvira, in South Kivu, where almost 220,000 Rwandan and Burundi refugees were reported to have found refuge, journalists present on the scene reported "a nascent ethnic cleansing (to be) unfolding."[37]

This is when "the Rwandans in disguise" sprang into action, bolstered by RPF units. Their familiarity with the geography of eastern Congo proved invaluable: one by one key localities came under their control, first Uvira on October 28, then Bukavu two days later, followed by Goma, Butembo, Beni and Bunia on December 25. With North and South Kivu virtually under control of the rebel army, the foot soldiers in black rubber boots – many teen-age child soldiers (the so-called *kadogos*) – proceeded to fight their way through the jungle, north to Kisangani and south to Lubumbashi, before finally entering Kinshasa seven months later.

Long before their victory lap, however, the insurgents had gained a sinister notoriety for their systematic "cleansing" of Hutu refugee camps. The story of what could be described as wanton mass murder has been told by in detail by a number of reliable observers. Among them Philip Roessler and Harry Verhoeven, who depicted in graphic terms "the magnitude of these crimes against humanity": "Refugees were strangled, their skulls bashed in, they were bayoneted, hacked to death or shot... The death toll, in all likelihood totals in six digits."[38] Of the 85,000 Hutu refugees sheltering at the Tingi-Tingi camp, few escaped alive. As one teenage participant in the butchery candidly recalled, "our objective was Kisangani, and Tingi-Tingi

---

[36] Ruhimbika, *Les Banyamulenge*, p. 30.
[37] Kirkpatrick J. Day and Paula J. Ghedini, "Another Forced Exodus," *The Washington Post*, October 1, 1996.
[38] Philip Roessler and Harry Verhoeven, *Why Comrades Go to War* (Oxford, 2010), p. 209.

was in the way. So we had to neutralize it. I was a *kadogo* (child soldier), only fifteen, our commander was Rwandan, General Ruvusha. He's a colonel in the Rwandan army now, but he was terrible. Laurent Nkunda was there too. Our Tutsi commander told us: they are *génocidaires*, they have to die... When I think back on it, it hurts so much. I regret it, but we were loyal to the AFDL."[39] Tingi-Tingi was not the only killing ground. Similar scenes of mass murder took place in Katale and Mugunga, both in North Kivu, sheltering 202,566 and 156,115, respectively. The British journalist William Shawcross spoke of "a vicious game of pursuit through the steaming jungles of eastern Zaire... a story as macabre as any other, involving genocidal attacks against refugees, some of whom were guilty of genocide themselves."[40] Even more appalling were the atrocities revealed in the so-called UN Mapping Report, the most thorough investigation of the mass atrocities committed by the RPA and its Congolese allies.[41]

The Congo kill zone

Widening the lens on the crimes committed against refugees, the UN report describes in agonizing detail the horrific slaughter that went on between March 1993 and June 2003 across the Congo. The evidence, collected by a team of 20 international and Congolese human rights professionals, is based on 617 cases of mass killings, sexual violence, attacks on children and other abuses committed by "armed actors," identified by the report as "foreign armies, rebel groups and Congolese government forces." It goes on to specify what the report is not – not an exercise "to establish individual responsibility nor lay blame," but "a first step towards the painful but nonetheless essential process of truth-telling after violent conflict."

Some of the most egregious human rights violations covered by the report had already been documented before by academics as well as the UN and several NGOs. Nonetheless, it is the first time that such crimes "have been comprehensively analyzed, compiled, and systematically organized by an official UN report." Especially noteworthy is the conclusion drawn by the UN that such crimes could conceivably qualify as genocide or crimes against humanity. Which raises the obvious question: Why has so little been done to bring to justice, or at least condemn by word and deed, those responsible for such abominations?

Page after page through 545 pages the reader is confronted with scenes of horror – from the killing by the AFDL/APR soldiers on March 14, 1997 of

---

[39] Van Reybrouck, *Congo*, p. 424.
[40] Cited in Filip Reyntjens and René Lemarchand, "Mass Murder in Eastern Congo, 1996–1997," in Lemarchand, ed., *Forgotten Genocides*, op. cit., p. 20.
[41] For the full text, see *Report of the Mapping Exercise Documenting the Most Serious Violations of Human Rights and International Humanitarian Law Committed within the Territory of the Democratic Republic of the Congo between March 1993 and June 2003*, United Nations High Commission for Human Rights, October 2010.

"at least 470 refugees in the two camps near Wanie Rukula in the Ubundu territory" (p. 104) to the killing of "at least 80 refugees including women and children at the Obilo camp on March 26 (p. 105) and the 200 people thought to have been killed in a massacre near Mbandaka" (p. 117). To go through the litany of such atrocities is all too facile; a more useful take for our purpose is to note how the Rwanda authorities reacted to the report. At first every effort was made to prevent the publication of the final version. Acting Foreign Minister Louise Mushikiwabo went so far as to threaten to pull Rwanda's 3,000 peacekeepers out of the African Union–UN peacekeeping mission in Darfur, but to no avail. The report's inconvenient truths were subsequently rejected by Mushikawabo as unacceptable and inaccurate from start to finish. The official statement issued by the Ministry of Foreign Affairs denounced the "DRC Mapping Exercise" as "malicious, offensive and ridiculous," and as "immoral and unacceptable" the accusations against a state that stopped the genocide, and as "shocking" and "in complete disregard for fundamental fairness" the failure of the Mapping Team to consult with Rwanda – "even though they had time to meet with over 200 NGO representatives."[42]

Rwanda's denial, echoed by Uganda and Burundi (then under Tutsi rule), is not surprising. More intriguing is the absence of a significant judicial follow-up to the report's disclosures. Jason Stearns gives us a clue: "for many the moral shock of the Rwanda genocide (of Tutsi) was so overpowering that it eclipsed all subsequent events in the region." He goes on to quote from an American diplomat, "Did we have prosecutions after the American civil war? No. Did the South Africans ever try the apartheid regime? Not really. Why should we ask them to do it there?"[43] Is this to say that failure to act on previous occasions, no matter how distant, is justification for not acting in the present?

While the scale of the Rwanda genocide is indeed beyond anything that could have been imagined, so also is the magnitude of the cold-blooded killings perpetrated by the RPF after the defeat of the Habyarimana regime, a point that has been convincingly argued by Judy Rever in her devastating expose.[44] One wonders whether the "overpowering" scale of one genocide can explain the silence surrounding another? To this we shall return in another chapter.

Going back to where we left off, even though the UN mapping report did not have the impact that some had expected, and others feared, the events described in its pages had a profound effect in the Congo long before they appeared in print.

---

[42] Rwanda Republic, Ministry of Foreign Affairs and Cooperation, *Statement by the Government of Rwanda on the Leaked Draft of UN Report on RDC.*

[43] Jason Stearns, *Dancing in the Glory of Monsters: The Collapse of the Congo and the Great War of Africa* (New York, 2011), p. 140.

[44] Judi Rever, *In Praise of Blood: The Crimes of the Rwandan Patriotic Front* (New York, 2018).

Switching sides

Among the several factors that have driven the Second Congo War (1998–2003) three carried dramatic consequences which seriously complicated the search for a solution and radically altered the parameters of conflict.

One is the involvement of no fewer than nine African states, each pursuing interests of their own and hoping to reap handsome economic and political dividends from their alignment with one or the other of the key players. The next relates to the drastic reconfiguration of the DRC's geopolitical map after the Congo government injected massive military aid into the hands of Mai-Mai warlords while Rwanda gave full support to its Congolese proxy, the Tutsi-dominated *Rassemblement Congolais pour la Démocratie* (RCD). Yet another stimulus to conflict stemmed from the sharp resentment felt by the population of Kinshasa towards Tutsi in general (and anyone looking like one), now seen as meddlesome occupiers rather than liberators. That almost none spoke Lingala, the lingua franca of the capital city, and many looked and behaved as triumphant interlopers didn't help either. As news of indiscriminate violence against Hutu refugees reached Kinshasa anti-Tutsi distrust turned into open hostility. Hundreds of Tutsi or Tutsi-looking individuals were killed because of their look – what the French call *le crime de facies*.

The tipping point came with the appalling butchery of Hutu civilians in refugee camps by units of the RPF assisted by AFDL elements. Kabila's disengagement from what now looked like an unworkable "unholy" alliance with Rwanda seemed unavoidable.

Faced with rising domestic and international outrage over the massive human rights violations committed by Kagame's army, Kabila felt he had no other option than to turn against his Rwandan patron, whose crimes he had long tried to conceal. The result was a spectacular shift of alliances: after sparing no effort to heap scorn on the atrocities of the *interahamwe* and Hutu *génocidaires* he now stood as their unrepentant supporter.

The crunch came with his decision on August 2, 1998, to rid himself of his most trusted Tutsi advisers, the first step towards reasserting control over his security forces. At this point the line-up between pro- and anti-Kabila states was clear: against Rwanda, Uganda, and Burundi, the hostile triumvirate, were two of Kabila's major allies, Zimbabwe and Angola, the first motivated by prospects of economic gain from Katanga's mineral wealth, the other by ideological affinities. Both saved the day when push came to shove in early August.

If anyone deserves a medal for presence of mind, tactical astuteness and sheer guts in the run-up to the war it is Kagame's chief of staff at the time, a youthful Uganda-born Tutsi named James Kabarebe. Immediately after Kabila's precipitous switch he flew back to Kigali, and then to Goma. Here, after meeting up with hundreds of crack RPA commandos, he hijacked four civilian planes and ordered the pilots to fly to the Kitona military base, some 200 miles west of Kinshasa. His plan was to fight his way back into the capital from the west, the most promising theater for a quick strike. The

plot would probably have succeeded had it not been for the swift intervention on August 21–22 of Angola's fighter jets and Zimbabwean helicopters,
both of which badly mauled Kabarebe's forces. The follow-through operations proved lethal. The tipping point came when "an Angolan mecha-
nized brigade and commando units poured across the border from Cabinda
engaging RPA and Congolese rebel forces throughout Bas Congo, including
Kitona, Moambe and Kasangulu."[45]

Why should Angola throw its lot with Kabila? The quick answer is the
proverbial adage that the enemies of our enemies are our friends. Given
the long-standing ties of friendship between Mobutu and Jonas Savimbi's
National Union for Total Independence of Angola (UNITA), President Dos
Santos's arch-enemy, it is easy to see why Kabila's credentials should attract
the sympathy of the Angolan president. Should it be allowed to happen,
Kabila's demise would probably resurrect Dos Santos's worst nightmare.

Another critical factor came into play: the resurrection of the Katanga
Tigers as one of Kabila's closest allies in ADFL coalition. The background
story is recounted by Philip Roessler and Harry Verhoeven: "When Kabila
visited Luanda in 1996 after the start of the ADFL liberation project, the
MPLA organized a meeting for Mzee with the Katangese diaspora. Lacking
Congolese soldiers who could balance the RPA and Banyamulenge, Kabila
charmed the Katanga Tigers whom he praised as professional fighters and
invited them to join him in eastern Congo... President Dos Santos endorsed
the idea of proxy warfare and organized for hundreds of Katanga Tigers
to be flown with Angolan intelligence and technical specialists to Kigali via
Zambia."[46] But if the Tigers' connection cannot be left out of the geopolitical equation, it also tells us something about their uncanny aptitude for
trimming their sails to the prevailing wind.

The Mobutist legacy

There is no point in parsing this cataclysmic Second Congo War into its
countless protagonists and participants – the multiple actors, domestic
and foreign, the shifting political arenas, attempted peace deals, spoilers
and traitors, warlords and mentors.[47] Suffice it to note some of the more
enduring traits inherited from the collapse of the Mobutist dictatorship: the
continuing presence from one dynastic regime to another, in one form or
another, of a state system based on vast networks of corruption, bolstered
by indiscriminate violence and predatory practices; the seemingly nev-
er-ending fragmentation of the Congo into a multitude of warring factions;
and as a consequence of the resultant weakness of the state, the ever-present

---

[45] Roessler and Verhoeven, *Why Comrades Go to War*, p. 375.
[46] Roessler and Verhoeven, *Why Comrades Go to War*, p. 227.
[47] This has been done with exemplary meticulousness by Filip Reyntjens in his classic work,
The Great African War: Congo and Regional Geopolitics, 1996–2006 (Cambridge,
2009).

threat of Rwandan intrusions, more often than not through neo-imperial, clientelist strategies designed to maintain a measure of control, direct or indirect, on the Congo's vast mineral resources.

Much ink has been spilled on the perils of Bula Matari: its propensity to crush human lives as well as rocks, and ignore or destroy of civil society organizations, its inability to transcend the appeals of patrimonial autocracy, its stunning lack of probity and efficiency. All of which conspire to create distrust and fear. Hence the proliferation of local factions aiming at protecting the local communities from the state, a phenomenon best exemplified by the Mai-Mai, which, for the most part, serve as locally-rooted substitutes for the state and its representatives. Distrust of the state extends to aid workers and, medical personnel, indiscriminately seen as vectors of a predatory state. At a time when health issues are of paramount importance the implications are clear. In the words of one medical expert familiar with the Congo-based Ebola epidemic, "the biggest impediment to containing Ebola in Congo is not its contagiousness, but suspicion of the state and of aid personnel. Since 2000 international agencies have spent more than $9 billion on aid in the country, with further $1.5 billion ought for humanitarian response in 2019. While some agencies manage to provide valuable services, they are also seen by many Congolese as having questionable ethics… Congolese are routinely subjected to extortion and violence by armed groups – the fallout of the regional wars sparked by the genocide in Rwanda –who compete for control of the illegal border trade in gold, timber, ivory, charcoal and drugs."[48] The sad irony is that many of the grassroots organizations claiming to protect the citizens against the state are among the worst offenders as far as violence, theft and extortion are concerned.

Into the void left by the disintegration of the Mobutist state rushed a variety of forces, some from abroad, others indigenous to the Congo. Of these the so-called Mai-Mai are still the most numerous. Locally rooted, ethnically-inspired, inherently distrustful of foreigners, first and foremost of anyone who looked or walked like a Tutsi, they came into existence as an improvised self-defense force. In the absence of a functioning police force, they served as the next best thing to insure the protection of their communities. Some of their best-known commanders, General Padiri around Bunyakiri, General Dunia around Fizi and Baraka, Lwecha in Shabunda, General Masunzu in the High Plateau area of South Kivu, are remembered for their commitment to the welfare and safety of their local communities. To view them as the expression of a culturally ingrained anarchic impulse is unwarranted. For all the violence that has accompanied their career paths they can better be seen as a rational response to the insecurities and threats arising from an endless war, a situation made worse by the implosion of the

---

[48] Annie Sparrow, "Ebola in Africa: What We're Getting Wrong," *The New York Review of Books*, October 24, 2019, p. 35. The author is assistant professor at the Department of Population Health Science and Policy at the School of Medicine at Mount Sinai Hospital in New York City.

state, the growing number of unemployed youth, and their ready enlistment into armed factions.[49] By 2010, by one count, the number of Mai-Mai warlords in North and South Kivu had grown to 16, prompting one observer to comment: "Armed groups in eastern Congo are like brooms in Disney's Sorcerer's Apprentice: they just seem to keep multiplying."[50]

While the proliferation of armed Mai-Mai factions could only lead to further fragmentation, some heavy hitters did not hesitate to carve out profitable spheres of influence. Consider the vicious infighting that broke out between Rwandan and Ugandan soldiers in 1999, 2000 and 2001, when each tried to push the other out of the mineral-rich region of Kisangani, in the process killing an estimated 1,000 civilians. Again, consider the alphabet soup of factions and subgroups spawned by the incessant splits within the *Rassemblement Congolais pour la Démocratie* (RCD) – RDC-G, RDC-K, RDC-ML, each in turn subject to intramural squabbles. Once seen as the most hopeful vehicle of Rwandan interests in the Congo, but more accurately portrayed by Van Reybrouk as a "phantom construction," the fate suffered by the RCD is a commentary on the obstacles met by Kagame in his efforts to re-enter the Congo through proxies.

For years the Kigali-based Congo Desk, once headed by the late Patrick Karegeya,[51] a division of Rwanda's External Security Operations, was the instrument of choice for coordinating political and military operations into eastern Congo. Large quantities of mineral wealth were extracted, transported, and commercialized through its wide-ranging subsidiaries and fair-weather clients, but this did not prevent the occurrence of bitter disputes over the distribution of benefits. Writing in 2002, Jim Freedman, a well-informed Canadian colleague, shared the following information on what he described as Rwanda's "most important and elusive" source of profits: "The Congo Desk turned the coltan trade into a truly efficient export business, working with the Russian mafia in particular, and it earned them considerable amounts. Their diamond scheme shave been plagued with difficulties. Onusumba [a former RDC secretary general] wanted the diamond trade to mature but there are too many crooks and unscrupulous players to make Rwanda – just one more crooked operator – a real competitor... I suspect the Rwandans played too rough in Kisangani and finally their attempt to

---

[49] For an excellent discussion of the internal dynamic behind the proliferation of Mai-Mai militias, including the opportunities for social reintegration into informal militarized networks offered to marginalized, alienated youth, see Koen Vlassenroot and Frank Van Acker, "War as Exit from Exclusion? The Formation of Mayi-Mayi Militias in Eastern Congo," *Afrika Focus*, vol. 17, nos. 1–2 (2001), pp. 51–77.

[50] Christian Bitela, personal communication, Author's files.

[51] After serving as the head of external intelligence in the Kagame government, and later a key opponent of the regime, Karegeya was found dead in 2013 in a Johannesburg hotel, the victim of a Kagame goon squad. Karegeya is the central figure in Michela Wrong out standing biography, *Do Not Disturb: The story of a political murderand an African regime gone bad* (Political Affairs, forthcoming). Her book stands out as a brilliant effort to critically re-examine the key episodes of the Kagame regime in a revisionist perspective.

create a monopoly through their Lebanese affiliate found the going very difficult."[52]

If the Rwandan army has been on the front lines of the Congo operations, it was first in line to cash in on the loot. It is estimated that in 2000 it made the equivalent of 20 million pounds sterling a month from mining coltan, and as recently as 2008 was said to be exporting quantities of diamond and gold mined in the Congo.[53]

The perverse effects of factionalism go beyond the siphoning of mineral wealth into foreign hands. Factional disputes lie at the heart of the repeated failures met by aspiring peace-makers. One only needs to recall its disastrous consequences on the Lusaka peace process. The Lusaka accords of July 1999 – signed by the key belligerents, the Congo, Rwanda, Zimbabwe, Angola, Namibia and Uganda – had raised great hopes. At long last a cease-fire agreement offered a genuine, though fragile opportunity for a regional settlement.[54] A report from the US Peace Institute cautiously warned the signatories: "The Lusaka agreement provides a last exit on the region's highway to hell." A number of armed factions missed the exit, thus reducing to naught the labors of the Lusaka negotiators. Incessant discords among RCD factions and between them and their parent organizations made sure that the road to hell would remain wide open.

Among the many factions that have consistently turned away from all attempts to negotiate a way into a modus vivendi one of the most obdurate has been, and remains, the *Forces Démocratiques* pour la *Libération du Rwanda* (FDLR), a loosely knit Hutu-dominated refugee organization which, despite its internal splits, never ceased to pose a major threat to peace processes. To this maverick outfit, which often served Kagame as a convenient pretext for invading the Congo, we shall return in a moment.

The emergence of proxies

Meanwhile, further contributing to the fragmentation of the political chessboard, new actors emerged on the horizon in response to Kagame's prodding, and in full awareness of the benefits they stood to gain from the reshuffling of diplomatic cards.

Since the application of force failed to reduce the Congo to a client-state, why not look for client factions to act as surrogates? Candidates ran a wide gamut. But two deserve mention: Laurent Nkunda and Bosco Ntaganda, equally brutal in dealing with their enemies, and ultimately defeated by their vaulting ambitions.

Both are Tutsi, the first from North Kivu, the other from north Rwanda. Both have earned for themselves a fearsome reputation for the odious

[52] Author's files.
[53] *The Economist*, August 21, 2006.
[54] See Filip Reyntjens, *The Great African War: Congo and Regional Geopolitics, 1996–2006* (Cambridge, 2009), pp. 247–262.

crimes they committed against scores of Congolese civilians. Nkunda reportedly trained as a psychologist before he became pastor of a Pentecostal church (hence his badge "Rebel for Christ" offered by a visiting delegation of US Pentecostalists)[55] ended up joining one Tutsi-dominated faction after another. He started his military trajectory as a member of the RPF in Rwanda; he later joined the AFDL rebellion in eastern Congo ultimately rising to the rank of military commander of the RDC. Though formally integrated into the Congolese army he never ceased to act on his own, regardless of the consequences.

He was the first to draw attention from Human Rights Watch (HRW) for his involvement in the massacre of scores of civilians in Kisangani in 2002. Summing up the HRW findings, this is how David Van Reybrouck described what happened: "Dozens of young people from the poor neighborhoods were murdered. At the bridge over the Tshopo, two hundred policemen and soldiers were slaughtered and thrown into the river. They were tied up and had a gag stuffed in their mouths. Some of them were shot and killed or decapitated, others had their necks broken or were bayoneted."[56] No less abhorrent was his 2004 raid on Bukavu, when, with the aid of another Tutsi, Colonel Jules Mutebutsi, he briefly captured the provincial capital, at the cost of hundreds of civilians killed and wanton looting of private property.

What happened next tells us much about the way violence, once ignited, spreads across boundaries in a tit-for-tat process. Days after the Bukavu "incident" scores of Banyamulenge residents, fearing acts of vengeance, left the city to seek safer grounds in Burundi: no sooner had they assembled in a UN refugee camp in Gatumba, near Bujumbura, than groups of Hutu killers (most probably belonging to the *Forces Nationales de Libération* [FNL]) mounted a night-time attack, killing over a hundred, men, women and children. Unmoved by his responsibility in the Gatumba massacre Nkunda was now determined to carve out a fiefdom of his own in North Kivu as the head of the *Congrès national pour la défense du peuple* (CNDP), an oddly misleading label in view of the narrowness of its base and thinly veiled pro-Rwandan orientation.

Not until January 2009 was a deal struck between Kigali and Kinshasa that paved the way for Nkunda's undoing. In what caught many by surprise elements of the Rwandan armed forces would join the FARDC in joint military operations in eastern Congo against the Hutu-led FDLR and in return Kagame would pull the rug from under Nkunda's feet. This, in brief, was the crux of the agreement reached at the Nairobi conference in November 2008, also known as *Umoja Wety* (our Unity). CNDP troops, meanwhile, would be integrated into the FARDC so as to prevent their resurrection,

[55] For an excellent account of Nkunda's background and multiple military engagements and human rights violations, see Colette Braeckman, *Vers la deuxième indépendance du Congo* (Brussels, 2009), pp. 211–218.
[56] Van Reybrouck, *Congo*, p. 52.

a move which turned out to be a pious wish. At any rate, on January 22 Nkunda was finally arrested in Kigali, but not soon enough to prevent him from killing of over a hundred civilians in Kiwanja near Goma, while UN observers looked the other way. As a result of *Umoja* Wety a number of FDLR elements were flushed out from parts of North Kivu (Walikale, Rutshuru and Masisi), but at great cost for the civilian populations. Basically, little has changed for the bulk of the Congolese population, caught as it is, to quote from two reliable observers, "in a dialectic of structural violence and privatized governance that forms an essential impediment to genuine change and peace-building."[57]

Ntaganda's saga has much in common with Nkunda's. He joined the RPF in 1990 and fought side by side with him in the battles that brought Kagame to power. During the First Congo War (1996–1997) he joined the AFDL, and then he RDC in Goma. By 2002 he was sent north in the Ituri district of North Kivu where Hema and Lendu were tearing each other apart. Culturally related to the Tutsi, the Hema found a valuable ally in Ntaganda, who soon joined hands with the pro-Hema *Union des Patriotes Congolais* (UPC). In his capacity as head of military operations he is reported to have engaged in horrific cleansing operations against the Lendu. True to his nickname, Terminator took no prisoners. Villages were set aflame, women raped, children forcefully inducted into the UPC, militias. One journalist described him as a Tropical Frankenstein. His military career ended when, against all odds, and probably under US pressures, he agreed to surrender to the tender mercies of the International Criminal Court (ICC), where he is awaiting trial.[58] Before his luck ran out he played an important role in the transfer of large quantities of gold and coltan from Walikale (North Kivu) to Rwanda and became a familiar figure among the movers and shakers of the Houston-based petroleum giant Camac Energy.[59]

While Rwanda's role in the Congo wars has often been underplayed by outside observers, notably in the US, the villainies attributed to Kagame and his allies are widely remembered among many Congolese. Although he

---

[57] Koen Vlassenroot and Timothy Raemaekers, "Kivu's Intractable Security Conundrum," *African Affairs*, May 2009, p. 484.

[58] On November 7, 2019 Ntaganda was sentenced to 30 years in prison by the ICC for war crimes, including murder, rape, and sexual slavery. According to the prosecution,

> he was one of the most ruthless and cruel of the Congo's rebel leaders. His army had conscripted children and outfitted them with ill-fitting uniforms and AK-47. Female fighters some under age were made sex slaves. He was also accused of personally shooting and killing a Catholic priest, and for being responsible for the massacre of a village, not sparing women or babies.

> (*The New York Times*, November 8, 2019)

[59] On February 5, 2011 a cargo of 480 kilos of gold, valued at $20 million, was seized by the airport authorities in Goma from the American crew of a Gulfstream V jet rented by the Houston-based Camac Energy. Originating from the mines of Walikale, then under the control of Ntaganda, the gold shipment was later confiscated by the Kinshasa authorities after a pro forma trial handled by Congolese judges. See "RCD: des affaires louches en or massif," *Slate-Afrique*, April 5, 2011.

human losses inflicted on civilian populations vastly exceed by their scale and atrocities anything previously encountered in the continent, disagreements persist about numbers. The International Rescue Committee (IRC) mentions a death toll of 4.5 million between 1998 and 2008, that is only for the duration of the Second Congo War; but this figure has since been revised downward by one half. Nonetheless, the IRC figure is probably a fairly conservative estimate if one adds the losses in Rwanda and Burundi since 1993. Admittedly, the overwhelming proportion of estimated deaths were caused by malnutrition, disease, physical exhaustion, but even if battlefield casualties account for a small proportion of human losses, the lethal impact of the Congo wars boggles the mind.

Statistics are abstractions. At best they only convey an order of magnitude. What they miss are the countless human dramas – the unspeakable sufferings inflicted on individuals by other human beings.

Is it any surprise in these conditions if Congolese memories of Kagame's villainies should have reached nearly pathological proportions? The depth of Congolese Rwandaphobia was brought home to me when I was invited to give a talk at the *Institut Supérieur de Développement Rural* (ISDR) in Bukavu. The topic was "*Le manque d'Etat*" (The lack of a state). That I happened to show up late owing to the innumerable potholes on the way seemed to underscore the relevance of the subject. I said that much while offering a few words of apology and then moved to the heart of the discussion before concluding with a few comments on the 2006 elections. Imprudently, I made the point that the weakness of the Congolese state led to all sorts of irregularities, making it impossible for the Banyamulenge minority to gain a significant share of seats in the provincial assembly, pushing them into a corner. This is when the audience showed visible signs of unease. Adding insult to injury I added that, once the chips are down, the real test of a healthy democracy was the manner in which it treats its minorities. This was met with palpable skepticism. During the question period the discussion came to the role of Rwanda as the chief villain in the Congo's troubles. While admitting that much I also stressed the part of responsibility of Congolese actors. This is when the room exploded: how could I hold the Congolese responsible for their fate when Kagame, acting in cahoots with the CIA and the State Department, reaped millions of dollars' worth of mineral wealth stolen from the Congo? Why is the State Department throwing its weight behind Rwanda's murderer-in-chief while turning a blind eye to the crimes committed by his proxies? Why was so little done to stop Rwanda from meddling into the domestic affairs of the Congo, at a huge cost in human lives and resources? All of which are, of course, perfectly legitimate questions. But by then the audience was in no mood for a dispassionate discussion. The only practical response to the incipient pandemonium was to discreetly ask for the way out.

***

The quote at the beginning of this chapter underscores the uniquely burdensome legacy of Belgian colonial rule. Today, most politically conscious

Congolese would probably agree that despite intolerable constraints, Belgian imperialism pales into insignificance compared to the relentless efforts of Rwanda to penetrate, control, manipulate and exploit its huge, mineral-rich neighbor. But if we zero in on the situation in Rwanda on the eve of independence much of the blame for its tragic destiny can be found in the extraordinary mix of incoherence, contradictions and underhand maneuvering that figures so prominently in the record of the Belgian tutelle. This is not meant to deny the part played by African actors – from Kayibanda and Habyarimana to Kagame – in bringing disasters onto themselves and their own people. Nonetheless, there is little question that the single most important element in the background of the genocide in Rwanda and the 1972 genocidal massacres in Burundi – along with the collateral damage in the Congo – can be traced to the manipulative policies and brazen illegalities that have presided over the regime change engineered under the auspices of Colonel Guy Logiest, Rwanda's military resident in 1959–1960. This is the subject of the next chapter.

2 Rwanda 1959–1962
Where it all began

One might roam the wide world over and never find a place that is quite so fascinating or where the world seems so much at peace. Peace and contentment, those rare elements in the world today, rest and brood over the lotus-land of Ruanda!

— Alexander Barns, *An African Eldorado*, 1926

By 1959 the Lotus-land had mutated into a war zone, with tens of thousands running for their lives. No other event has had a more devastating impact on Rwanda's destinies than the Hutu revolution of 1959, a fact which is by now common knowledge among students of the Great Lakes. Not nearly as well known is that it carried far-reaching consequences beyond the boundaries of Rwanda. I for one never imagined that, besides sowing the seeds of genocidal violence in neighboring Burundi, the events of 1959–1962 would carry in germ as it were the violent upheavals set in motion by Kagame's refugee warriors. Nor, of course, could he have anticipated his stunning political destiny as a four-year-old toddler following his mother's footsteps to evade revolutionary violence.

Although there are many threads leading to the 1959 insurgency, its genesis is inseparable from the abrupt shift of policies that marks the terminal phase of Belgian rule in Rwanda. Since much of this sequence of events has been dealt with at some length in my book on Rwanda and Burundi, I shall limit myself here to a brushstroke summary.[1]

For 36 years – first as a Mandate under the League of Nations and later as a Trusteeship under the UN – Rwanda was administered according to the principle of indirect rule, which in effect meant not only the recognition of traditional authorities as the only viable intermediary between the colonial state and the "native" populations, but, more importantly, the

---

[1] René Lemarchand, *Rwanda and Burundi* (London and New York, 1970). Although the book received the Melville Herskovits Award from the African Studies Association, it received scant attention from the wider public, which, given the less than inspiring title, is not surprising. Who would want to curl up with a 562-page monograph on two little-known minuscule states in Central Africa? The title I had initially suggested to my editor, Colin Legum, was *A Tale of Two Kingdoms*, but this was promptly turned down on the grounds that the book was part of a series running from Algeria to Zimbabwe.

preservation – or, more accurately, the refashioning – of Tutsi supremacy. Only in 1957, with the proclamation of the *Manifeste des Bahutu*, did the prospect of a significant policy change come into view. It would take another two years for the Belgian tutelle to take concrete steps to put in practice the agenda suggested in the list of grievances set forth in this pivotal document. By then, however, Rwanda was already in the early stages of a bitter civil war. By coming out squarely on the side of the nascent Hutu elites, and turning a blind eye to the sufferings of tens of thousands of Tutsi civilians pushed out of their homes, the Belgian authorities sowed the seeds of a seemingly endless regional conflict between Hutu and Tutsi. The 1994 genocide is perhaps the most tragic illustration of the unforeseen consequences of the decisions made by the Belgian authorities on the ground (as distinct from the Brussels-based decision-makers). Nor would it be the last.

This is admittedly an oversimplified picture. To speak of a straight Hutu–Tutsi conflict is to gloss over important nuances and differences of attitude and ideologies within each group; the options facing the Belgian administration were not taken in a vacuum, independently of local pressures and circumstances, or free of the constraints arising from the international context; and if the plight of the Tutsi expellees cannot be left out of the accounting, they were evidently not the only victims. So were the Hutu killed in retaliation. To these and other considerations we shall return. But first a few comments about the change of course initiated by the colonial authorities during the last years of their trusteeship.

Sins of omission

The most serious criticism any one can make of Belgian policies in Rwanda is their failure to respond constructively to the surge of new social forces in the years following WWII. No serious effort was made to bring Hutu and Tutsi closer together within a common institutional framework; nothing was done to promote a measure of social integration, to facilitate the recruitment of Hutu elements in existing advisory councils, or to alter the long-standing official perception of Hutu elements as inherently incapable of meeting minimal standards of administrative competence. The guiding principle for such policies was tersely summed up in 1936 by Msgr. Classe, a highly respected and influential figure, in a stern admonition against any attempt to eliminate "the Tutsi caste." "A revolution of that nature would lead the entire state directly into anarchy and to bitter anti-European Communism... Generally speaking we have no chiefs who are better qualified, more intelligent, more active, more capable of appreciating progress and more fully accepted by the people than the Tutsi."[2] His statement carries, retrospectively, a prophetic ring: no other group was seen as more dangerously left-leaning and anti-Belgian than the small group of radical Tutsi

---

[2] Lemarchand, *Rwanda and Burundi*, p. 73.

elites who stood at the forefront of the anti-colonial crusade in the late 1950s and early 1960s.

The pioneering role played by Tutsi politicians in the awakening of a nationalist consciousness is hardly surprising. As the privileged recipients of Western education, they possessed the intellectual tools to challenge the colonial authorities on their own terms. They represented the majority of the indigenous clergy and served as the backbone of the "native administration." And while the first *mwami* (king), Musinga, did not quite meet the moral standards of the Catholic Church, and ended his life in exile in eastern Congo after being replaced in 1931 by a more pliant candidate, the monarchy as an institution stood as a critically important symbol of legitimacy.

What the Belgians introduced under the guise of "indirect rule" was in fact a radical restructuring of the traditional society. For what used to be a highly complex, more subtly nuanced set of social hierarchies, emerged a rigidly racialized society. Unmindful of the disparities of wealth and status among Tutsi, ethnicities were calcified into rigid categories. Where the Tutsi were treated globally as a separate high-status group, the Hutu were similarly lumped together as an undifferentiated laboring mass of hewers of wood and drawers of water.

Although European misperceptions and prejudices played a determining role in hardening the Hutu–Tutsi fault line, the rift was present in Rwanda long before the advent of European rule. This is brilliantly demonstrated by Jan Vansina. What really crystallized ethnic tensions was the imposition under *mwami* Rwabugiri of corvée labor (*uburetwa*) on the Hutu as a group, but not on the Tutsi herders. This, writes Vansina, "was the straw that broke the camel's back. Very soon it provoked a rift that was to divide society from top to bottom into hierarchical and opposed social categories, henceforth labeled Hutu and Tutsi."[3] What European rule did was to formalize, distort, and calcify a mode of stratification that was already in evidence in the mid-twentieth century.

Contributing significantly to such misperceptions were the writings of European missionaries, whose views of the Tutsi were strongly influenced by nineteenth-century ethnographic speculations about "Hamitic races." Typical in this regard is Father Pagès's book, *Le Rwanda. Un royaume Hamite au centre de l'Afrique*, published in 1933, which inspired a number of administrators, missionaries and journalists. In this world of fantasy Tutsi are defined as Hamites whose ancestral roots were in Abyssinia; their foreign origins give us a clue to their cultural superiority.

The imaginings spawned by the Hamitic hypothesis covered a wide gamut, from Catholic clerics to colonial administrators and journalists, but the underlying theme remained unchanged. In the words of Léon Classe, Vicar Apostolic in 1927, "the Batutsi are superb men, with fine and regular

---

[3] Jan Vansina, *Antecedents to Modern Rwanda: The Nyiginya Kingdom* (Madison, 2003), p. 134.

features, with something of the Aryan and the Semite." Johannes Van den Burgt, an eminent linguist and missionary, was equally impressed: "We can see Caucasian skulls and beautiful Greek profiles side-by-side with Semitic and even Jewish features." Another missionary, Francois Ménard, noted, "The Tutsi are closer to the White man than the Negro... He is a European under a black skin." As for Pierre Ryckmans, the first Belgian governor of Burundi and later Governor General of the Congo, "The Batutsi are destined to reign... over the inferior races that surround them."[4] To put it in a nutshell, the Tutsi are a people apart physically and culturally, exceptionally gifted and intellectually more advanced than the backward "indigenous" masses over which they are destined to rule.

The Hamitic myth became a standard feature of colonial literature, projecting a conception of authority patently at odds with historical realities. While reinforcing the racial preconceptions of the Church, and by implication of the colonial state, the Hamitic frame also shaped the views of the indigenous clergy. A case in point is the late Abbé Alexis Kagame (no relation to Paul Kagame). Though reluctant to endorse the more outrageous versions of the Hamitic vulgate, his sympathy for its underlying premise is clear. In his private correspondence he gives free rein to his nationalist urgings. His plea for hastening the pace of independence is inscribed in the title of one of his most widely read contributions, *Le code des institutions du Rwanda pré-colonial* (Brussels, 1946). The juridical phrasing is no coincidence. Traditional Rwanda was already a highly sophisticated political system long before the advent of colonial rule. The country's legal codes were already in place. All that is needed to insure a successful transition to independence is to unearth these long-buried institutions, all of which contain within themselves the seeds of political modernity. Again, the message conveyed by his *Inganji Karinga* (The Sources of Progress) is straightforward: if

---

[4] The long-standing attribution of Jewish roots to Tutsi identities received a fresh impetus after the 1994 genocide, and found expression in a variety of ways. One example is the email I received from a Christian visitor to Rwanda, Donna Bosn, who, after congratulating me on my article titled "Disconnecting the Threads: Rwanda and the Holocaust Reconsidered" (see Chapter 8 in my collection of essays, *The Dynamics of Violence in Central Africa*, 2009), wrote

> I have to tell you that I am convinced the threads can never be disconnected, because after what I have learned I believe that the Tutsi really are God's chosen people... They should go home to Israel the land given to the Jewish people by the God of Israel.

(Author's files)

Even more bizarre was the creation in 2005 of a formal organization, the Havila Institute, headed by a self-described prince from Burundi, Yocanan Bwejeri, whose proclaimed objective was to demonstrate the Jewish origins of the Tutsi via their Kushite ascendency in Ethiopia. See *Havila Annals*, June 2006, "Havila Revolutionary Paradigm: Deconstructing the Hamitic Myth as CounterHistory." See also *Chroniques de Havila*, Organe d'information de l'Institut, Mai 2010, "La Question des Juifs Batutsi." Each of the quotes in the paragraph above are borrowed from Nigel Eltingham's excellent discussion of the Hamitic hypothesis in "'Invaders Who Have Stolen the Country': The Hamitic Hypothesis, Race and the Rwandan Genocide," *Social Identities*, vol. 12, no. 4 (July 2006), p. 432.

any lesson can be learned about the pathways to progress it can only come from Rwanda's age-old traditions and institutions.

By the mid-1950s the winds of change were beginning to be felt across a wide spectrum, including the core institutions of the Catholic Church. A whole new set of attitudes about the responsibilities of the European clergy began to take root. Christian social democracy introduced a new ethos, based on democracy, social justice, and political equality. A new generation of missionaries, anxious to put into practice a more generous conception of their evangelic message, replaced the older phalanx of conservative prelates. Their immediate objective was to ease the constraints of Tutsi predominance to facilitate access to education for Hutu elements. For this they could rely on the militant support of the newly appointed bishop of Kabgaye, Msgr. Perraudin, whose Swiss origins appeared entirely in synch with his deeply held democratic values. The gospel of democracy also found a receptive echo in the higher reaches of the colonial administration. With the appointment of Liberal civil servants (in the European sense of the term) who, for the most part, were more than willing to hold in check their anti-clerical biases, a new basis was found for the Church to work hand in hand with representatives of the state.

Cautiously at first, Rwanda's democratic opening made it possible for a growing number of Hutu elites to make their mark in life as journalists, medical auxiliaries, clerks, civil servants, and members of the clergy. Under the editorship of Grégoire Kayibanda, the monthly newspaper, *Kimanyateka*, became the sounding board for the grievances shared by the Hutu community. Social justice was the theme that resonated through its pages, giving ample coverage to the abuses associated with the monopoly of power exercised by Tutsi chiefs, sub-chiefs and judges. As the social climate became more permissive, freedom of expression found new outlets.

The Bahutu Manifesto of March 24, 1957 had the effect of a bombshell. Its full title seemed innocuous enough, "Note on the social aspect of the indigenous racial problem in Rwanda" (*Note sur l'aspect social du problème racial indigène au Rwanda*), but the depth of grievances set forth, and the remedies proposed, sent tremors through the colonial establishment.[5] At the root of the discrimination suffered by the Hutu, we are told, is a two-stage system of colonialism, one exercised by Europeans and the other by the Tutsi over the Hutu. Of the two the latter is the more oppressive, reflecting the age-old prejudices of the Hamitic minority. The problem is both social and racial. As long as they are denied access to education the Hutu will continue to suffer discrimination, but an even more daunting obstacle is racial prejudice. The antagonism that separates one race from the other defies a quick solution for the differences are of a biological nature. The Tutsi are settlers of Hamitic origins, which in effect means that the Hutu are doubly

---

[5] For the full text of the manifesto along with additional documents and commentaries, see Les Dossiers du CRISP, *Rwanda Politique, 1958–1960*, Documents présentés par F. Nkundabangenzi (Brussels, 1961).

colonized. All things considered, the biggest menace facing the Hutu is the risk of an all-too-hasty dismantling of Belgian overrule that would leave them at the mercy of a Hamitic minority. By a curious twist of fate the Hamitic myth, once cited as a reliable cultural trait in support of indirect rule, had now morphed into a threatening Hamitic yoke.

The counter-attack came on May 17, 1958, in the form of a vehement rebuttal of the manifesto by group of Tutsi hard-liners closely connected to the court. Self-described as *bagaragu bakuru b'i Bgami*, the "high-ranking servants of the court," the gist of their message is best captured in the following phrase, "The relations between us (Tutsi) and them (Hutu) have since time immemorial been based on bondage. There is therefore no basis for friendship between us and them." Again, "since our kings have conquered the country of the Bahutu, killing their kinglets, and thus turning the Bahutu into slaves, how can they pretend to be our brothers?"[6]

Radically different in their inspiration and conclusions the two statements give us a sense of the social distance between the representatives of the two groups. They evidently do not reflect the range of ideas and sensibilities within each community. But they are suggestive of the parameters around which the ensuing civil strife unfolded, pulling the protagonists into opposite camps, and confronting the Belgian authorities with a Hobson's choice.

A peasant revolt gone awry

What became known euphemistically as Rwanda's "social revolution" began as a *jacquerie*, in short, a peasant revolt; it quickly developed into a Hutu–Tutsi conflict, and ultimately into a Belgian-assisted regime change, leading to the forced expulsion of tens of thousands of Tutsi families.

The term *jacquerie*, borrowed from the lexicon of French peasant rebellions, is generally used to underscore the contrast with revolutionary movements. The former have "strictly limited aims," writes Chalmers Johnson, such as "the restoration of lost rights or the removal of specific grievances… A jacquerie is rebellious rather than revolutionary… it aims at the restoration of legitimate government rather than making unprecedented structural changes."[7] Typically, the Hutu uprising did not seek the overthrow of the monarchy but the return of their *mwami* to take the defense of their legitimate rights against the "abuses of the bad chiefs" and the evil-minded Belgians.

Only if we recall the earth-shaking events of 1959 can we begin to understand the roots of the Hutu *jacquerie*. On July 25, 1959 the Rwandans learned over the radio the devastating news of the death of *mwami* Mutara

---

[6] Cited in Jean-Pierre Chrétien and Marcel Kabanda, *Rwanda: Racisme et Génocide* (Paris, 2016), p. 133; for a summary of the key points in the Bahutu Manifesto, see Ibid., pp. 128–132.

[7] Chalmers Johnson, *Revolution and the Social System* (Stanford, 1964), pp. 31–32.

Rudahigwa in Bujumbura, immediately after a routine medical examination by a Belgian doctor. Received as a shock by the population, the announcement unleashed immediate suspicions among Tutsi politicians that "the Belgians killed our king!" The atmosphere of uncertainty surrounding the *mwami*'s death continued unabated long after his burial on July 28. On that day occurred another game-changing event, the unexpected nomination, like a bolt out of the blue, of his successor, Rudahigwa's half-brother, Jean-Baptiste Ndahindurwa, better known as Kigeri. Present at the funeral were scores of Hutu and Tutsi who had come to pay their last respects to their deceased sovereign. A host of pressing questions arose: how would the Belgian governor, Jean-Paul Harroy, react? Would the Mwima *coup de théâtre* be accepted for what it was intended, a unilateral transfer of power? What of the future relationship between the new *mwami* and the Belgian authorities in Kigali and Brussels?

It was in this highly volatile climate that the Hutu uprising broke out on November 1, a day remembered as All Saints' Day. The spark that set off the explosion was a relatively minor incident, involving a popular Hutu sub-chief from Gitarama, Dominique Mbonyamutwa, reported to have been attacked by Tutsi militants affiliated to the newly created *Union Nationale Rwandaise* (Unar); this was enough to ignite a violent reaction from the Hutu population. From Gitarama, violence and arson spread to other areas. Thousands of Tutsi *rugos* (huts) were pillaged and set aflame. This is how a UN report described the scenes: "The incendiaries set off in bands of ten. Armed with matches and paraffin which the indigenous inhabitants use in large quantities for their lamps, they pillaged the Tutsi houses they passed on their way and set fire to them. On their way they would enlist other incendiaries to follow the procession, while the first recruits too exhausted to continue would give up and return home. Thus day after day the fires spread from hill to hill."[8] (In contrast with this spontaneous, uncoordinated display of violence, the Tutsi repression was not only better organized, but more specifically related to political aims. The main target was the Hutu leadership, and more specifically the leaders of the newly founded Hutu parties, widely regarded as the principal trouble-makers.)

Already in 1957 Grégoire Kayibanda had launched the *Mouvement Social Hutu* (MSH), which did not prevent one of its key members, Joseph Gitera, from creating a dissident, somewhat less restrictive organization, the *Association pour la promotion sociale de la masse*, in short *Aprosoma*. In 1959, sensing the need for a more tightly organized movement, Kayibanda transformed the MSH into a more explicitly labeled *Parti du mouvement de l'émancipation Hutu* (Parmehutu).

With the emergence of ethnically based parties, the peasant rebellion moved into a new phase, signaling a more sustained, ideologically oriented face-off between Hutu republicans and Tutsi monarchists. It began with

---

[8] Cited in Lemarchand, "The Coup in Rwanda," in Robert Rotberg and Ali Mazrui eds., *Protest and Power in Black Africa* (New York, 1970), p. 904.

the rapid absorption of many of the rural insurgents into the ranks of the *Parmehutu*, followed almost immediately by a brutal Tutsi-led repression organized around the *mwami*'s court, in Nyanza.

A man with a mission: orchestrating regime change

Confronted with scenes of violence instigated by the growing militancy of Hutu party activists and the rise of vehemently anti-Belgian feelings among a large segment of the Tutsi population, it didn't take long for Governor Jean-Paul Harroy to appoint a military proconsul to act as Military Resident. The man picked for the job was Colonel Guy Logiest, who served in the Congo as a *Force Publique* officer but whose knowledge of Rwanda was virtually nil, limited, we are told, to what he learned from Father Pagès's 1933 Hamitic gospel, *Un royaume hamite au centre de l'Afrique*. His legacy, as will be seen, has been immensely more consequential than had been anticipated when he assumed the responsibility of restoring order to a country bordering on chaos.

In the interest of full disclosure let me say that my first and only encounter with Guy Logiest was the shortest I've ever had with any Belgian official. As I came into his office I tried to explain the purpose of my visit. Given that I was writing a book on the history of Rwanda and Burundi I would be grateful if he could educate me on his involvement in the transfer of power to a Hutu government in the months immediately preceding independence. His answer, in one word, brought my visit to an abrupt end: "Sortez!" (Get out!). If what follows bears traces of this unsettling contre-temps, the reader will know why.

The newly appointed *Résident Militaire* explains the purpose of his mission in his *apologia pro vita sua*, titled, tellingly, *Ma mission au Rwanda: Un blanc dans la bagarre Hutu-Tutsi* (Brussels, 1988). What he called a *bagarre*, a scuffle, turned out to be a conflict of a far more serious and complex nature. Treating it as a "scuffle" speaks volumes for his mission's shortcomings. Just as revealing is the iconography of the cover: a representation, in vivid colors, of the royal drum, the so-called Kalinga, symbol of the monarchy, bearing the blood-stained wrappings which, according to legend, contained the genital remains of the Hutu chiefs defeated by Tutsi conquerors. A quick glance at the image is enough to disabuse the reader of all illusions about the author's choice in discriminating between friends and foes.

His aim was twofold. To quote from Professor Stengers's sympathetic preface, the immediate priority was "to bring to an end the Hutu's *grande jacquerie* unleashed against the Tutsi, and by the same token stop the retaliatory moves by Tutsi against Hutu." The means employed by this "pure neophyte," to use Stengers's phrase, were as simple as they were drastic. On November 17, 1959, addressing a meeting of territorial administrators he announced his decision to dismiss in one fell swoop all Tutsi chiefs and sub-chiefs and replace them, "systematically, en masse," by Hutu elements. Had a different choice been made, Stengers continues, more in line with

Belgium's age-old policies, "the Tutsi would have remained in control of Rwanda's transition to independence, and it is under their domination that today's Rwanda would be living, the Rwanda of 1988."[9] The Rwanda of 2019 is back under Tutsi domination, but had a wiser decision been made in 1959 could it conceivably have been spared the agonies of 1994?

In any event, the appointment of some two hundred Hutu chiefs and sub-chiefs – provisionally called interim authorities – inaugurated a period of great uncertainty, marked by considerable incompetence and mutual ethnic provocation. Countless examples of administrative incapacity were reported, along with rising levels of violence. Hundreds of *rugos* were set aflame, their owners killed or expelled. Faced with a situation that threatened to get out of hand, Logiest made his position clear in January 1960: "What is our goal? It is to accelerate the politicization of Rwanda... We must undertake an action in favor of the Hutu who live in a state of ignorance and under oppressive influences. By virtue of this situation we are led to take sides. We cannot stay neutral or and sit."[10] Far from being neutral or passive, the territorial administrators promptly took note of Logiest's instructions. The result was a major uptick in the flight of Tutsi refugees from their native regions. From about 7,000 at the end of November 1959 their number rose to 22,000 by April 1960. In premonitory previews of what happened in 1994 many sought refuge in mission stations, churches, or government buildings, or wandered across the countryside in a vain quest for food and security. The mere presence on the hills of thousands of Tutsi refugees, most of them lacking the barest necessities of life, had a multiplier effect on ethnic tensions. Incitements to violence from the *Parmehutu* zealots encouraged Hutu extremists to go on the rampage, while supporters of the stridently anti-Belgian *Union Nationale Rwandaise* (Unar) did everything they could to exploit to their advantage the refugee situation.

Traveling through Astrida (Butare) in September 1960, one scene in particular is etched in my memory. A Hutu-led raid had just been launched against Tutsi civilians. Two children had been killed, speared to the ground near a smoldering hut. The Belgian paratroopers in charge of rounding up the assailants were assisted by helicopters flying at low altitude over the hills. In the course of the operations one of the helicopters crashed over a hill-slope, only a short distance from the main road. A few minutes later, a crowd of some 500 Hutu was gathered on the scene of the accident. Aside from the sympathy shown by the Hutu helpers to the injured crew, what was remarkable was the rapidity with which hundreds of Hutu virtually materialized out of thin air. From the evidence, insuring the protection of hundreds of Tutsi families dispersed in the countryside proved impossible, notwithstanding the presence of Belgian paratroopers in charge of maintaining "peace and order."

---

[9] Guy Logiest, *Mission au Rwanda: Un Blanc dans la Bagarre Hutu-Tutsi* (Brussels, 1988), p. 2.

[10] Lemarchand, "The Coup in Rwanda," p. 909.

In an effort to move the transfer of power a step further, Logiest was now entrusted with another mission, this time as Special Resident invested with almost unlimited powers to handle the local elections in ways that would leave little doubt about the outcome. The aim was to replace the hastily appointed interim authorities with elected mayors (burgomasters) and local councilors (*conseillers communaux*). Predictably, the communal elections of June and July 1960 saw a landslide victory of Hutu candidates, with the Parmehutu claiming 70 percent of the votes and the majority of the 229 seats of burgomaster. No effort was spared to cast discredit upon Unar candidates, seen as the incarnation of racial hegemony and monarchical oppression.

By then, however, another threat loomed on the horizon: the UN. The triennial visits the Trusteeship Council were viewed with undisguised contempt by the Special Resident. On his visit to Rwanda shortly before the elections the head of the UN mission, Mason Sears, was derisively dismissed by Logiest as a naively anti-colonial bumbler – "like every good American he is plagued by an anti-colonial virus in his veins... When it comes to Rwanda he just doesn't get it (*manifestement il n'a rien compris à la situation*)."[11] What infuriated the Special Resident was the UN's recommendation to postpone the date of the elections so as to make a last attempt at encouraging reconciliation between Hutu and Tutsi, a legitimate worry considering the continuing bloodshed and destruction of Tutsi property.

The forthcoming legislative elections, to be held in early 1961, prompted similar concerns on the part of the UN, some of which were also shared by Brussels. In a display of goodwill the Special Resident held consultations with the minister of African affairs, and this was followed by pro forma attempts at reconciliation during conferences in Brussels and Ostend, from which nothing tangible emerged. As it turned out, other plans were afoot.

The coup of Gitarama

The most brazenly illegal move taken by Logiest occurred on January 21, 1961 in the town of Gitarama, in central Rwanda. Since the early hours of the morning dozens of trucks converged on the main square, where they disgorged their passengers, some three thousand recently elected communal councilors and burgomasters, summoned, they were told, to discuss matters concerning the maintenance of peace and order before the legislative elections. But many of those present suspected, with reason, that a more momentous decision was in the offing. The first speaker, Joseph Rwasibo, gave more than a hint of what was about to happen when, after a long diatribe against the monarchy, he asked rhetorically, "what will be the solution given to the problem of the monarchy? When shall we abandon the realm of the provisional? It is incumbent upon you, burgomasters and councilors, to answer these questions." The answer they gave was unambiguous. Not

[11] Logiest, *Mission au Rwanda*, pp. 129–130.

only did they unanimously vote to abolish the monarchy and proclaim the republic, but, sitting as a constituent assembly, they proceeded to co-opt among themselves the members of the Legislative Assembly. The next order of business was to elect the president of the republic and a prime minister, along with a cabinet of ten members. With Grégoire Kayibanda co-opted as prime minister, later to become president of the republic, the coup of Gitarama – in defiance of the UN recommendations, and in total disregard of the consequences – concluded the regime change process set in motion in November 1959.

The plotters succeeded brilliantly in circumventing the recommendations of the UN. No longer would they have to worry about postponing the date of the elections in the interest of a cooling-off period (which they feared could only play to Unar's advantage), or declaring amnesty measures for political prisoners. As Logiest later admitted, while the idea of a de facto proclamation of the republic by way of a coup came from Kayibanda, without his help Gitarama would never have happened: "I promised to help organize the operation, the transport of the participants, the construction of a podium, the setting up of loudspeakers, and I asked him to swear never to reveal what we had agreed on." In short, mission accomplished: "my active role was about to come to an end. I was no longer indispensable."[12] Except for one thing – the decisions taken at Gitarama would have to be formalized through legislative elections and a referendum on the future of the monarchy, both to be held in September 1961. On both counts the Special Resident could help. Not only would he have to account for his actions to the metropolitan authorities in Brussels, whose sense of dismay was no secret, but also to the UN.

Even more decisive was his role in ensuring a Hutu victory at the polls. With 2,200 metropolitan troops on the ground, half of them paratroopers," assisted by seven helicopters and eight transport planes, the maintenance of order" meant in effect throwing the full weight of the tutelle behind one group of electors against another. The results came as no surprise. With 35 of the 44 seats in the legislative assembly, against seven for Unar, the Parmehutu enjoyed unfettered control of the legislature. Though predictable, their electoral triumph, with 83 percent of the votes, did not go unchallenged from the international media. The UN Trusteeship Council, outmaneuvered, "could only bleat," wrote Colin Waugh, "albeit with prescience that an old oppressive regime had just been replaced by another one."[13]

Just how oppressive the new power-holders could become is made clear in the press reports covering the 1961 elections. At every polling station, in every commune, scenes of mayhem were depicted. This is how the correspondent of the *Sunday Times* (London), Richard Cox, described what he saw: "Between August and September 1961 gangs of Parmehutu youth

---

[12] Logiest, *Mission au Rwanda*, pp. 190–192.
[13] Colin M. Waugh, *Paul Kagame and Rwanda: Power Genocide and the Rwandan Patriotic Front* (London, 2004), p. 237.

roamed the steep hills of Rwanda intimidating nationalists, threatening any-one who voted in the referendum to keep the monarchy with death, burn-ing huts. In the Astrida (Butare) region alone there were over 150 deaths, three thousand huts were burnt, and 22,000 refugees came into Astrida. The violence spread to Nyanza, traditional seat of the king, to Kigali and finally, in a wave of terror on the eve of the elections, to the northeast region of Kibungu. Despite the vast troop reinforcements, despite armed police, despite every modern method of control, the administrators and officers on the spot were 'unable' to bring the trouble to a halt... Whatever (Minister of Foreign Affairs) Spaak may have ordered, it is clear that the lower ranks of the administration disobeyed. Even the country's governor and senior officials deliberately allowed the intimidation against the nationalists and the monarchists to continue and made certain of the republican victory they wanted... On the election day I visited a catholic mission inside Kigali where 4,000 refugees were sheltering. Less than 24 hours earlier the Par-mehutu told the Fathers that after the election they would not hesitate to attack the mission and root out the refugees... Even before the elections the Parmehutu declared their intention to run all the nationalists and monar-chists out of the country. Within a week of the results hundreds were pour-ing across the borders of Tanganyika, Uganda and Burundi. Racial hatred has been stirred up with a vengeance... It is unforgivable that a power administering on behalf of the UN should have conspired to leave behind such a terrible legacy."[14]

The fallout

There is nothing in the history of colonial rule comparable to the violent regime change engineered by the Belgian authorities on the eve of Rwanda's independence. The consequences have been earth-shaking both within and outside Rwanda, resulting in tens of thousands of civilians killed because of their suspected ties with or sympathy for those Tutsi refugee warriors who became known as *inyenzi* (cockroaches).

How many Tutsi families were forced to seek asylum in neighboring states is impossible to tell. The most reliable figures are those available from the UN Economic Commission for Africa. By 1964, two years after Rwan-da's independence, Uganda was host to 54,000 refugees, the Congo 54,000, Burundi 34,000, Tanzania 12,000. Out of the total of 154,000 refugees, the overwhelming majority were Tutsi, though a few Hutu did follow their "patrons" [*shebuja*] in exile, as I found out on a trip to North Kivu in 1965. How many became actively involved in refugee movements, where, and with what consequences is again impossible to determine. What is clear is that none of those early resistance movements succeeded in wresting control from the new Hutu-dominated government. Some nearly did, as

[14] Richard Cox, *Sunday Times*, November 1961, quoted by Barnabas Bahizi at the 1270th meeting of the UN Fourth Committee, XVI, 1962).

happened in December 1963, when a group of armed refugees pushed their
way northwards from Burundi, before being intercepted and defeated by
the Rwandan National Guard (RNG). The revenge killings inside Rwanda,
as we shall see, suggest a frightening parallel to the 1994 bloodbath.

For all the rave reviews received by Scholastique Mukasonga's
heart-breaking autobiographical narrative,[15] the term *inyenzi* has yet to
become a household name. There is no point in challenging the uncritical
use of the term (cockroach), imputed to Hutu politicians to cast discredit
on all Tutsi civilians inside Rwanda. Contrary to a common belief, however,
the term was is by no means intended as an insult to vilify the Tutsi as a
group. It is an acronym of *Ingangurarugo yiyemeje kuba ingenzi*, meaning
"Combatant of the royal militia *Ingangurarugo* whose motto is we are the
best," a term borrowed from Rwanda's dynastic folklore by Tutsi to refer
to those refugee combatants, most of them members of Unar, who engaged
in armed raids across borders in hopes of bringing down the Kayibanda
government.

From March 1961 to November 1966 no fewer than eight major *inyenzi*
attacks were launched from Tanzania, Uganda, Burundi, and the Congo.
The deadliest was organized from Burundi on December 21, 1963. The
assailants overran the military camp at Gako, stoking up on arms and
ammunition, and went straight to the refugee camp at Nyamata, where
they received an enthusiastic welcome from the Tutsi refugee population.
According to some observers, they wasted precious time when they decided
to pause for celebrations, and he libations offered for the occasion probably did not improve their marksmanship either. By then their ranks had
swollen to well over a thousand. But by the time they came almost within
reach of Kigali they were confronted with several units of the Rwandan
National Guard (RNG) armed with mortars and semi-automatic weapons
and under the command of Belgian officers. In a matter of hours, the attack-
ers were routed, suffering heavy casualties. Far more devastating were the
losses suffered by Tutsi civilians at the hands of Hutu burgomasters in the
days ahead.

The killings began on December 23, in the prefecture of Gikongoro, a
bastion of Tutsi opposition in central Rwanda, at the instigation of a local
prefect, André Nkeramugaba, who, addressing a meeting of burgomasters,
is reported to have said: "We need to defend ourselves. The only way to do
it is to paralyze the Tutsi. How? They must be killed!"[16] This was the signal
for the slaughter. Armed with clubs, machetes and spears, Hutu killers proceeded to exterminate every Tutsi in sight, men women and children. In the
prefecture of Gikongoro an estimated 5,000 Tutsi were wiped out. Worse
was yet to come. According to the World Council of Churches, between

---

[15] Scholastique Mukasonga, *Cockroaches* (New York, 2016), translated from the French,
Inyenzi ou les cafards (Paris, 2006).
[16] Lemarchand, *Rwanda and Burundi*, pp. 223–224.

10,000 and 14,000 Tutsi were killed during these appalling outbursts of ethnic hatred – and fear.

Writing years later, I tried to capture the horrifying scenes related by eyewitnesses. "One missionary later recounted how a group of Hutu hacked the breasts of a Tutsi woman, and as she lay lying forced the dismembered parts down the throats of her children, before her eyes. Robert Conley of the *New York Times* wrote that on one Tutsi hilltop the massacre went on all night, prompting one missionary to say – still stammering from shock – "it was beyond belief – screams, it went on hour after hour." "In one locality more than one hundred Tutsi women and children were reported to have voluntarily drowned themselves in the Nybariongo river in a suicidal attempt to escape the clutches of attacking mobs of Hutu The impression from various eyewitness reports is one of unspeakable brutality. Popular participation in violence created a kind of collective catharsis through which years of pent-up hatreds seemed to find an outlet."

In words that have since been repeatedly quoted – more often than not out of context – I turned to the British philosopher Bertrand Russell: he described the events as "the most horrible and systematic human massacre we have had occasion to witness since the extermination of the Jews by the Nazi." The Holy See echoed his statement in a broadcast of February 10, 1964, referring to "the most terrible and systematic genocide since the genocide of the Jews by Hitler."[17] Clearly, the official estimate of 750 casualties cited by the Rwanda Radio was patently inaccurate. Nor was any mention made of the summary execution of a number of remarkably talented Tutsi politicians in the sinister jail of Ruhengeri, in northern Rwanda. Though largely unremembered, this episode is one of the saddest consequences of the aborted invasion. Over a dozen were executed – some say on orders of Belgian officers – most of them affiliated to the Unar or to the moderate *Rassemblement Démocratique Rwandais* (Rader), including Etienne Afrika (Unar), Joseph Rutsindintwarane (Unar), Michel Rwagasana (Unar), Prosper Bwanakweri (Rader), Lazare Ndazaro (Rader). Their deaths marked the end of the non-violent opposition to the Kayibanda dictatorship.

Most surprisingly, coming from the man who claimed to have liberated the Hutu from the yoke of an oppressive, feudalistic minority, not a word is said in Logiest's memoir of the tragic sequence of events that followed his experiment in regime change. Nor indeed of the overthrow in 1973 of a regime, whose birth owed so much to his personal efforts to legitimize the illegal.

The part of responsibility borne by Logiest in opening the way to this "terrible and systematic massacre" is, of course, shared by Jean-Paul Harroy, the resident general, whose complicity is undeniable. This is how he explained his decision to look the other way: "Let me now make a half-confession (*des demi-aveux*): I never made a major effort to know. If something was going on (*si quelque chose se tramait*), I preferred not to know. That

---

[17] Lemarchand, *Rwanda and Burundi*, p. 224.

sums up the nature of my contacts with Guy Logiest. I just listened to what he wanted to tell me. I honestly believe that he sensed that I'd rather not know all that he knew, and that it suited him perfectly to satisfy my tacit wish. Thus, let me be clear, from him I learned nothing."[18] Quite aside from the level of cynicism conveyed by Harroy's comment, there can be no question that he alone is responsible for the patent illegality of the methods used to implement the transfer of power, a fact that did not go unnoticed by Minister of Foreign Affairs Spaak. "Colonel," asked Spaak disingenuously in the course of an informal exchange at his home in 1961, "how did you manage to organize the revolution in Rwanda? I've always been curious to know how revolutions break out and above all why some succeed and others fail," in turn eliciting a similarly ambivalent response: "Did Mr. Spaak really imagine that I could single-handedly lead the Hutu people to revolt against their Tutsi masters?"[19]

Yet nothing was done to investigate how Logiest's behind-the-scenes maneuverings, so patently counterproductive, have contributed, directly or indirectly, to the blood-stained trajectory beginning with the events of 1963. Again, while their ample reasons to believe that his role in Rwanda created the conditions that led to the 1972 genocidal bloodshed in Burundi, at no time did the Belgian government seriously envisage a judicial inquest to shed light on the connection between the two. One wonders, however, whether anyone in the government was even aware of the existence of any such relationship.

For an insight of how the Rwanda tragedy impacted on Tutsi perceptions in Burundi, it is interesting to turn to the memoir of Albert Shibura, who gained notoriety as chief of staff and minister in the Burundi government during the 1972 killings of Hutu in Burundi, and is remembered today as one of the most rabidly anti-Hutu organizers of the carnage. Writing in July 1993, he recalled his student years at the *Groupe Scolaire* in Astrida (now Butare): "When the massacres began in 1959 I was in Rwanda, a grown up, and therefore I know what I am talking about. One thing is beyond doubt, there has not been a Hutu revolution in Rwanda. What happened, quite simply, are massacres organized by the (Belgian) administration... The responsibility of the Belgian administration is overwhelming. It alone is responsible for inventing the false Hutu–Tutsi problem, for organizing and perpetration the massacre of innocents, for continuing to stimulate hatreds, for deceiving international public opinion." And finally, this statement, outrageously at variance with the facts on the ground, written four months before the assassination of Melchior Ndadaye, Burundi's first popularly elected Hutu president: "Today I can assure you that the quarrels between ethnic communities do not exist."[20]

---

[18] Jean-Paul Harroy, *Rwanda: De la féodalité à la démocratie (1955–1962)* (Bruxelles, 1984), p. 416.
[19] Logiest, *Mission au Rwanda*, p. 7.
[20] Albert Shibura, *Témoignages* (Bujumbura, 1993), pp. 23, 28.

Even more momentous, in retrospect, was the fallout of 1959 on the second and third generations of Tutsi refugees in Uganda. The first generation of Unarist militants emerged from the revolution chastened and disheartened. Their ill-fated cross-border raids all failed; if anything they drove the Kayibanda regime further in the direction of anti-Tutsi extremism, at enormous costs in human lives. The next generations learned valuable lessons from the mistakes of their elders. In terms of organizational skills, access to financial resources, political and military experience, they stood as a group apart. Aside from their more impressive performance as a warrior class, sheer luck also played a role. With Museveni's rise to power in 1986 new opportunities came into view. By then the sons and daughters of the "fifty niners" had come of age. Many would emerge as key players in the deadly confrontation with the Habyarimana regime.

Fast-forward to Kigali, on January 28, 1994. The celebration of the 33rd anniversary of the Gitarama coup has attracted large crowds. Two of the most viscerally anti-Tutsi leaders, Donat Murego and Frodouald Karamira, both associated with the Hutu Power movement (also known as Pawa), seize the mike to address the audience: "Power means Hutu! If someone says you are Power it means you are Hutu!... The date of January 28 1961 will never be forgotten by the Hutu, a date which left us overjoyed, and the Tutsi in consternation. On that occasion let the Hutu share their joy with the founding fathers of that historic moment of 1961, and let the Tutsi know that any attempt on their part to restore the monarchy and feudalism will jeopardize the spirit of concord and reconciliation inaugurated by the unforgettable date of January 28, 1961."[21] A little over two months later, the genocide of Tutsi erupted.

Before turning to the Burundi tragedy, it is useful to make clear where it differs from Rwanda's Belgian-engineered transition. Aside from the fact that the scale of the 1972 massacres in Burundi far exceeded the casualties exacted by the revolution in Rwanda, the victimized group in Burundi were Hutu, and the perpetrators were Tutsi. Measured by this yardstick the case of Burundi is the reverse of what happened in Rwanda. Furthermore, life-and-death decisions were made by African officials, not by European bureaucrats. Again, while in Burundi lip service for minority rights served as the ostensible motive to justify the use of violence against the majority, in Rwanda the rights of the majority were consistently held up to legitimize the wanton use of force against a "feudalist" minority. Seen in this light the two cases are polar opposites.

A more useful approach is to focus on the contagiousness of the fears and grievances harbored by the refugees. There is an obvious connection between the brutal uprooting suffered by the Tutsi minority in Rwanda and the fear many refugees felt that the same haunting scenario might again materialize in Burundi. Some of this is graphically captured in the letter

---

[21] Cited in Valens Kajekuhakwa, *Rwanda: De la terre de paix a la terre de sang: Et après?* (Paris, 2001), pp. 296–297.

written by an acquaintance of mine, Thierry De Coster, to the editor of
the Belgian newspaper *Le Soir* on July 28, 1973: "You've lost sight of the
fact that the genocide began in Rwanda in 1959, and that the massacres
that happened then are no less bloody than those in Biafra, Bengal and
elsewhere. It is from that moment that was born the terror between the two
communities. And if I use the word terror it is by design because if terror
translates into violence it is in fear that it finds its origins. For more than
ten years the Tutsi feel threatened, for more than ten years they've been
living in fear. They are the least numerous and they have good reasons to
believe that the day they will face a major confrontation it is they who will
be massacred to the last man."[22]

By way of a footnote to this all too prescient commentary: the potential
impact of the Tutsi refugee community in Burundi is inscribed not just in
history, but in the UNHCR statistics on the relative size of refugee flows. By
1964 336,000 Rwandan Tutsi had fled their homeland; *the vast majority,
some 200,000, went to Burundi*, 78,000 to Uganda, 36,000 to Tanzania,
and 22,000 to the Congo.

Considering what they went through in Rwanda is it any wonder that
many felt the urge to enlist the support of their Burundi kinsmen in keeping
their Hutu enemies at bay?

In his preface to Logiest's memoir Professor Stengers offers this arresting
commentary, penned in 1987: "In order to understand why there has been
a Congo, you need to understand Leopold's II's psychology; to understand
why there is a Hutu Rwanda you need to understand Colonel Logiest."[23]
This heavy legacy could extend even further, raising the question of his historic responsibility in the chain of events leading to the genocidal killings in
Burundi and Rwanda.

---

[22] Author's file.
[23] Logiest, *Mission au Rwanda*, op. cit., p. iv.

3 Burundi 1972

A genocide too far?

A visitor can find few Hutu in Bujumbura. It is a little like entering Warsaw after World War II and looking for Jews... In Burundi something terrible has happened. A year ago the government run by the minority Tutsi tribe tried to eliminate, in a chilling and systematic way, the entire elite class of the Hutu people – all those with some education... Since then there has been even more killing, the latest in May and June of this year.
   Stanley Meisler, "Rwanda and Burundi," The Atlantic Monthly, September 1973
   Ukuri guca mu ziko ntigusha (Truth passes through fire without burning).
                                                                 – Kirundi proverb

As I reflect on the avalanche of public attention surrounding the Rwanda genocide, I am astonished by just how little press coverage and even less scholarly interest was given to Burundi at a time when a huge segment of its population was being decimated. Not much has changed in our perceptions of the Burundi tragedy. Could it be that these events are too distant, too far from our immediate interests?

There was one notable exception, however. It came from someone I would never have guessed could be moved, much less politically upset, by the terrible news filtering out of Burundi. This is how Richard Nixon, of all people, reacted to a memo from Henry Kissinger, his national security adviser, stressing that the events in Burundi posed no serious threat to US interests and thus required no immediate attention. His handwritten response, scribbled on the memo, conveys something of his anger:[1]

This is one of the most cynical, callous reactions of a great government to a terrible human tragedy I have seen. When the Paks try to put down a rebellion in East Pakistan the world screams. When Indians kill a few thousand Paks no one cares. Biafra stirs us because of Catholics; the Israeli Olympics because of Jews, the North Vietnam bombings because

---

[1] I am grateful to Christian Desroches, a former graduate student of mine at Concordia University (Montreal) for sharing with me this extraordinary document. I also want to record my indebtedness to Michael Hoyt, who served as the US deputy chief of mission in Burundi, for giving me access to the cables sent out from the embassy to the State Department.

of Communist leanings in our establishment. But when 100,000 (one third of the people of a black country) are murdered we say and do nothing, because we must not make blacks look bad (except of course when Catholic blacks are killed). I do not buy this double standard. Tell the weak sisters in the African Bureau of State to give a recommendation as to how we can at least show moral outrage. And let's begin by calling our Ambassador immediately for consultation. Under no circumstances will I appoint a new Ambassador to present credentials to these butchers.

Never mind the off-the-wall demographics: assuming that the conservative estimate of 100,000 deaths is correct, this would by no means translate into a third of a population of about seven million. Nonetheless, Nixon's angry scribbling is notable for being one of the rare official gestures of reprobation elicited by the killings. Just as noteworthy is the absence of a significant follow-up to his colorful admonition, other than the recall of the ambassador. The phrasing of Kissinger's memo downplayed causes for alarm, observing that "the Tutsi (decided) to exterminate all Hutu with any semblance of leadership, i.e. who could read and write, or those who wore shoes." The death toll reached "possibly 100,000, and (resulted in) nearly half-million Hutu widows and orphans." "Our interests in Burundi," Kissinger added, "are microscopic (we buy some coffee). We have 150 citizens there mostly missionaries. There has never been any threat to the safety of Europeans." However, "microscopic" US interests, the death toll makes the mind reel.

In her widely applauded block-buster, *A Problem from Hell*, Samantha Power shows how, in the face of irrefutable evidence of widespread genocidal atrocities from Bosnia to Rwanda and beyond, US policymakers, pretending not to know, sat on their hands.[2] Conspicuously missing from her list of states drenched in genocidal blood are the mass murders in Burundi in 1972, 30 years before her book appeared in print.

What is one to make of this near-universal indifference to what I would not hesitate to describe as the first genocide to take place in independent Africa?

The answer lies in part in the timing of the tragedy, unfolding at a time when human rights issues had yet to emerge as a significant source of public concern. To this must be added the singular complexity of a society all too readily defined as the carbon copy of Rwanda. While sharing with Rwanda some basic features, including a population consisting of two major ethnicities, Hutu and Tutsi, the two groups are divided into distinctive sub-categories, and to further complicate the equation at the top of the social pyramid stood a category of chiefs unknown in Rwanda, the *ganwa*. Often referred to as "princes of the blood," the *ganwa* were the sons of the reigning *mwami*, and as such held considerable authority as chiefs. Though often exhibiting

[2] Samantha Power, *A Problem from Hell: America and the Age of Genocide* (New York, 2002).

a typical Tutsi phenotype, they were considered as a group apart, neither Hutu nor Tutsi. Exactly how to navigate this complicated landscape is a daunting enterprise. Undeterred, a few scholars rose to the challenge, at the risk of further muddying the waters: the radically different interpretations pawned by the Burundi carnage are yet another reason why, to this day, it remains one of the most neglected – and controversial – themes in the recent history of the continent.

But perhaps the single most important factor has been the enormity of the 1994 genocide in Rwanda, which to this day tends to eclipse all others in the continent. Just as in the post-Shoah years some commentators stubbornly refused to apply the g-word to any genocide other than the one leading to the death of six million Jews in WWII, so also with regard to Burundi: only in Rwanda does the killing of over half a million Tutsi qualify as genocide. This is not to deny that massacres have occurred, many horrific in their scale, but none qualify as genocide. I hope to disabuse the reader of this highly debatable point of view.

Refugees are never neutral. Nor is their political involvement necessarily peaceful. This is the principal lesson to be learned from the presence in Burundi of tens of thousands of Tutsi refugees from Rwanda. By creating intense fears among their kinsmen that a Hutu-led rebellion might be the thin edge of the wedge for a Rwanda-like revolution, the stage was set for something resembling a self-fulfilling prophecy. No matter how fanciful a perception may seem at any given point, it may take on a measure of reality by the mere fact that it becomes internalized and ends up being seen as "real." In a word, the contagiousness of ethnic distrust served as the most powerful force driving Burundi towards the abyss.

In order to grasp the dynamics of mass murder it is useful to remind ourselves of the sequence of events preceding the catastrophe.

A troubled transition

"Rwanda and Burundi have a lot in common but they are very different from each other." This is the trope I remember most distinctly from the conversations I had on my first trip to Burundi in September 1960. Just how similar and yet unlike the two countries are is perhaps best illustrated by the vision held by the Belgian authorities on the eve of independence – and their resounding setback when they tried to implement the Logiest scenario.

As the Belgian journalist Guy Poppe pointed out, the Rwanda model was ever-present in the minds of Belgian officials as they went about the task of preparing the ground for a democratic transition to self-government. "Given that a number of high-ranking officials, such as Harroy, Regnier and Reisdorff had spent time in Rwanda," writes Poppe, "it is not surprising that they believed and hoped that a similar model could be installed: a revolution would overthrow the monarchy, the *mwami* and his entourage, including (the mwami's son) Rwagasore, thus ushering a regime dominated by the Hutu majority, which would be supportive of Belgium."[3] Much as they may have tried, the Rwanda model could not be replicated.

Burundi in 1960 experienced none of the ethnic spasms that brought Rwanda to the brink of civil war. The central issue had little to do with Hutu and Tutsi. The main fault line revolved around dynastic rivalries identified with two different groups of *ganwa*, the Bezi v. Batare, identified respectively with the *Union pour le Progrès National* (Uprona), led by the *mwami*'s son, Rwagasore, and the *Parti Démocrate Chrétien* (PDC), whose two leading personalities were the sons of a well-known *ganwa* family, the Baranyanka. Unlike Rwanda, where the monarchy and its representative were the centerpiece and symbol of Tutsi supremacy, the Burundi monarch was a distinctly modest figure, politically and otherwise,[4] but there can be no denying that, as the head of the Uprona, the only significant vehicle of nationalist aspirations Mwambutsa's son enjoyed a popularity unmatched by his father.

On October 13, 1961, Rwagasore was shot dead at a lakeside Bujumbura restaurant by a Greek gunman in the pay of the PDC leaders, thus eliminating from the political scene the man who stood as the most prestigious nationalist leader, equally respected by Hutu and Tutsi, only months before independence – a loss from which the country never recovered.

At the root of the tragedy lay the age-old antagonism between two leading *ganwa* families, but it also implicated, if only indirectly, some leading Belgian colonial officials. This is the subject of Poppe's inquest, which offers enough evidence to demonstrate that the authors of the crime knew they would enjoy virtual impunity from the *tutelle* authorities. Without going into the details of how Belgian officials became involved, there is little question that the colonial authorities were widely seen as a key element behind Rwagasore's death. This fact alone is enough to explain why, in the months following independence, the Uprona emerged as the standard bearer or nationalist ideology.

---

[3] Guy Poppe, *L'assassinat de Rwagasore, le Lumumba Burundais* (Bujumbura, 2012), p. 211.

[4] I can think of no better illustration of the contrast between the two kingships than the strikingly different poses struck by their respective sovereigns, Musinga (Rwanda) and Mwambutsa (Burundi), in a photograph dating back from the 1920s – Mwambutsa wearing an open shirt in an ill-fitting cotton suit, and a bush hat, and Musinga ramrod straight, resplendent in his colorful traditional regal attire, next to an equally elegant *mwamikazi*. The contrast was by no means diminished after the replacement of Musinga by his successor, Mutara Rudahigwa. I remember meeting Mwambutsa once, by chance, at the swimming pool of the Club Nautique in Bujumbura, where he often joined his European courtiers. I approached His Majesty in swimming trunks with all due respect, hoping to wrangle an informal impromptu interview, but no sooner did I articulate my request than I was politely referred to the Grand Maréchal de la Cour, Henri Kana, a notorious scoundrel, at which point our dialogue ended. For the photo mentioned above, and further fascinating insights into the early history of Burundi, see Charles Baranyanka, *Le Burundi: Face à la Croix et à la Bannière* (Bruxelles, 2009), p. 341. The author, son of the legendary Pierre Baranyanka, who acted as a powerful *ganwa* notable under German and Belgian rule, served as his country's first ambassador to Belgium after independence.

Rising ethnic tensions

The unifying bonds created by Rwagasore's assassination proved short-lived. The Hutu revolution in neighboring Rwanda could not but sharpen the asperities of incipient ethnic divisions. It is hard to imagine how Hutu elites in Burundi could have remained indifferent to the implications of majority rule, or for that matter how the Tutsi minority could have turned a deaf ear to the dangers inscribed in the "tyranny de the majority." With tens of thousands of Tutsi refugees from Rwanda entering the country with tales of horror on their lips about their homes destroyed, relatives killed, cattle destroyed, the ethnic temperature spiked to dangerous levels.

Among Belgian officials some did not hide their preference for the Rwandan model. Even though they failed in their initial efforts to make it happen, some became actively involved in the promotion of Hutu interests. After giving their blessings to the ephemeral *Association des Progressistes et Démocrates du Burundi* (Aprodeba), they later gave their support to the pro-Hutu *Parti du Peuple* (PP). One of the personalities closely associated with the PP was a Belgian settler named Albert Maus, who, upon learning of the Uprona victory in the 1961 elections, committed suicide.

Little wonder if in this climate of rising anxieties and mutual suspicion ethnic rivalries threatened to tear asunder the fabric of society. First came the Kamenge riots in 1962, pitting a handful of militant Hutu trade unionists against elements of the predominantly Tutsi Uprona youth group, *Jeunesses Nationalistes Rwagasore* (JNR), followed by a serious leadership crisis within the ruling Uprona. Contesting each other's claims were two aspiring figures – thoroughly cross-grained from the standpoint of their backgrounds and personalities – André Muhirwa, an aristocratic *ganwa*, and Paul Mirerekano, a Hutu agricultural assistant from Muramvya where he helped organize a highly successful rural cooperative. I remember meeting him in Kigali in 1964, some time after reading a translation of his pamphlet, *Mbwire gito canje*,[5] better described as an ode to the monarchy. I simply could not recognize the apologist of the mwamiship in the firebrand he had become. By the time I met Mirerekano in Rwanda the struggle for the leadership of the Uprona was in fact a symbolic competition between Hutu and Tutsi, a fact readily understood by all observers.

But the most critical factor behind the crystallization of ethnic tension was the assassination of Pierre Ngendandumwe, Burundi's first Hutu prime minister on January 18, 1965, by a Tutsi refugee from Rwanda employed at the US Embassy. The circumstance of his death is a metaphor for the part played by Tutsi refugees in sharpening the edges of conflict. Not only was the assassin never brought to justice, but the Tutsi community as a whole showed remarkably little compassion for the victim (much the same

---

[5] The title of the pamphlet are first words of a well-known proverb, meaning roughly "I am talking to my rascal of a son hoping some else will get the message" (*Mbwire gito cnje git c'uwundi yumvireho*).

indifference was on display after the assassination of Melchior Ndadaye in 1993).

In such conditions, the stunning electoral victory scored by Hutu candidates during the legislative elections of May 1965 is hardly surprising. With a total of 23 seats out of 33 in the National Assembly they had every reason to expect the appointment of a Hutu prime minister. But instead of appointing a Hutu as prime minister, the king turned to a famous *ganwa* of Bezi origins, Leopold Bihumugani, better known as Biha. By making a mockery of the constitution, and concentrating all power around the throne, Mwambutsa's decision infuriated the Hutu elites. The explosion came on October 19, 1965, when a group of Hutu army and gendarmerie officers drove to Biha's residence and greeted him with a volley of bullets. Amazingly, Biha survived; the monarchy didn't.

Having dealt with the prime minister the rebels drove to the royal palace, only to be met with unexpected resistance from the king's personal guard.

Reinforcements were called in, under the command of Capt. Michel Micombero. Caught in the crossfire, the mutineers surrendered. The coup that almost was carried momentous consequences. The mutineers took a huge gamble and lost, but the losses involved more than the extermination of thousands of Hutu elements within the army and gendarmerie; it led to the physical elimination of every Hutu leader of any standing, including Mirerekano. As 1965 drew to a close power was exclusively in Tutsi hands.

King Mwambutsa, meanwhile, panic-stricken, left his country for a more peaceful retreat on the shores of Lake Geneva, leaving to his younger son, Charles Ndizeye, later known under the dynastic name of Ntare, the responsibility of assuming the mwamiship. His reign was probably the shortest in the kingdom's history, lasting from his formal coronation on July 8, 1965 to his deposition less than five months later on November 28, followed by the proclamation of the First Republic. His assassination in 1972, at the hands of Tutsi elements, is a commentary on the depth of the transformation experienced by the country at the time of the 1972 bloodbath.

April 1972: the Hutu revolt

Between the birth of the republic in 1965 and the 1972 carnage, the Burundi political landscape changed in another fundamental sense: along with the emergence of Michel Micombero as president of the republic and head of the armed forces, power passed from one Tutsi sub-group to another, from Banyaruguru to Hima.

Each have their roots in pre-colonial history, the first as a community close to the seats of monarchical power, and thus held in high regard, and the other as a low-status group, often derided in the oral literature. In the context of the 1960s the rift took on some ominous dimensions. The Banyaruguru, largely concentrated in the north, around Ijenda and Muramvya, the royal capital, became the target of deep suspicions in the late 1960s; many were seen as undeclared monarchists, secretly plotting to overthrow the republican regime. Their Hima opponents, most of whom lived in the Bururi province in the south, were identified with the "Bururi lobby." The Hima v. Banyaruguru division took on a nasty turn when charges of sedition were brought against a number of Tutsi elites from Muramvya suspected of manipulating Hutu elements in order to bring about the restoration of the monarchy. In a sense in the minds of many Hima the Hutu threat was the flip side of the monarchical peril.

In a parody of justice, reminiscent of Soviet show trials, on January 14, 1972, a military tribunal issued nine death sentences (four officers and five civilians) and seven life sentences. On hearing the verdict, the public prosecutor, Leonard Nduwayo, himself a Tutsi from Bururi, resigned after requesting that the case be dismissed. He was immediately arrested. On February 4, however, under the pressure of domestic and international opinion, the death sentences were commuted to life imprisonment, and five of the defendants previously sentenced to serve prison terms were set free. The principal conspirators behind this incredible judicial masquerade were two key government officials whose mere mention of their names would soon sow intense fears among Hutu, and not a few Tutsi: Artémon Simbananiye, minister of foreign affairs cooperation and planning, and Albert Shibura, holding two major portfolios, interior and justice. Simbananiye (now a born-again Christian) emerged as the most powerful figure in the Micombero government, and Shibura as the man who, in all probability, ordered the killing of mwami Ntare.

But the Hutu menace did in fact become a tragic reality, and the brutality of the repression, besides conjuring the immediate danger, served as a powerful source of intra-Tutsi solidarity in the face of a common peril.

On April 29, a violent insurgency exploded in the normally peaceful lakeside towns of Rumonge and Nyanza-Lac. In a matter of hours, terror was unleashed by Hutu against Tutsi, causing thousands of deaths among civilians. In the town of Bururi all civilian and military authorities were killed. A short-lived Martyazo Republic was proclaimed in Vyanda in early May, an experiment quickly ended by the government troops.

The US deputy chief of mission in Bujumbura, Michael Hoyt, reported the shadowy presence of Mulelistes: "Bands of Mulelist Hutu entered Burundi during the past week [from the Congo] and started slaughter in Nyanza-Lac and particularly Rumonge." But the use of the term Mulelist, to refer to followers of Pierre Mulele, the organizer of the Kwilu rebellion in the Congo in 19641965, is misleading. What is more plausible is that remnants of the ill-fated Kabiliste insurrection in eastern Congo could have joined the rebels, but this is mere speculation. Of the horrific killings committed by the rebels, there can be no doubt. The number of victims among Tutsi can only be guessed, but one missionary source – Bishop Bernard Bududira, a Tutsi, who agreed to share his views with me in the months following the carnage – evaluated their number at some 5,000. While this may well be an overestimation, it is a far cry from the 50,000 claimed by the government white paper later published by the Burundi delegation to the UN. Even more problematic is the assessment of the human losses resulting from the ensuing repression.

The genocidal response

The response of the government was immediate. On April 30, while counter-attacks were launched against the insurgents, elements of the armed forces began to coordinate their attacks to eliminate all Hutu suspected of having taken part in the uprising. In charge of the operations were the hard core of the Bururi military "lobby," as it came to be called, including the chief of staff, Thomas Ndabemeye, the notorious Albert Shibura – author of the only memoir written by a leading participant[6] – André Yanda, Joseph Rwuri, all of whom went about the task of eliminating Hutu suspects with ruthless efficiency.

The next phase is where repression mutated into genocide. It is best described as a systematic, nationwide slaughter of Hutu civilians. Purges affected every segment of the civil society. The carnage went on unabated until August. Day after day Hutu were rounded up by elements of youth militias, now renamed "revolutionary" (*Jeunesses Révolutionnaires Rwagasore*) and handed over to the army. As Jeremy Greenand reported, "the government radio broadcasts encouraged the population to hunt the python in the grass," an order readily interpreted by Tutsi as a license to exterminate all educated Hutu, down to the level of secondary and even primary school-children. Tutsi pupils prepared lists of their Hutu classmates. Administrative personnel of Hutu origins, not only local civil servants but chauffeurs' clerks, semi-skilled workers, were rounded up, taken to the nearest jail and either shot or beaten to death with rifle butts or clubs. In Bujumbura alone an estimated 4,000 Hutu identified as educated or semi-educated, including university and secondary school students were loaded upon trucks and taken to their graves.

Boniface Kiranganya, an eyewitness of *ganwa* origins, who once served as deputy director of intelligence, later confided his sense of dismay: "If I should one day lose my sanity, it will be in large part because of what I saw during the events of April–May 1972. I would have given anything for not being a witness. It was beyond anything I could imagine… *C'est le paroxysme de la démence.*"[7] Michael Hoyt's cables to the State Department spell out the scenes of horror: "No respite, no letup. What apparently is a genocide continues. Arrests going on around the clock. Chargé d'affaires laundry boy fled JRR bands last night, says they are killing most Hutu on the spot… Tutsi reprisals unabated in interior but have slackened somewhat in Bujumbura… In north Hutu take cover upon arrival of any vehicle, reflecting pervasive fear… Repression against Hutu is not simply one of killing. It is also an attempt to remove them from access to employment, property,

---

[6] Shibura, *Témoignages*, op. cit.
[7] Boniface Fidel Kiraranganya, *La vérité sur le Burundi* (Sherbrooke, 1977).

education and the general chance to improve themselves... We have clear report mass graves near airport again utilized at beginning of week."[8]

If Shibura stood as the orchestrator of the military repression, the man who bears the heaviest responsibility for organizing the killing of Hutu civilians was Artémon Simbananiye. Wrongly identified in some Belgian newspapers as the architect of "le plan Simbananiye," a plot to surgically equalize Hutu and Tutsi, by eliminating as many Hutu as necessary to bring them on par numerically with Tutsi, he did, however, play a major role in plotting the return of King Ntare from Uganda, where he lived in exile; as minister of justice during the killings he never flinched from ordering the elimination of a large number of highly educated Hutus; he saw to it that the JRR militias would play a major auxiliary role in identifying and rounding up suspects. Nor did he ever contemplate to bring under judicial scrutiny the extensive plundering of Hutu property by their murderers. It was Simbananiye, I might add, who also invited me to Burundi in 1973 with the clear intention of clueing me in on "what really happened" (of which more in a moment).

As also happened in Rwanda, the anticipation of material gains from the seizure of the victim's property – his cows, his land, his bicycle, his house, even his bank account – was a major inducement to violence. The incident reported by Jeremy Greenland is only one example among others: "In May 1972 a certain Hutu teacher was arrested late at night and subsequently killed. A Tutsi friend accompanied his wife to the bank when it opened the next morning to draw the family's savings, only to find the account already closed and the money gone. In countless cases the furniture was removed from the homes of arrested Hutu, with the widows and orphans sitting on the bare floor. The cars and lorries of wealthier Hutu became the property of those who arrested them. A considerable sum of money was raised by private subscription for 'victims of the events,' but I know of no Hutu who ever received a franc of that money; only the Tutsi along Lake Tanganyika who had suffered in the original Hutu attack benefited."[9]

In his compelling reassessment of the first ten years of Burundi's independence Aidan Russell takes a fresh look at the 1972 tragedy, drawing a wealth of original insights from archival materials covering the northern border with Rwanda. He shows how the repression dovetailed from individual arrests to entire social categories. After Micombero's urgings on May 8, the killings spread through much of the northern prefectures. Deogratias Ntavyo, a magistrate from Ngozi, played a pivotal role in cutting through the subtleties of individual indictments: "the logic of repression extrapolated from chains of individuals to define and indict entire groups."

---

[8] Cited in Lemarchand, "Le génocide de 1972 au Burundi. Les silences de l'histoire," *Cahiers d'Etudes Africaines,* no. 167 (2002), p. 557.
[9] Quoted in Lemarchand, *Burundi: Ethnic Conflict and Genocide* (Cambridge and Washington, DC, 1995), pp. 102–103.

First came "the *fonctionnaires*, members of the administration itself"; then came Protestants, including, said Ntavyo, "the pastors and catechists of the Pentecostal Church (who) make use of their religion to preach division... Ntavyo then specifically noted the dangers of teachers including several at Catholic institutions... they were condemned by association with early targets and complaints from the pupils' parents." Finally came merchants: "their relatively greater access to wealth equipped them for a mission to use gifts in cash or in kind in order to persuade people and lead them to conviction. Thus money finally emerged as a unifying thread." The JRR played, of course, a central role in delivering their targets to the execution squads. But the rounding up and execution of the suspects is better seen, according to Aidan Russell, as a "joint process penetrating society through the collaboration of society itself."[10]

From this calculated, deliberate extermination of Hutu civilians – resulting in the deaths of anywhere from 100,000 (a conservative estimate) to 300,000, the figure cited by Boniface Kiraranganya – emerged a maimed society, in which the only elites were Tutsi elites.[11] Summing up the thoroughness of the operation, Michael Hoyt noted, "In area after area no educated Hutu male is believed to be alive. This is particularly true in the south where we have word from growing number of villages that no Hutu males remain at all." For the next 20 years, the Burundi state remained a Tutsi-dominated state, where what was left of the Hutu were systematically excluded from access to the army, the civil service and the university.

In a report to the Minority Rights Group (MRG) written in 1973 titled *Selective Genocide in Burundi*, I underscored the fact that the victims were virtually all males, most of them claiming some degree of education. By eliminating the elites and all potential elites, the aim was to restore long-term stability to the country. "At least we'll have peace for the next 30 years," Simbananiye is reported to have said.[12] This macabre triage helps explain why today many of those who grew up as orphans, who were told of what happened to their fathers, uncles, brothers, and relatives, and now occupy high-ranking positions in the government, are acutely conscious of themselves as a martyred community. Their determination to avert at all cost a return to Tutsi rule is easy to understand.

An unanticipated invitation

On a more personal note, my report was written on the basis of data collected during a trip I made in the summer of 1973, under unusual circumstances.

---

[10] Aidan Russell, *Politics and Violence in Burundi: The Language of Truth in an Emerging State* (Cambridge, 2019), p. 242.

[11] See Kiraranganya, *La vérité sur le Burundi* (Sherbrooke, 1977).

[12] René Lemarchand and David Martin, *Selective Genocide in Burundi*, Minority Rights Group Report No. 20 (London, 1973).

I came to Burundi at the invitation of Artémon Simbananiye, in hopes that I would set the record straight. He welcomed me to his home, kindly mentioned my recently published book on Rwanda and Burundi, and informed me that a dinner has been planned in my honor by President Micombero; among the guests were the French ambassador, Henri Bernard (I was not yet a naturalized American citizen), and Father Gabriel Barakana, a Jesuit, rector of the university, who later served as my escort as we traveled through several cities in the north. After shaking hands with President Micombero, and much to my surprise, and with no little embarrassment, I found myself enlisted in an order I had never heard about *L'Ordre de l'Amitié des Peuples*. There was something wonderfully absurd about getting a medal commemorating the "people's friendship" from a man who should have been sent to the guillotine. Going from the absurd to the ridiculous, what I remember most vividly is my brief tete-à-tete with Micombero, during which he told me, looking at me in the eye, in all seriousness, "*Monsieur le Professeur, écoutez moi bien, le Burundi aussi, un jour, aura sa bombe atomique!*" ("One day Burundi will also have its atomic bomb"). I remained tonguetied. After this surreal exchange I was promptly ushered to the reception hall to share in a much-needed libation.

The next day I was met at my hotel by Father Barakana and his chauffeur, and off we went to our first destination, Gitega, where I was able to meet my friend and colleague, the late Jeremy Greenland, a British scholar and teacher with months of experience in Burundi, who discreetly slipped into my hand a listing of the Hutu losses recorded during the killings at the Bujumbura University, in a number of technical and secondary schools (*athénées*) and professional institutes.[13] As we drove from Gitega to Muramvya and Ngozi – towns normally alive with crowds of schoolchildren, artisans, peddlers, beggars, traders – I couldn't help noticing the unseemly silence, the all-pervasive sense of fear, the unsmiling faces. Barakana's business-as-usual remarks sounded hollow. So did the greetings from the hotel clerk. Never before had the country seemed more somber.

Revisionist takes

My report to the MRG was intended as an interim assessment, a brief discussion of what I saw as the key elements behind the slaughter, the scale of the human losses, and the consequences. The most illuminating part of the report, I thought, were the statistics offered by Jeremy Greenland. Little did I expect that it would trigger a barrage of criticisms from some of my French colleagues for its alleged inaccuracies. One such colleague, Jean-Pierre Chrétien, whom I invited to collaborate on the report, declined the offer, saying, comically, that I misinterpreted the significance of the Hima–Ruguru division, by confusing a social division with areas of geographical

---

[13] See *Selective Genocide in Burundi*, Appendix II, Losses of Hutu students in secondary schools and university as of July 1972, p. 27.

concentration. Be it as it may, this is not the place for settling personal scores. A more useful exercise is to take a critical look at how the events of 1972 have been interpreted by academics, journalists and indeed political actors.

Among the latter Albert Shibura deserves pride of place. Not only because his anti-Hutu sentiments are so clearly inscribed into his familiarity with the events surrounding the Hutu revolution, but because it reflects the official interpretation of why a genocide happened. According to him, a genocide did happen. But it was a genocide of Tutsi. Only the Hutu are perpetrators. Had the army not intervened to kill the killers, the hecatomb would have been much worse. The plot had been concocted years before, at least since 1965, with the active participation of the CIA and the Belgian-based Christian trade unions; what happened in 1965, with the attack on the king's palace, was only the first phase. The aim was to assassinate the *mwami*, the secretary of state for national defense, the prime minister and all the Tutsi officers present in Bujumbura. The second phase would be the proclamation of a Hutu republic; the third involved the "liquidation of all Tutsi army men, gendarmes, civil servants, clerics and businessmen"; the fourth and final phase would have resulted in "the liquidation of all Tutsi peasants."[14] In plain language, every Tutsi in sight was to be killed in order to prevent the worst from happening. Hardly more nuanced is the scenario outlined in the government white paper. "When confronting aggressors seeking not only to overthrow the republic but to systematically exterminate all the Tutsi, the authorities had no other choice than to inflict a severe punishment on those responsible for this genocide." Just how severe remained unsaid.

A welcome respite from the repetitive "blame the victims" theme inscribed in official documents – all Hutu are perpetrators; all Tutsi are victims – can be found in the important contribution by Jean-Pierre Chrétien and Jean-Francois Dupaquier.[15] This is the richest source of documentation available anywhere; particularly illuminating are the scores of interviews with eyewitnesses, and the effort to situate the tragedy in its historical context. This said the title is strangely ambivalent: *Burundi 1972: On the brink of genocides*. In other words although the country came close to the abyss, it managed to avoid not one but two genocides.

I have elsewhere indicated why I have some reservations about their handling of the data,[16] but it may help to sum up the nub of my criticisms. Thirty-two years after the fact one could have expected some degree of circumspection concerning the reliability of the testimonies told by local informants, especially those coming from persons closely associated with the Micombero regime. A case in point is Emile Mworoha, who served

---

[14] Shibura, *Témoignages*.

[15] Jean-Pierre Chrétien and Jean Francois Dupaquier, *Burundi 1972: Au bord des génocides* (Paris, 2007).

[16] René Lemarchand ed., *Forgotten Genocides: Oblivion, Denial and Memory* (Philadelphia, 2011), p. 46.

as general secretary of the infamous *Jeunesses Révolutionnaires Rwagasore* (JRR) during the killings. Though frequently cited as an authoritative source (his name is mentioned 17 times in the index), nowhere is there as much as a hint that he could have played a central role in the killing of innocent civilians. The standard argument set forth by Mworoha is to brush off responsibility to local officials, over whom he presumably had no control. Consider the following exchange: "Who do you think are the JRR's bosses? Mworoha: The real bosses of the JRR are the governors, the administrators, the zone heads (chefs de zone). They are the ones who send out orders to arrest such and such... I have no control over them. Didn't you give instructions to JRR militants? The instructions are general guidelines, like vigilance, and denounce the enemies." Asked about a notorious killer with the unlikely name of Aimable, Mworoha replies, "Yes, Aimable was one of the great militants of the repression. But me, even in my capacity as Secretary General of the JRR. I couldn't even talk to him. Which goes to show you how much authority I had."[17] Evidently, there is every reason to wonder whether it could have been in Mworoha's interest to adjust his testimony to the circumstances of the interview.

Just as questionable is the handling of the documentary evidence. To treat as solid proof of genocidal intent the text of an anti-Tutsi tract cited in a government white paper full of lies and inaccuracies is hard to accept. The tendentiousness of their argument is nowhere more evident than in the section of the book titled "Hypothesis of a global plan to eliminate the Tutsi." In addition to relying heavily on the misleading government white paper, the "hypothesis" is almost entirely based on anecdotal evidence, much of it irrelevant to their intended purpose.

Only in the last pages of the book does their argument take on a measure of clarity: the massacre of Hutu civilians can indeed be described as genocide, but it occurred as a response to another genocidal "project," revealed by "the massacre of Tutsi men, women and children, and simple peasants as well as notables, because of their supposed feudal nature." At the root of this tragedy, we are told, is not a "retributive" reaction, to use Helen Fein's phrase, but "the choice of a policy of death, where the key words are race and blood."[18] Numbers make no difference. Whether we're dealing with a few thousands on one side, and anywhere from 200,000 to 300,000 on the other, is immaterial. Both are equal in their choice of a policy of death; their common adherence to an ideology of blood and race is what brings them together at the cusp of a double genocide.

Rather than tarry over the merits or demerits of their stance, here a word or two of self-criticism is in order. To help me turn a critical eye on my own shortcomings I rely on Aidan Russell's important recent contribution, from which I pilfered at some length in a previous section.[19]

---

[17] Chrétien and Dupaquier, *Burundi 1972*, p. 252.

[18] Chrétien and Dupaquier, *Burundi 1972*, p. 478.

[19] Aidan Russell, *Politics and Violence in Burundi: The Language of Truth in an Emerging State* (Cambridge, 2019).

The bane of a binary frame?

I cannot think of any other work on Burundi that is quite as compelling, and more carefully researched. Thanks to his familiarity with the Kirundi language, a prolonged immersion in archival materials, countless interviews with eyewitnesses, and an uncanny ability to extract fascinating new insights from his field work in the borderland with Rwanda, the author brings out the multiplicity of "truths" inscribed, spoken or whispered in political exchanges among political actors. From his painstaking scrutiny of new materials – including the seldom consulted newspaper *Ndongozi* (The Guide), a crucial source of information for the post-independence period – he paints a remarkably diverse, fluid, and ultimately many-sided picture of Burundi politics in the decade following independence. Unsurprisingly, the author takes me to task for endorsing a "binary" narrative,[20] thus missing the rich complexity of the language of politics as the embodiment of different kinds of truths, and hence involving a plurality of possibilities. It is difficult to disagree. Yet I wonder if we are not operating at different levels of truth – to use his favorite metaphor – and therefore looking at politics through different analytic lenses. If I am indeed captive of a binary framework, this is for the sake of sifting out the essentials out of an already exceedingly complicated concatenation of forces. Whichever way you may want to look at the rapidly changing landscape of Burundi politics after independence one can hardly miss the binary rhythms of the Batare–Bezi competition, the shift to a monarchist vs. republican rift, the rise of a Hutu v. Tutsi conflict, simultaneous with the Banyaruguru v. Hima factions, only to fall back to a Hutu v. Tutsi bloodbath. Admittedly, this does not rule out the spectrum of truths, opinions, confrontations and nuances that the author has so ably analyzed. What I tried to do is to give the reader a framework through which to make sense of what remains to this day a situation of puzzling and potentially violent complexity.

As we move on to the next question in this narrative – what has been its impact of the 1972 bloodbath on subsequent events – the binary frame is again difficult to avoid.

The assassination of Melchior Ndadaye: murder as a game changer

The assassination of Melchior Ndadaye, on October 21, 1993, marks a tragic turning point in Burundi's recent history. Not just because of the victim's personality, hugely popular among Hutu and not a few Tutsi, but because of the context in which it occurred, and what happened next.

Along with him four of the most promising political figures were killed: Pontien Karibwami and Gilles Bimazubute, president and vice-president of the National Assembly respectively, Juvénal Ndayikeza, minister of territorial administration, and Richard Ndikumwami, head of national security. In one fell swoop disappeared the core leadership of the *Front Démocratique*

---

[20] Russell, *Politics and Violence in Burundi*, p. 10.

du Burundi (Frodebu), the clear winner of the 1993 elections. The void they left would never be filled, and their murderers never brought to trial.

Ndadaye's death shocked me more than I could have imagined. Over the years a solid friendship developed between us; in our conversations we quickly moved from the formal "vous" to the "tu," as might be expected of old friends; we met on a number of occasions, within and outside Burundi. My encounter with Ndadaye owes much to his long-time friend, Jean-Marie Ngendahayo – a brilliant *ganwa* politician who played an important role in the birth of the Frodebu and later, while serving as minister of foreign affairs made a name for himself as a vocal critic of the abuses committed by the Tutsi-dominated army.

Ndadaye was the antithesis of a sectarian, exclusionary leader. His massive frame concealed gentle dispositions, an openness to dialogue, a capacity to listen to differing opinions, and a determination to do all he could to build bridges between Hutu and Tutsi. His attitude of tolerance came across frequently in his public statements, but also in the diversity of ethnic, gender, regional, and political strands apparent in the composition of his government. Just over half of his ministers were from the Frodebu, others from the pro-Tutsi Uprona, including the prime minister, Sylvie Kinigi. This opening to the opposition is all the more generous when seen in the light of the Frodebu's overwhelming victory: in a 97 percent turnout, the Frodebu won 64 percent and 71 percent of the vote respectively in the presidential and parliamentary elections In contrast to previous elections, the 1993 poll was applauded by international observers as remarkably free and fair. As a further token of a smooth passage to parliamentary democracy, Ndadaye's opponent, President Pierre Buyoya, publicly acknowledged his defeat as he warmly embraced the victor. And yet, as Nigel Watt, observed, "in reality Buyoya was angry and bitter."[21]

This brief experiment in pluralist democracy was abruptly brought to an end on October 21 by the army chief of staff, Jean Bikomagu, a key figure in the small group of hard-line politicians gravitating around Buyoya. Little did they suspect the scale of the revenge killings they were about to unleash. By their fateful decision to reverse the verdict of the polls Ndadaye's assassins hoped to turn the clock back to the post-1972 situation of undiluted Tutsi hegemony. Except that in the meantime a new generation of Hutu elites had emerged, determined to resist. However, much Tutsi extremists tried to submerge it, the new reality turned up to confront them. The stage was set for a long and vicious civil war that took the lives of an estimated 100,000.

The surge of horrific mutual killings of Tutsi by Hutu and Hutu by Tutsi, causing the death of some 50,000, was only the opening phase of a broader conflict. The butchery went on for weeks and months. I remember most vividly the systematic ethnic cleansing of Hutu elites, including university students, by Tutsi militias – made famous by the infamous *Sans échec, et sans*

---

[21] Nigel Watt, *Biography a Small African Country* (New York, 2008), p. 43.

défaite and equally brutal *Solidarité Jeunesse pour la défense des minorités* (Sodejem) – led inexorably to further confrontations. In his autobiographical narrative, Alain Aimé Nyamitwe, later to become one of Nkurunziza's close aides, gives the reader a harrowing depiction of the systematic assassination of Hutu students on the campus of the university by armed Tutsi students, acting with the complicity of the army or the Sodejem.[22] The scenes of violence reported in the Amnesty International report appended to the book convey something of the horror that swept across the university and the Lycée du Saint Esprit in Bujumbura: "Alexis Ndayisaba (a Hutu) was killed by the students using knives and iron bars. Tutsi students then went on rampage attacking their Hutu colleagues using machetes and knives, fire arms and grenades. Some of the Hutu students were taken to the Nyakabiga suburb, a Tutsi stronghold, where they were killed and buried in a mass grave... At least fifteen students were killed. Some sources in Bujumbura said that at least 98 students were killed."[23] Of the scores of victims killed by the *Sans Echec* few shocked me more painfully than the death of Ernest Kabushemeye, minister of mines and energy, gunned down in broad daylight as he stepped out of his office. A brilliant mind and friendly personality I had met him a few days before when he invited me to interview him in his office. At the end of our *tour d'horizon* I couldn't help thinking that as long as men of his caliber remained in office there were still reasons for hope... Unbeknownst to me at the time, Evariste Ndayishimiye, the incumbent president of the republic, had more luck: he is among the few who survived the campus massacre of 1995.

The simultaneous bloodbath in Rwanda acted as a powerful stimulus to the killings in Burundi, thus accelerating he growing polarization that now propelled Burundi into civil war. The relentless ethnic killings that went on from 1993 to 2000, during which the Tutsi-dominated army played a central role, go far in explaining why, 18 years later, the Nkurunziza government's thinly-veiled anti-Tutsi sentiment seriously threatens the fragile ethnic balance reached through the power sharing deal signed at Arusha (Tanzania) in 2000.

More puzzling is the less than neutral attitude of some international organizations, such as the World Bank, in seeking to chart a new course towards peace and reconciliation, or for that matter the personal tiffs that have accompanied the diplomatic efforts of State Department officials.

Intra-mural discords

In a paper commissioned by the World Bank in early 2008, where we tried to pin down the nexus between politics and the economy, Julien Nimubona, a well-known political scientist at the University of Bujumbura,

---

[22] Alain Aimé Nyamitwe, *J'ai échappé au Massacre de l'Université du Burundi, 11 juin 1995* (Paris, 2006).

[23] Nyamitwa, *J'ai échappé au Massacre de l'Université du Burundi*, Appendix V, p. 172.

and I summarized the impact of the civil war on the challenges faced by the country: "Economic development is problematic where insecurity is an everyday phenomenon; nor are the prospects for improved security any brighter where severe poverty affects the lives of millions. Furthermore, the profits derived from chronic violence, and the vested interests they create among insurgent groups and government officials alike help explain its self-perpetuating character. In such circumstances creating an environment compatible with economic development becomes a Sisyphean task."[24] The 31-page paper, based on scores of interviews during a two-week stay in Bujumbura, never made it to the desk of policymakers. A few months late I learned by a phone call to the World Bank field office in Bujumbura, that the topic discussed in the paper was "too sensitive" to be communicated to the persons for whom it was intended. Needless to say, I was taken aback by a decision that seemed so counterproductive to the objectives of the Bank, and detrimental to the interests of the country. I shouldn't have been, however, looking back at what the mission director, Vincent Fruchart, had to go through before I received the green light to join our flight to Bujumbura. On learning that I was a member of the mission, intense pressures were put on the Bank antenna in Bujumbura, presumably from its Tutsi affiliates, to veto my participation. Given that I had expressed in no uncertain terms my sense of outrage over the 1972 killings in a number of academic publications, there was little doubt in my mind about the source of the obstruction. Only after the mission director threatened to resign was I admitted back to the mission.

This was not the first time the Bank objected to my take on Burundi. In 2006 I was approached by colleagues at the Institute of Development Studies (IDS) in the UK, who had been commissioned by the Bank to write a series of papers on transitions to democracy in a number of developing countries. I was asked to contribute an in-depth analysis of on the impact of extreme poverty on the prospects for a transition to democracy in Burundi, a subject that I found sufficiently challenging to be worth the effort. After several revisions, I was finally informed of the Bank's decision by my colleague at IDS, Andrew Rosser: "We were informed that the Bank's office in Burundi had objected to the publication of your paper... We have not been provided with any explanation from the Bank about why the country office rejected your paper, but a colleague (CL) said the country office was concerned that the publication of the paper could somehow derail the peace process. It seems rather far-fetched but this is the reason we were given. We tried several different arguments with the Bank about why the paper should be published... but to no avail" (Letter of January 23, 2006, from Andrew Rosser, author's archives). Flattered though I was by the implication that I could single-handedly derail the peace process, I, too found the reason "far-fetched." The unstated reason, of course, was that the Bank office in

---

[24] René Lemarchand and Julien Nimubona, *Burundi Political Economy Scoping Study*, Bujumbura, May 1, 2008, p. 7 (Unpublished manuscript).

Bujumbura was yielding to the pressure of its Tutsi advisers, as it happened again two years later when asked to join a Bank project in Bujumbura.

Trifling though it may sound, the incident is illustrative of the rancorous disagreements that sometimes-plagued policymakers on issues related to the civil war and its aftermath. This is nowhere more evident than in the discord that broke out between State Department officials and Ambassador Robert Krueger during the latter's term in Bujumbura, from 1994 to 1996. The story has been told in his compelling memoir, co-authored with his wife, Kathleen Tobin Krueger.[25] In it the authors convey a frightening picture of the killings of civilians by the Tutsi-dominated army during the civil war. In page after page the reader is confronted with grisly crime scenes, graphically illustrated by horrific photos of murdered men, women, and children. Even though Hutu-led *bandes armées* are not exonerated from blame, Krueger's statements to the press left no doubt as to who was responsible for such atrocities. He was promptly identified among some government officials as the enemy of the Tutsi. Recriminations from army brass were followed by death threats. Ultimately, in June 1996, the State Department recalled the ambassador for consultations. He never came back.

A former senator and congressman, I first met Ambassador Krueger in 1984 at the US Embassy in Bujumbura, and many years later in Texas, at the Texas Lutheran University, where I was invited to present a paper. On each occasion he struck me as a highly competent, warm-hearted, outgoing personality, as well as a principled diplomat (this is not an oxymoron). His courage as ambassador was legendary, insisting on driving his 4-wheel vehicle to scenes of mayhem, at great risk to his life, visiting the bereaved, reaching out to missionaries, and never hesitating to point the finger at the murderous rabble aka the Burundi Defense Forces. Not everyone in Foggy Bottom was pleased with his performance. To put it crudely, many were more concerned about covering their asses than uncovering the truth.

Nor is this attitude unique to the US. Consider the case of the French cabinet minister Bernard Debré, who, shortly after landing in Bujumbura, volunteered the following astonishing comment about Colonel Bikomagu (whose role in planning Ndadaye's murder is only one example among others of his military prowess): "Bikomagu is an extraordinarily decent man," adding in the same vein, "the Burundi army opposes extremists (and) have decided to preserve[26] order while respecting political authorities," prompting Krueger to comment, "this was the most extraordinarily misinformed statement by any high-level visitor to Burundi during my entire time there."

One of Krueger's most dedicated critics, the late Howard Wolpe, stands out in my mind, if only because of the curious warning he sent me in 2008, years after being appointed by President Clinton as Special Envoy to the Great Lakes. My cordial relation with Krueger apparently set off alarm

---

[25] Bob Krueger, *From Bloodshed to Hope in Burundi: Our Embassy Years during Genocide* (Austin, 2007).

[26] Krueger, *From Bloodshed to Hope in Burundi*, pp. 207–208.

bells. His email is worth quoting: "Frankly René, State was hugely embarrassed by Krueger's conduct, and felt that they had to remove him from the scene. He became so identified with a pro-Hutu perspective, and so demonized all Tutsi that he became dysfunctional as a diplomat. He was removed before I began my role as Special Envoy. When I did take over in June 1996, principal policy making responsibility became mine, working closely with Assistant Secretary, with Ambassador Bogosian, and later with the various Ambassadors that served following Krueger. My deputy Jim Yellin, became my principal resource; none was more knowledgeable or nuanced about the Burundi situation." This mail came like a bolt out of the blue, given that I never solicited his opinion about Ambassador Krueger's performance. I needed no assistance on that score.

I should have known better. My fallout with Wolpe is traceable to a talk I gave at the Carnegie Foundation on the situation on Burundi, attended by a fair number of interested Africanists and policy wonks, the Burundi ambassador and Wolpe himself. After some off-the-cuff remarks about Madeleine Albright's less than prophetic tribute to the "New Leaders" of the Great Lakes, holding aloft the promise of democracy, I proceeded to explicate the complexity of Burundi politics, which I said seemed largely beyond the ken of US policymakers. I ended by presentation with a note of caution about the unwisdom of appointing special envoys whose views may conceivably clash with those of accredited ambassadors. Wolpe never forgot. Whether he forgave I am not sure.

At any rate I am still at a loss to figure out how a Democratic Congressman, undoubtedly well-intentioned but with little knowledge of French, and even less of the history and politics of the Great Lakes, could end up holding a key policy-making position in a largely Francophone, and extraordinarily complex, region of the continent. After serving as Special Envoy, Wolpe served as director of Africa Program and Leadership Project at the Woodrow Wilson International Center for Scholars. His main claim to fame in this role was to have inaugurated and pushed through one the most expensive fiasco in the history of international peace initiatives: his Leadership Workshop for Burundi Military Commanders, a project funded by the World Bank, the UK Department of International Development, and the European Commission for Conflict Prevention Unit, became a by-word for waste and mismanagement. The ill-fated program was later extended to the DRC, with equally dismal results, but at an even higher cost. Sadly, as the continuing threats to civilian lives tragically demonstrate, the Leadership Workshop experiment never lived up to its promise.

Nkurunziza's ambivalent legacy

Looking back at the country's turbulent trajectory since President Nkurunzia's election in 2005 and his unexpected death (of cardiac arrest) on June 9, 2020, the peace deal brokered by Nelson Mandela at Arusha, officially known as the Arusha Peace and Reconciliation Agreement (APRA) of

August 2000,[27] stands as a watershed. Even more consequential, however, is the 2015 crisis ushered by Nkurunziza's decision to run for a third term in defiance of the constitution. His fateful gesture helps us understand his strikingly mixed record in the course of his 15 years in office.

There are two Nkurunzizas. One is a symbol of national reconciliation, the other a symbol of division; one is the embodiment of power-sharing, the other of Hutu hegemony; one pays tribute to the Arusha-inspired constitutional guarantees, the other seeks to destroy them. The more positive image – all too often ignored by commentators fixated on the "bad guy" trope – cannot be shoved under the rug. Even the devil must be given his due.

To be frank, I've never been more upbeat about the future of Burundi than during the early years of Nkuruniziza's mandate. No other statesman anywhere in the continent seemed more committed to make the Arusha-based power-sharing formula the basis of the new state. Concretely, this meant that Hutu elements would control 60 per cent of governmental and parliamentary positions and the Tutsi 40 per cent. Crucially, the army was now thoroughly reorganized on the basis of an equal number of Hutu and Tutsi. Furthermore, of the two vice-presidents one was a Hutu, the other a Tutsi, each belonging to different parties. While Rwanda remained firmly under the rule of a Tutsi-dominated dictatorship buttressed by a constitutionally sanctioned ethnic amnesia, Burundi appeared headed in a distinctly more promising direction, where the recognition of ethnic differences would serve as the best guarantee of political stability.

The disenchantment came in 2015. First came Nkurunziza's earth-shaking announcement that he would run for a third term, regardless of constitutional obstacles. Then came the insurrectionary response: the abortive, Hutu-led coup of May 13, 2015 brought the country to the edge of the abyss, reducing to naught what few promising steps had been made towards a multi-ethnic, pluralist democracy. In the days following the coup some 1,200 civilians were killed, some by the police and security forces, others by the predominantly Hutu youth militia, the *imbonerakure*. A number of journalists, human rights activists and politicians, Hutu and Tutsi, were targeted or forced to seek refuge in neighboring states. Of these Rwanda ended up being host to some 300,000, mostly Tutsi refugees.

As 2015 drew to a close, the political landscape changed utterly. The architect of this drastic shift to autocracy was Nkurunziza himself, but this could not have happened without the institutional tools forged during the devastating civil war (1993–2000) at the cost of an estimated 300,000 deaths. The ruling party played a key role. Propelled by its own revolutionary zeal as the spearhead of the Hutu rebellion, the *Conseil National pour la Défense de la Démocratie/Forces pour la Défense de la Démocratie*

---

[27] Not to be confused with the ill-fated Arusha Peace Accord of August 4, 1993, between the Rwanda government and the RPF, under the auspices of the UN and the Organization of African Unity (OAU), which was intended to lay the groundwork for national reconciliation.

(CNDD/FDD) quickly displaced the Frodebu as the standard bearer of Hutu aspirations; from the ashes of its more tolerant predecessor emerged an immensely more coercive apparatus.

Among those who defected some did not hesitate to denounce the ominous trend towards dictatorial inquisition. Commenting on the effect on its leadership of years spent in the bush as a rebel organization, Gervais Rufyikiri, a former vice-president of the Nkurunziza regime now living in exile, gives a frightening picture of the party's modus operandi, especially as it applies to its armed wing, the *Forces pour la Defense de la Démocratie* (FDD): "Torture and other inhuman treatments were also meted out to punish fighters found guilty. They were often sequestered in a kind of dugout also known as *ihandagi*... The prisoners were subjected to a regime of up to 50 lashes three times a day for weeks or months. Worse, many combatants suffered and died from cruel torture particularly in cases of upright partial burial alive... Several sources claim that internal conflicts caused more FDD's officers' deaths than were killed by the opposing camp."[28] As I found out in the course of conversations with asylum seekers, this legacy of brutality is still painfully evident in the methods used by the police or the security apparatus to deal ith suspected dissidents.

That some of the most competent and democratically inclined higher-ranking civil servants felt they had no other choice than to seek asylum abroad is hardly surprising. Besides Rufyikiri, the list includes Leonidas Hatungimana, the president's official spokesman, Pie Ntahovyohanyuma, president of the National Assembly, Onesime Nduwimana, the CNDD-FDD spokesperson, Geneviève Kanyange, president of the CNDD-FDD's Women's League, Moise Bucumi, minister of public works. All of them are now living in Belgium or Germany.

Since 2015, the ruling party has been remarkably adept at consolidating its authority through parallel organizations under the sway of hard-liners.

The most striking feature of the new system is the extent to which the army top guns have been retooled as the "big men" in an all-encompassing network of coercive hierarchies. As of late 2019 The top brass included the following generals: Alain Guillaume Bunyoni (minister of public security), Etienne Ntakarutimana (head of the security services), Evariste Ndayishimiye (secretary general of the CNDD-FDD), Gabriel Nizigama (chef de cabinet of the president), Godefroid Bizimana (chargé de mission), Prime Niyongabo (army chief of staff), and Gervais Ndirakobuca (chef de cabinet of the head of police).[29] This rise to power of the military is succinctly captured in Tomas van Acker's excellent analysis of the evolving party–state relationship he sums up the emergent system as resting on "a

[28] Gervais Rufyikiri, *The Post-Wartime Trajectory of CNDD/FDD Party in Burundi: A Façade Transformation of Rebel Movement toPolitical Party*, Institute for Development Policy and Management (IOB), University of Antwerp, 2018.

[29] I am grateful to Gervais Rufyikiri for mentioning these names to me.

double dictatorship: a single party system, and within the party a military dictatorship."[30]

Under a military rule that doesn't say its name the state has developed into a tightly controlled set of command structures. The police force rose from 2300 in 2000 to somewhere between 15,000 and 20,000 by 2007; ten years later, its size has increased to 30,000. Organized into three Rapid Mobile Intervention Groups (*Groupements mobiles d'intervention rapide*) intended to combat crime, it has developed into a powerful political tool. Its propensity to engage in arbitrary arrests and violence is well established. The ruling party youth militia, *imbonerakure* (those to see from afar) can best be described as an auxiliary police force, and like the regular police consists of a vast majority of Hutu elements. Even more fearsome is the *Service National des Renseignements* (SNR), the all-powerful intelligence apparatus, which operates totally outside the law and has a free hand to arrest, incarcerate, torture or kill. Since 2015 hundreds of suspected enemies have been killed, and thousands of others arbitrarily arrested and tortured.

Meanwhile the regime has gone through great lengths to split opposition parties, a strategy associated with a practice known as *nyakurisation*, from *nyakuri*, "truth." In short, the only "true" opposition parties are those recognized and manipulated by the state. Conferring or withholding authenticity is the key to the government's divide and rule strategy, as it implies favors, including exemption from police brutality or worse. In the ideological context of Burundi politics, the truth label confers legitimacy and thus protects party leaders from the shame of betrayal. Betrayal is indeed the standard accusation leveled at all *bajeri* – meaning roughly "rabid dogs that need to be killed" – as opponents to the regime are generally described, in contrast to the heroic virtues inherent in the *abagumyabanga*, the name given to the members of the CNDD/FDD. In her illuminating discussion of the Burundi crisis, Anne-Claire Courtois translates the term as "those who can keep a secret," or "those who walk a straight line." As she goes on to show, seen in the context of the rebellion this language has a deeper connotation, evocative of the courage and trustworthiness of the CNDD/FDD combatants, united in the same struggle against a common enemy.[31] It is at this level, brilliantly explored by Aidan Russell, where language adds a moral dimension to politics,[32] that one can best understand the aura of near-sanctity claimed by Nkurunziza.

God's truth is an altogether different kettle of fish. But there is a significant connection between divine truth and the *nyakuri* phenomenon, well summed up by Courtois: "there is no way to challenge religious rhetoric: to

---

[30] Tomas Van Acker, *From Bullets to Ballots and Back? Arenas, Actors and Repertoires of Power in Post-War Burundi* (Ghent, 2018), p. 84.

[31] Anne-Claire Courtois, "Le Burundi en crise: 'Pirates' contre 'Vrais Combatants'," *Fondation pour la recherche stratégique*, Note no. 11/17, p. 3.

[32] Russell, *Politics and Violence in Burundi*.

engage in political opposition is tantamount to challenging God Himself, which is unthinkable."[33]

The messianic dimension of Burundi politics finds its clearest expression in, *The Power of Hope*, the autobiographical narrative of Nkurunziza's wife, in which she reveals her "true" identity as an Evangelist: "Above all I am one of God's servants, an ordained Deacon since 2001 and an Evangelist since 2005. And since 2011, Pastor. Becoming a Pastor is not a sudden desire that enters you and to which you respond. It is a calling, *umuhamagaro*, in Kirundi."[34] The call came in April 1997 at the Protestant Church of the Good Shepherd in Mutanga-Nord: "That day the pastor who was preaching took his sermon from Matthew 11:28: 'Come to me, all you who are tired of carrying a heavy load...' From then on, every time I came home from work, I went to this soothing place, for a little word. The pastor said to me 'God loves you' and I would go home appeased."[35] Presumably her husband's political engagement stemmed from the same divine inspiration, as when he heard God's call to become a Born-again Christian, and serve as the *ndongozi* (guide) leading his flock out of darkness through the light of a God-given mandate. Make no mistake about it: he was elected to execute God's mission, and knew about his victory from prophecies way back before his election in 2005.

Born-again Christians make odd bedfellows. Thus shortly after his election to the presidency, and to the shock and consternation of onlookers, Nkurunziza welcomed Artémon Simbananiye, the orchestrator of the 1972 bloodbath, with a big hug and a warm handshake! The photo of the two killers, one Tutsi, the other Hutu, embracing each other, circulated widely on social networks. From all evidence unrepentant murderers can get along fine as long as they share a common faith in Born-again Christianity.

If this can be seen a bizarre an avatar of the 1972 bloodbath, others are more somber reminders of what happened. In early 2017 a mass grave was discovered in central Burundi that contained the skeletal remains of some 1,000 victims, most probably all of them Hutu. More recently, the Burundi-based Iwacu News network revealed the existence fourteen mass graves in Ruvubu containing the remains of 7,000 bodies. According to the chairman of the Truth and Reconciliation Commission (TRC), Pierre-Claver Ndayicariye, the victims "are from Gitega, Karuzi, Ruyigi and Muyinga provinces and were killed in the 1972 crisis. The victims include teachers, civil servants, soldiers, small traders, more or less well-off peasants, pupils, religious people and Burundians of all categories and ethnic groups... They were first killed in Gitega prison before being thrown in mass graves dug by mechanical devices overnight near Ruvubu bridge."[36]

[33] Courtois, "Le Burundi en crise," p. 7.
[34] Denise Bucumi-Nkurunziza, *The Power of Hope* (Paris, 2013), p. 149.
[35] Bucumi-Nkurunziza, *The Power of Hope*, pp. 80–81.
[36] Diane Uwimana, "7000 Bodies Identified in Fourteen Mass Graves," www.IWACU-Burundi.org, January 29, 2020.

Tragically linked to such grim reminders is the presence in Burundi of a large number of orphans, some of whom are now holding positions of considerable authority. Their influence on the future destinies of the country is hard to exaggerate.

The orphans' revenge

"The problem of orphans is enormous," writes Nigel Watt: "there are estimated to be up to 900,000 in Burundi, about one third of this number due to AIDS."[37] An unknown proportion are the product of the 1972 killings; many were brought up in an environment where they learned at an early age why they mourned the absence of a father, grandfather or uncle. Among them are a large number of high-ranking Hutu officials and politicians. Two of the most prominent, now deceased, were Nkurunziza, and the former head of SNR, Adolphe Nshimirimana (killed in 2015). A third is Nkurunziza's successor, Evariste Ndayishimeye, elected to the presidency of the republic on May 20, 2020, just in time to fill the vacancy left by the self-styled Eternal Leader and Supreme Guide of Patriotism.

As one reflects on the rising tide of anti-Tutsi sentiment in the wake of the abortive 2015 coup, the enduring legacy of 1972 becomes evident. Could it be that one genocide is ushering in another?

This is the question I raised with my exiled friend, Gervais Rufyikiri, Nkurunziza's former vice-president. His commentary is worth summarizing: A surprisingly high proportion of orphans can be found among political and military decision-makers. And their influence on how the past impacts on the present is considerable. Remembrance of 1972 is inseparable from the vision of Hutu elites, some of whom make no effort to conceal their determination to seek vengeance. Derogatory expressions intended to vilify the Tutsi are commonplace among the ruling organizations, notably he *imbonerakure*. The term *mugeri* (a rabid and very dangerous dog), is one example among others of how such terms are used to whip up Hutu support for the CNDD-FDD.

Of course, nothing is ever said of the countless abuses committed against Tutsi civilians by the security agencies, the police and the SNR, with the aid of the pro-government militia, *imbonerakure*. Nonetheless, the 1972 cataclysm stands as the irreducible single common denominator behind the venomous climate of anti-Tutsi sentiment that figures so prominently in today's political equation.

In his gut-wrenching biographical narrative of Aloys Niyoyita's career as an orphan turned journalist-in-exile Antoine Kaburahe – himself a journalist forced into exile after a near-fatal attempt on his life – gives us a sense of the terrifying void experienced by orphans as they tried to find their

[37] Watt, *Burundi*, op. cit., p. 142.

bearings. In his preface to the book Gael Faye[38] asks: "What happens when orphaned children no longer have access to the stories of their parents? What happens when words no longer say anything and the tears of the living take refuge in their bellies like a swallowed scream?" This is Aloys's reply: "Papa disappeared. Literally and figuratively. I have retained a few vague if not fleeting images that accompany my nights of insomnia. My young brain couldn't' hold on to an image of papa. I was only four when he disappeared. No one will ever know how to evaluate the damage caused by such trauma in the head of a kid my age. The need for security, the lack of affection. Until the age of fifteen I could only fall asleep on the still firm breast of my poor mother. She let me snuggle up to her and calmed my nightmares. Instinctively she understood my malaise. Mothers feel things like that. 1972 didn't' just take papa. It also stole the candor of our child-hood... 1972 crushed my childhood. The broken dreams of a whole family."[39] Aloys's thoughts should give us pause, especially when you consider that they could be shared by hundreds if not thousands.

Although there is no denying their influence, one of the many unknowns in Burundi's political equation is the precise role the grown up orphans now at the helm are likely to play in shaping the perceptions and policies of the state.

Another is what changes, if any, one can expect from the emergence into the public space of their most prominent representative, the newly elected president of the republic, Evariste Ndayishimiye.

The Ndayishimiye enigma

Not a great deal is known of his career path and personality, except that he was among the first to join the CNDD-FDD armed rebellion. Born in 1968 in Gitaga, in central Burundi, he became an orphan at the age of four. Years later, he enrolled as a law student at the University of Bujumbura. He miraculously survived the targeted killing of Hutu students in March 1995, an operation code-named "Take down the monster" (*Déboulonner le monstre*), the latter being the soon forced to resign Hutu president Sylvestre Ntibantuganya. He hastily joined the armed rebellion. By 1997 was commander in chief of the CNDD-FDD combat units, and from 2001 to 2003 served as president of the *Conseil national ses patriotes*, the party's core policymaking organ. He rose further up in the ladder after being appointed minister of interior and public security from 2006 to 20007, and ultimately as the Secretary general of the CNDD-FDD.

---

[38] Gael Faye, now living in exile, is the author of the award-winning novel *Petit Pays* (Paris, 2019), a brilliant effort to illuminate Burundi's turbulent history through the misadventures of his friends and family.

[39] Antoine Kaburahe, *Hutsi: In the Name of Us All*. Editions Iwacu (Bujumbura, 2019), pp. 16, 63–64. Like a great many orphans, Aloys Niyoyita is of mixed origins, his father was Hutu and his mother Tutsi. Hence the book's title, *Hutsi*.

As one Nkurunziza's hand-picked successors Ndayishimiye's victory at the polls was unsurprising. By winning 69 percent of the vote against his nearest CNL opponent, Agaton Rwasa, his score seemed plausible, at least compared to the Stalin-like percentages repeatedly registered in Kagame's Rwanda.

Doubts arise though when you consider the massive fraud that has been reported by impartial observers on the ground. Ballot stuffing, giving votes to people incarcerated or dead was not infrequent. "When I saw the same person voting for the third time I complained, said one voter; he was sent packing by officials and told to stop creating problems."[40] This is not the first time that fraudulent elections have been reported, or that electoral results remained unchallenged by the courts. Again, the abuses reported by the *Ligue Ibuka*, a reliable watchdog now operating in exile, raised few eyebrows among those familiar with earlier elections. More than 400 supporters of Rwasa ended up in prison in the run up to the polls, along with some 200 arbitrary arrests, 67 killings and 20 cases of torture.[41]

What is new is the broad sweep of powers now conferred on the president, and the limits placed on parliamentary controls. Both are conspicuous features of the new 2018 constitution under which Ndayishimiye will rule.[42] Gone are the minority veto guarantees inscribed in the two-thirds parliamentary majority for passing legislation. A simple majority is all that is needed, thus rendering almost meaningless the maintenance of ethnic quotas. The vice-presidents are simply eliminated, and instead a prime minister has been introduced whose party affiliation and ethnic identity will likely be the same as the president's. As head of the government the prime minister is largely eclipsed by the enhanced authority of the head of state. Besides being elected for a seven year term instead of five as was the case in the previous constitution, the president can appoint and dismiss government ministers; any piece of legislation not promulgated within 30 days automatically lapses; and only the president has full control of the national intelligence agency (SNR). In such circumstances, the survival of ethnic quotas is puzzling. Coalition governments are unlikely to materialize, and so are the ethnic checks and balances so carefully calibrated in the Arusha accords. Admittedly, those had already been virtually dismantled by Nkurunziza after 2015, when every effort was made to strengthen the grip of control mechanism headed by generals. The new arrangement makes plain what until then had been a thinly veiled maneuver.

It is still too early to predict what the future may hold in store, but with the elimination of those few constitutional hurdles that stood in the way of despotic rule nothing will prevent Ndayishimiye from emulating Kagame's

---

[40] As reported by *The Economist*, "Burundi's Sham Elections," May 20, 2020, p. 38.

[41] *Economist*, "Burundi's Sham Elections."

[42] For the information in this paragraph I am indebted to Stef Vandeginste's excellent analysis, "Burundi's Institutional Landscape after 2020," *Africa Policy Brief*, no. 30, April 2020.

ethnic dictatorship. There are too many signs pointing in this direction not to be concerned by this ominous convergence. This is made plain in the open letter addressed to President Evariste Ndayishimiye by the Burundi Human Rights Initiative, an independent international human rights project. After taking note of his "public condemnations of political violence and commitment to ending impunity in (his) inauguration speech of June 18, 2020," the letter goes on to draw attention to "the cases of six Burundian s who were killed because of their political affiliations between October 2029 and May 2020": "According tour investigations members of the youth league of the party you headed for the last four years, the *Imbonerakure*, were responsible for most of these crimes. In Ngozi province, they attacked a 22-year-old bar owner, Evariste Nyabenda, when he tried to stop them from beating his fellow CNL members in October 2019; he died in November from his injuries. A month later, in Bujumbura province, Desiré Ntahondabasigiye, a local CNL representative, was shot dead through a window of his house while he was eating dinner with his wife and children; two *Imbonerakure* with guns were seen near his house. More recently, in May, only two weeks before the elections, *Imbonerakure* abducted Richard Havyarimana, a local CNL representative in Mwaro province. He was found dead in a river three days later, with deep gashes on his head. He left behind a young widow and a three-month-old baby. In some of these cases Imbonerakure acted in collusion with – or with the apparent support of – local government officials or local CNDD-FDD representatives... In other cases, state agents are reported to have carried out killings themselves. In March 2020 Albert Niyondiko, who was suspected of supported the armed opposition was shot dead on the doorstep of a shack in Bururi province, in an operation by the police and intelligence services, who ordered his immediate burial... Evariste, Désiré, Richard, Jean-Bosco, Fauzia and Albert are just a few of the victims of political violence that has swept through Burundi in the period leading up to the 2020 elections."[43] Given Ndayishimiye's consistently repressive track record in his earlier incarnation any trend towards a genuine democratic opening is highly unlikely.

At a time when the "Black Lives Matter" movement has reached an unprecedented world-wide visibility following George Floyd's martyrdom, how would one wish to hear an echo, faint as it might be, resonate across the Great Lakes, as in Tutsi lives matter, Hutu lives matter. In Rwanda the phrase has no meaning; there are, constitutionally speaking, no Hutu or Tutsi, only Banyarwanda. In Burundi a semblance of ethnic power-sharing is written into the constitution, a make-believe afterthought that fools no one. In both cases, though, while the past continues to haunt collective memories the present is pregnant with potential violence.

What stands out in Burundi is the persistence of a memorial legacy that feeds mutual hatreds, cutting across generations, deepening ethnic fault

---

[43] Burundi Human Rights Initiative (BHRI), "An Open Letter to President Evariste Ndayishimiye," July 9, 2020.

lines. Will the grown-up orphans now in charge of the country's destinies lay to rest once and for all the ghosts of 1972? The opacity surrounding the state of Hutu–Tutsi relations makes it hard to predict. A Kirundi proverb puts it in its own idiosyncratic way: *Umurundi aguhisha ko akwanka nawe ukamuhisha ko ubizi.* A Murundi hides the fact that he hates you, and you hide the fact that you know it.

4 The view from Uganda

Refugee warriors at the gates

Early on the afternoon of October 1, 1990, a group of armed men wearing Ugandan army fatigues crossed the border with Rwanda at the Kagitumba border post, opening the way for hundreds of others. In the next few hours some four thousand members of the Rwanda Patriotic Front (RPF) entered the Mutara region of northern Rwanda, determined to fight their way back into their ancestral homeland. Little did they realize the magnitude of the cataclysm they were about to touch off, or, as a harbinger of worse to come, the terrible costs of the three and a half years of the war that soon engulfed both invaders and resisters. Nor did anybody else.

Though duly reported in the press, the news of the invasion went almost unnoticed in the US. Not only was Rwanda a virtually unknown entity in the minds of most Americans, but mere mention of Tutsi and Hutu seemed to evoke little more than polite smiles. Expressions of concern from the Rwandan Embassy in Washington stirred few anxieties in the State Department. The Voice of America (VOA) was the exception. In the interview I gave to the VOA in early November I made it a point to emphasize the risks involved: after pointing out that the invasion could only be described as a flagrant violation of the most elementary principles of international law, I went on to draw attention to serious threats it posed to the Tutsi civilian population in Rwanda, now held hostage and a potential target of *revanchiste* moves. The interview – relayed in Kinyarwanda in the pages of *Impuruza*, the pro-Tutsi newspaper edited by Alexander Kimenyi in California – sealed, if not my fate, at least my reputation. Rightly or wrongly, I was now firmly identified as a friend of the Hutu and an enemy of the Tutsi.

I found some doors wide open, others slammed shut. Rwanda's embassy, predictably, proved especially welcoming. Ambassador Aloys Uwimana soon called to thank me for the interview, adding that public opinion in the US needed to be much better informed about the possible consequences of the Uganda-backed invasion. How about coming to Washington to alert the *Time Magazine* correspondent of the gravity of the situation? I agreed. After meeting the Washington bureau chief, we explained the reason for our visit, at which point he admitted having no clue where Rwanda was on the map of Africa. A map was promptly supplied, but did little to awaken his interest in our story.

"I honestly don't think our readers would be interested," he concluded, while politely showing us the exit.

But as the crisis moved from a cross-border clash to something resembling a full-scale invasion accompanied by daring raids – such as the January 1991 raid on the Ruhengeri prison, resulting in the liberation of scores of inmates, including the (in)famous Lizinde (of which more later) – it attracted growing international attention.

Inyenzi and Refugee Warriors

Parallels with the border raids made by the *inyenzi* 30 years earlier inevitably come to mind, perhaps most notably among readers of my 1970 book on *Rwanda and Burundi*. But if Chapter 7, The *Inyenzi* at the Gates, rhymes with the title of this chapter, that is as far as the analogy goes. With the benefit of hindsight, seen from the perspective of their leadership, fighting skills and resource base the refugee warriors of the 1990s could not have been more different.

Much has been written on the prehistory of the Rwanda Patriotic Front (RPF), starting with its nascent embryo, the Rwanda Refugee Welfare Foundation (RRWF), later becoming the Rwanda Alliance for National Unity (RANU), then joining Museveni's Front for National Salvation (FRONASA) and finally mutating into the RPF. Readers of Gérard Prunier's early historical account[1] are familiar with the twists and turns of the movement's early trajectory. But a closer look at the factors that have contributed to the RPF's military and political success may be useful when compared with other refugee communities.

The vast majority of the RPF cadres were sons or grandsons of *Unar* politicians. Their ancestral roots were in Rwanda; their mother tongue is Kinyarwanda; their political consciousness is inseparable from the setbacks suffered by their elders as they vainly tried to fashion the *Unar* into an effective politico-military organization. They learned important lessons from the past. First and foremost, the need to build a coherent organization, which is the one thing the Unarists never was able to achieve, torn as they were between monarchists opportunists, and left-leaning socialists. The list of associational ties preceding the birth of the RPF is a commentary on the hands-on experience gained by the refugees long before they became warriors. They were able to stitch together a vast network connecting links with their kinsmen not just in Uganda, but also across the Great Lakes region and Europe. Associations made financial resources available, and by the same token facilitated access to higher education at Makarere College, where ad hoc meetings among Tutsi students became more frequent; education went hand in hand with rising prospects for social promotion.

If organizational skills proved crucial to gain access to resources, both were essential for expanding the reach of the RPF and establishing its

[1] Gérard Prunier, *The Rwanda Crisis: History of a Genocide* (New York, 1995).

credentials as a rebel movement. But one thing more than anything else made the difference: luck.

Only by an extraordinary combination of circumstances were Fred Rwigyema and Paul Kagame able to rise to the top echelons of the NRA military establishment, the first as Chief of Staff (and later Deputy Minister of Defense), the other as acting head of military intelligence. Both fought side by side against Obote's forces, eventually scoring a decisive victory at Kabamba, in the Luwero triangle, in 1981. Only by their iron-clad commitment to their long-term agenda, and unflagging self-confidence were they able to overcome their early setbacks, and cash in at a later date on their signal contribution to the NRA's victories in the years following the fall of Idi Amin in 1979. Nonetheless, luck also helped.

Their change of fortunes began with Amin's overthrow and Obote's rise to power following rigged elections in 1980. Neither were cause for rejoicing among Rwandan refugees. Many had been supporters of Amin; if for no other reason they fell foul of the new regime, and in time the entire Banyarwanda community found itself in Obote's cross-hairs.

The early 1980s were the worst of times – not just for Tutsi refugees but for Banyarwanda in general, including Hutu and Tutsi, non-citizens as well as long-established residents. Everywhere in Africa refugee communities are casualties of power struggles within host countries, but if the fate that befell the Tutsi refugees in Uganda is by no means unique, the political backlash of the pogroms inflicted by Obote's youth squads and the special forces police units is hard to exaggerate. After the forced displacement of tens of thousands their decision to fight their way back to their homeland became an existential choice. Going back was no option.

The flight to Rwanda – and back

Between October 2 and December 31, 1982 an estimated 80,000 Banyarwanda, most of them Tutsi, were expelled from their homes in south-west Uganda. Of these some 40,000 fled to Rwanda. One eyewitness, Jason W. Clay, describes what happened: "The displacement was carried by force. People who resisted were beaten; women were raped. Some people were killed; others committed suicide rather than leave their homes. Others died from neglect or exposure. Many displaced citizens were stripped of their IDs. The roofs, doors and windows, as well as anything else of value, were removed from the houses, which were then burned or pushed to the ground. Some of the displaced people travelled five to seven days before reaching Uganda or Rwanda."[2]

By October 1982, 1,500 refugees a day were seeking shelter in Rwanda. At the end of the day the presence of an estimated 40,000 Banyarwanda – a majority of the Hutu – confronted the Habyarimana government with

[2] Jason Clay, *The Eviction of the Banyarwanda: The Story Behind the Refugee Crisis in Southwest Uganda, Cultural Survival*, August 1984, p. 3.

difficult choices. Aside from the additional pressure on an already densely populated region, the flow of thousands of Banyarwanda would likely trigger a dangerous spike of ethnic tensions. In the end 13,000 refugees and 50,000 cattle were allowed to settle in the Kagera National Park, a tsetse-infested region, that made a permanent settlement improbable. Only a fraction of the 30,000 that Rwanda had reluctantly agreed to host effectively stayed within its borders. The real breakthrough came with the overthrow of the Obote regime in November 1985, which cleared the ground for the repatriation of 30,000 expellees.

The breakthrough

In January 1986 the triumphant NRA entered Kampala. According to Mahmood Mamdani, a close observer of the Uganda scene, roughly a quarter of their ranks of 16,000 were composed of Banyarwanda. From then on, many young Tutsi, and not a few Hutu, enthusiastically cast their lot with the NRA. But if the future of the NRA looked brighter than at any time since its birth, that of the Banyarwanda remained uncertain. Anti-Banyarwanda sentiment grew steadily in the late 1980s, fueled by a sense of deprivation in the face non-citizens rising to high-ranking positions within the army, and, at the other end of the spectrum, at the sight of thousands of Banyarwanda herders squatting the land owned by indigenous ranchers. Both sets of grievances were aired publicly and repeatedly by the anti-Banyarwanda lobby in Parliament. Legislators made every effort to bar Banyarwanda elements from land ownership, and, even more ominously, to remove them from the army. Their call did not go unheeded. Museveni responded by removing Rwigyema from his position as Chief of Staff in 1989, and, for good measure, relieving Kagame of his duties as head of military intelligence, sending him for training to Fort Leavenworth, Kansas. It is ironic to recall that Kagame was thus following the footsteps of Guy Logiest when, some 30 years earlier, he attended the US Command and General Staff College at Fort Leavenworth, though mistakenly located in Missouri in his *apologia pro vita sua*.

Sensing that the time had come for some sort of breakthrough Museveni made a deal with his fair-weather Rwandan allies, in the form of a quid pro quo. For the quid of logistical and military support from the NRA Museveni received the quo of their promised exit from Uganda. As soon as the circumstances seemed right, the Banyarwanda combatants would push on into Rwanda with the blessings of their commander in chief.

Thus began, on October 1, 1990, an invasion described by many as a return to their homeland. The operation did not begin under the best of auspices. The death of the charismatic Rwigyema, killed on the first day of the invasion, was received with shock and sadness among RPF rank and file. Opinions differ as to whether Rwigyema fell under an enemy's bullet or by intended unfriendly fire. Whatever the case may be, the posthumous homage paid by Alexandre Kimenyi in his long eulogy, penned in the style of Rwanda's dynastic poems, is a measure of the respect he enjoyed during his short life.

The resolve of his companions remained undiminished. After years of exile, alienation and homelessness, at long last the promised land was within reach. Or so it seemed.

The rising tide of Hutu radicalism

Their buoyant sense of triumphalism is what I remember most distinctly from the contacts I had with my few Tutsi friends in the days following the invasion. One of them was Charles Murigande (later to become Minister of Foreign Affairs and Secretary of the FPR in the Kagame government), who at the time had found employment as a research assistant at Howard University. He and his wife had invited me for dinner at their Washington home, and the conversation immediately zeroed in on the news from the battlefront. Concerns about the deterioration of Hutu–Tutsi relations inside Rwanda were groundless, he assured me. Unlike the Habyarimana regime, the FPR once in power will spare no effort to install a genuinely democratic system, free of ethnic discrimination; we have no intention of replacing one form of dictatorship by another. Premature though it was to predict how things might turn out, I had my doubts. What seemed most likely, I thought, was a surge of extremism at both sides of the ethnic spectrum.

The tragi-comic scenario put in place by the Habyarimana government immediately after the invasion is sadly illustrative of how ethnic tensions were manipulated for political benefits. By staging a fake attack on Kigali by RPF troops, the aim was to project a dramatic picture of the gravity of the menace posed by the Tutsi enemy so as to pressure the French and Belgian governments to substantially increase their levels of military aid. The shooting directed at the imaginary assailants went on through much of the night of October 4, prompting the French ambassador, Georges Martres to send an alarming report to Paris about heavy fighting in the capital, thereby, as Prunier observes, "achieving the desired effect in Paris."[3]

The monstrous ineptitude of the Habyarimana blowhards was on full display the following day when thousands of predominantly Tutsi suspects were rounded up and herded in the Kigali stadium. Among them was a close Tutsi friend of mine, Landoald Ndasingwa, whose restaurant, Chez Lando, was a favorite watering hole of the international community. News of his arrest made my blood boil. I immediately sent a wheedling letter to President Habyarimana to convey "my sense of anguish over the fate of my long-time and dearest friend, Lando," imploring him to set him free. Instructions to that effect promptly followed. Glad though I was to have gotten him out of the clutches of the security, my sense of elation was short-lived. Lando was among the first to be assassinated in April 1994. Nor did my intercession on his behalf help assuage the fear and sufferings of

[3] Prunier, *The Rwanda Crisis*, p. 102.

thousands of innocents held captive in inhuman conditions. Nothing could have done more to deepen the Hutu–Tutsi rift.

As the conflict dragged on, prospects for peace vanished. By early 1991 the Rwanda Patriotic Army (RPA) had become a force to be reckoned with. This was made dramatically clear by the spectacular raid launched on the Ruhengeri prison in January 23, 1991, setting free dozens of prisoners, including Theoneste Lizinde, Habyarimana's former security chief, then serving a life sentence for allegedly ordering the killing of 56 former high-ranking personalities of the First Republic between 1973 and 1979.[4]

Besides causing a huge psychological shock, the Ruhengeri raid dispelled all doubts about the RPF's military capacity. While French military assistance rose to new levels, immediate steps were taken by Habyarimana to enlist fresh recruits into the army. From a small outfit numbering 5,200, the *Forces Armées Rwandaises* (FAR) reached a total of 15,000 in 1991 and 50,000 a year later. France, meanwhile, stepped up its military assistance. In March 1991 Agence France Presse announced the decision of the French government to send fresh troops to Rwanda to beef up its boots on the ground commitments. Which caused Charles Murigande – by now self-styled "Representative of the Rwandan community in Washington" – to write a strongly worded letter on March 17 to President Mitterrand, his prime minister Michel Rocard and the president of the National Assembly, Laurent Fabius. After reminding them of President Habyarimana's recent ultimatum to the FPR demanding its combatants to lay down their arms within 15 days, notwithstanding the recommendation of the summit meeting of the heads of state of Uganda, Tanzania, Rwanda and Burundi of February 18 to engage in peace negotiations under the mediation of President Mobutu, Murigande wonders whether Habyarimana's excessive self-confidence (*excès de confiance*) is not the consequence France's rising levels of military assistance in support of "a man who never ceased, over the last 17 years, to trample upon the values of liberty, equality and fraternity that are the foundation of the French Republic" (Author's archives). Unsurprisingly, Murigande's letter remained unanswered. But the questions it raised about the objective of France's military assistance to Rwanda did not go unnoticed.

Enters Rusatira

It is useful at this point to give voice to Colonel Leonidas Rusatira, one of the FAR's most lucid senior officers, known for his courage and professionalism.

---

[4] Lizinde was assassinated in Nairobi in October 1996, by courtesy of the RPF, perhaps a belated retribution for his stridently anti-Tutsi book, The *Discovery of Kalinga*. It is clear that Lizinde could never have authorized the appalling assassination of the entire batch of the First Republic revolutionaries – *les révolutionnires de* la *première* heure – without Habyarimana's approval. But this was a convenient pretext for putting in the clink one of his most dedicated opponents.

I met him for the first time in Kigali in 1990. He and I became close friends. I have kept the many letters he sent me not just as a reminder of our exchanges over the years but because of the light they shine on the impact of the country's venomous politics on the gradual deterioration the situation on the battlefield. Even more dangerous, as it turned out, was the venom distilled by the Kagame regime after the genocide when Rusatira, eager to turn the page, joined the RPA. In a letter of August 23, 1991, he expressed his qualms over the "official truth" about the war: "As somebody said the first casualty in a war is truth. Neither camp is totally right nor totally wrong. Whoever ends up with a monopoly on truth is the winning party. My dearest wish, which I fortunately share with most of my compatriots is that victory will belong to the real victor, the people of Rwanda." The tone of his March 27, 1992 letter was distinctly somber. "Too numerous are the victims on both sides. Thousands of displaced people are living in indescribable conditions. Even in the remotest corners you frequently find land mines and other devices likely to explode... This war has changed the country's physiognomy, as well as the stakes. It is mutating more and more into a civil war... At first what was at stake was our national sovereignty, threatened by an outside invader, and which every citizen owed to himself to combat. But that war has now ended. It has transformed itself into a conflict involving indefensible special interests, connected to the same people who are soliciting an outside intervention. Herein lies the explanation for the recent massacre in the Bugesera region, officially evaluated at 192 killed but in fact certainly a lot more... The Rwandan people are much in need of international solidarity to give aid and comfort to the many persons of good will seeking to bring to an end the massacre of innocent populations inside and outside the combat zones... Absent national unity this border war will spill over inside the country and beyond through the entire sub-region, already beset by countless problems."[5] Rusatira's prophetic words fell on deaf ears within and outside Rwanda. In a letter of October 22, 1997, informing me of his decision to seek asylum in Belgium, he wrote, "the massacres and manhunts are still going on"; he mentioned the killing of his three brothers, their wives and ten children, sarcastically adding, "good governance is finally in sight!" Turning to the political situation in Rwanda, the picture he draws is worth quoting: "The regime in Rwanda has won a military victory, but has lost the peace. What used to be a political problem when parties were allowed has become a purely ethnic problem. The FPR has lumped together all Hutu without exception, including those with the best of intentions, and thrust them in the same bag, thus missing the opportunity to reconstruct the country. Its first priority has been to get it over with the Hutu as a whole, beginning with those who had the misfortune of knowing how to read and write, among whom future leaders could be recruited. Dire consequences followed, including the continued massacres of the so-called 'infiltrated' [*ibyitso* in Kinyarwanda, the term was often used to designate

---

[5] This and other quotes from Rusatira's correspondence are from the author's files.

the Tutsi living in Rwanda before the 1990 invasion, many of whom were suspected of spying and dealt with accordingly]. But in fact most of the time what we have are cleverly orchestrated *mises en scène* by the regime's extremists to justify the elimination of thousands of poor innocent people whose only crime is their ethnic identity" (Author's archives).

What became known as "the Rusatira affair" reveals another frightening aspect of the Kagame regime: its capacity to target and ferret out a number of Hutu politicians and intellectuals living in exile. At the height of the genocide in early April 1994 Rusatira saved the lives of dozens of Tutsi by taking them to his residence in Kigali; on April 11, he went out of his way to rescue a dozen relatives of Alexis Kanyarengwe, a well-known Hutu opponent of the Habyarimana regime, whose lives were at risk; and on July 6, as Thierry Cruvellier reminds us, "he and a handful of other officers issued the so-called Kigeme declaration, in which they explicitly condemned the genocide and called for the creation of a tribunal to try the perpetrators."[6] Neither his courage in saving Tutsi lives, nor his decision to join the new regime, prevented Tutsi extremists from accusing him of actively participating in the genocide; even more astonishing was the receptivity of the International Criminal Tribunal for Rwanda (ICTR) to such aberrant charges. On February 22, 2002, the chief prosecutor Carla del Ponte brought an indictment against him in Brussels, charging him with the crime of genocide. Not until August 9, after mounting pressures from several well-known experts, notably Filip Reyntjens, Alison Des Forges, and André Guichaoua, all of them outraged by this travesty of justice, did the Chief Prosecutor withdraw the indictment.

The case of Rusatira casts a lurid light on the handling of justice under Kagame. But this is by no means the only one. The "disappearance" of Augustin Cyiza, a Lieutenant Colonel in the FAR who later served as Deputy President of the Supreme Court in the Kagame government, is even more abhorrent. Like Rusatira, he was a graduate of the *Ecole Militaire Supérieure* (EMS); he shared with him a strong personal and professional commitment to human rights and justice, made all the more convincing by his law degree, and both took a firm stand against the 1994 killings. But he also served on the infamous military commission appointed in 1991, which in its confidential report defined as an enemy of Rwanda every Tutsi or Hutu opponent to the regime, and whose senior member was none other than Théoneste Bagosora, the driving force behind the genocide.[7] Unlike Rusatira, however, Cyiza had a law degree, which propelled him to the top echelons of the Supreme Court. But under Kagame no court is ever supreme.

---

[6] Thierry Cruvellier, *Court of Remorse: Inside The international Criminal Tribunal for Rwanda*, copyrights of Board of Regents of the University of Wisconsin System. Reprinted by courtesy of the University of Wisconsin, Madison 2010, p. 147.

[7] See Thierry Cruvellier's vivid portrayal in "Par delà le glaive et la balance" in the fine collection of articles dedicated to Cyiza's memory, *Augustin Cyiza: Un homme libre au Rwanda* (Paris, 2004), pp. 7–15.

Of this his friend and supporter Joseph Sebarenzi became fully aware during his term of office (1997–2000) as speaker of the National Assembly,[8] before he too came into Kagame's cross-hairs and had to run for his life. His encounter with Colonel Frank Mugambage, chief of staff in the president's office, charged with explaining why Cyiza had to go, is not untypical of the government's modus operandi. To quote from Sebarenzi's autobiographical narrative: "We had to remove Augustin, he told me. It was for the good of the country... It's unconstitutional I said. Only the National assembly has the power to remove a justice of the supreme court, and then only with a two thirds majority vote... He shook his head. 'We didn't remove him because we disagreed with him... We took action because he was making decisions alone. He wasn't following procedures.'"[9] Neither did Sebarenzi. He and Cyiza were men of principles. They never allowed their professional conscience to be swayed by political considerations. Which is why, resisting pressures from above, Sebarenzi insisted on asserting his constitutional authority as speaker of the National Assembly, and exercised his right to become a member of the opposition *Parti Libéral*. Only by an extraordinary stroke of luck was he able to leave Rwanda in the nick of time to evade threats to his life.

Cyiza's commitment to a form of justice unconstrained by political motives was simply not acceptable. Like many others before and since Kagame's security agents made sure he would be "disappeared." On the evening of April 23, 2003, after giving a lecture at the Adventist University, he was arrested by agents of the Directorate of Military Intelligence (DMI) and never seen again. Between 1994 and 2006, according to André Guichaoua, and to mention only cases that have been verified, 21 high-ranking ex-FAR officers were assassinated, and 15 disappeared or put in prison.[10]

An invitation that turned sour

In July 1991 I received two memorable back-to-back invitations, one from Joseph Nzirorera, the all-powerful secretary general of the ruling party, *Mouvement Révolutionnaire National* pour le *Développement* (MRND), and the other from President Habyarimana. Both left me with a sense of watching a train wreck in slow motion. The first because of the unmistakably uncompromising, hard-line message that came out of the meeting, the other because of the pathetic helplessness conveyed by my interlocutor.

I met Nzirorera in November 1990 in Washington, through Ambassador Uwimana who insisted that I should join them for a drink. I was happy to comply. Nzirorera had just flown in from Paris on a Concorde supersonic

---

[8] The National Assembly replaced the *Conseil* National de Développement (CND) in 2003, until then often used as a synonym for the Senate.

[9] Joseph Sebarenzi, A *Journey of Transformation: God Sleeps in Rwanda* (New York, 2009), pp. 143–144.

[10] André Guichaoua, "Une disparition annoncée," in *Augustin Ciza, un homme libre*, p. 45.

plane to attend a World Bank conference. Coming from one of the poorest countries on earth, his chosen mode of transport struck me as bizarre. Short of stature, bright-eyed, intense, with an easy way with words, he also earned the reputation of an extremely corrupt politician. Sometimes referred to as "Mr. ten per cent," it was an open secret that he made his fortune from the bribes exacted from prospective buyers of real estate after he was appointed minister of public works.

His political clout owed much to his geographical origins in the Gysenyi prefecture, in a commune (Mukingo) that was also Habyarimana's birthplace. Not only was he a northerner (a Kiga in Kinyarwanda) who shared ties of proximity with the president; thanks to his wide network of strategic contacts and manipulative skills he quickly rose to the top of the MNRD as one of heavy weights in the *mouvance présidentielle* (a catch-all phrase widely used to refer to Habyarimana's entourage).

Guichaoua's outstanding inquest into the roots of "criminal politics" in Rwanda describes in considerable detail how Nzirorera "widened the scope of popular support for Habyarimana: by expanding the reach of the *mouvance présidentielle*" through satellite organizations, such as the rabidly anti-Tutsi Coalition for the Defense of the Republic (CDR), by coordinating financial operations on behalf of the party,[11] by facilitating the recruitment of hard-liners into the party militia (*interahamwe*), a term borrowed from the days of the monarchy to refer to those closest to the hub of power.

Of Nzizorera's claims to fame I knew little before accepting his invitation. We had met in Kigali a couple of times over glasses of champagne – a de rigueur ritual chez Joseph – in Kigali, and though I was aware of his wealth and influence, only after meeting the dozen or so MNRD top dogs did I take the full measure of my captive audience. Present at the champagne and chicken dinner were among others, Elie Sagatwa, Habyarimana's brother in law and unofficial chief of staff, Laurent Seruguba, deputy chief of staff of the armed forces, Deogratias Nsabibama, army chief of staff, Habyarimana's son, and his personal physician. The atmosphere was informal and relaxed, but as is customary on such occasions the host took pains to introduce me as a faithful friend of Rwanda, a French citizen whose love of Rwanda deserved to be acknowledged, and who would some day undoubtedly make his home in Rwanda (he would help me pick a suitable spot, on a lakeside parcelle). The message was clear: Being French I was by definition a friend of Rwanda, and I could be counted on to support the "good fight" by word or by deed. After all, was not France the one country in Europe that was most actively involved in aiding the besieged government, militarily, financially and politically? Except that (a) I was also an American citizen, (b) I had no appetite for engaging in propaganda activities, (c) I found the

---

[11] By enlisting the support of the notorious financier Félicien Kabuga, a long-time fugitive from international justice recently arrested by French authorities in his hide-out in Asnière. Correctly identified as a millionaire tied to the genocide Kabuga played a key role in funding the hate-spewing Radio Mille Collinnes during the killings.

killing of his opponents, Hutu or Tutsi, deeply objectionable, and (d) had no personal sympathy for Nzizorera as a person. After thanking my host and making plain my sincere and long-standing attachment to Rwanda and its people, I went to great lengths to drive home to my audience the grave dangers posed by a single-minded recourse to violence as against the merits of a compromise solution based on a cease-fire followed by peace negotiation. My modest proposal went up like a lead balloon. A tense silence followed, interrupted by Nzirorera's terse good-by and a head sign to his chauffeur to drive me back to my Mille Collines hotel. This was the last I saw of Mr. ten per cent.

My next stop, a few days later, was at Habyarimana's splendid Kanombe residence, overlooking manicured lawns and leafy spaces. I had met him once before in early 1990 in Kigali, at a conference on refugees, where I made a fool of myself; in response to his query as to whether he should be concerned about refugee movements I replied, "Mr. President I am sure that the refugees are more afraid of you than you of them." Now the political context was entirely different; a constitutional amendment had just authorized the introduction of multi-party elections, and a flurry of new parties were about to challenge the MRND's hold on power. The changing political climate seemed to have left its mark on the president's mood, as if he had a premonition of just how calamitous the consequences would be. As he paced the floor of the huge living room he looked distraught, at a loss for words to engage the conversation. But as he made clear his sense of being at an impasse over what steps to take to restore a measure of stability to the country, I ventured a counsel of prudence. Given that he was a frequent target of criticisms for accumulating too much power I suggested, the phrasing of which I still remember. "*Monsieur le président, vous portez trois casquettes, président de la république, président du parti MRND et ministre de la défense. Vous devriez laisser les deux dernières au vestiaire.*" ("Mr. president, you're wearing three hats, president of the republic, president of the MNRD and head of the army. You should leave the latter two in the cloakroom.") He remained dubious. We discussed at random a variety of issues, including the range of possible candidates for the prime ministership; I mentioned the name of Lando Ndasingwa, which he quickly dismissed, saying that Lando's closest associate in the Liberal Party, Justin Mugenzi, was – correctly as it turned out – a very distasteful character ("*infréquentable*"). An hour went by before we parted ways. The impression I was left with was that of a singularly indecisive mind. Hamlet in Kanombe. As I try to reconcile this image with the one projected by the media – a ruthless taskmaster of genocidal violence – I must confess my doubts. While there is little question about his subservience to hardliners, and his inability or unwillingness to keep them on a tight leash, I find it hard to see him as the uncompromising orchestrator of the killings. If either of my two distinguished hosts fits that picture, it is Nzirorera, whose subsequent career path made him a central figure among the growing cohorts of Hutu extremists.

The backlash of multi-party competition

How did the advent of multi-party competition, ushered in by Mitterrand's famous speech at La Baule in 1990, end up injecting an added stimulus to violent extremism?

The key to this paradox lies in the unforeseen consequences of proliferating youth militias. Until they became a tool of mass murder the *jeunesses* groups acted as the single most important source of violence within and among parties.

No sooner had parties been recognized, following the constitutional amendment of June 1991, then they found themselves drawn into an intense competitive struggle for popular support. Besides the MNRD, the principal newcomers were the Democratic Republican Movement (MDR), the Liberal Party (PL), the Social Democratic Party (PSD), and the Christian Democratic Party (PDC). In most cases, their bases of support were defined by regions and personalities not by ideologies. Once identified with regional loyalties, or pre-existing parties – such as the MDR whose roots in the south-central region coincided with the zone of influence of Kayibanda's Parmehutu – party rivalries became fierce. This is best illustrated by the so-called *ubukohoza* ("to liberate") campaign that pitted the MDR militants against the MRND, and wrought havoc in the south-central region, once a MRND stronghold. The aim, in short, was for the MDR to recover ownership of the properties – buildings, land, public spaces – owned by the ruling party, which they felt were part of the ill-gotten gains taken away from their legitimate owners.

The operation soon turned violent. The spearhead of the campaign consisted of the MDR youth militia, *inkuba* ("thunder"), the first such armed militia to be identified with a party. Others followed, the PSD spawned the *abakombozi* ("liberators"), the CDR *impuzamugambi* (those who share the same goal), the Liberal Party the *jeunesses du PL*, and, most notably, the MNRD the *interahamwe* ("those who work together"), headed by a Tutsi (Kajuga), and soon to become a synonym for genocidal terror. The relationship of the youth wings to their parent organizations varied, but many ended as loose cannon. This was especially true of the *interahamwe*, which many did not hesitate to hold responsible for the Bugesera massacre on March 1992. In an orgy of violence lasting from March 4–7, an estimated 300 Tutsi civilians were killed (182 according to government sources). In protest, Tutsi members of the MNRD, according to one observer, left the party in droves, leaving the PL as the only shelter where Hutu and Tutsi were able to co-exist more or less peacefully. But this was not the first-time anti-Tutsi violence threatened to get out of hand. On January 27, 1991, in response to the RPF's raid on Ruhengeri, scores of Bagogwe – a Tutsi subgroup in the north of Rwanda – were killed in and around Kinigi commune. Violence also erupted in other localities. The net result has been to transform the youth wings into more or less autonomous self-defense entities, and the *interahamwe* ultimately into a killing machine.

How to re-establish effective control over the youth militias became the central issue facing party organizations in the months ahead, a task made all more complicated by the behind-the-scenes efforts of the RPF to divide and rule.

Spies and informants: The *ibyitso* threat

If there is one face among scores of others I met at the Mille Collines Hotel that I remember vividly it was Zozo's, the ever-friendly, smiling receptionist at the desk. Diminutive, slightly above 5 feet tall, but fleet of foot and always ready to help, I could always count on him when I had to look up a phone number, chart my way across Kigali, leave a message, confirm or cancel an appointment. He knew how to make himself indispensable. Years went by after my 1991 visit and when I saw him again in December 1994, the normally affable Zozo had turned into a stern, distant figure. As I soon found out, his Hutu phenotype notwithstanding,[12] he was a Tutsi informant in thrall to the RPF. My every move at the hotel, every phone call, every rendez-vous with government officials, were duly reported to whoever had to be informed. I don't know whether Zozo's monitoring had anything to do with Kagame's distinctly frosty reaction when I met him for the first and last time in Washington in early 1991. But my encounter with Zozo, banal as it is, tells us something about the RPF's uncanny ability to pick up information where its presence seemed most unlikely.

Informants are not spying, and neither are they killers. But all three can conveniently be subsumed under the rubric *of ibyitso*, rendered in French as *infiltrés*, or more generally as accomplices of the RPF. All three played an important role after the advent of multi-party politics. Recruiting informants was no problem. In Kigali alone, the number of *infiltrés* on the eve of the genocide was estimated by a group of ONGs at 4,000. What to do with the information they conveyed was trickier, but seldom did the RPF miss an opportunity to play its enemies off one another. Murder was the weapon of choice.

Among the political assassinations credited to the FPR the names of Emmanuel Gapyisi, a leading MDR personality, Félicien Gatabazi, executive secretary of the PSD, Martin Bucyana, president of the CDR, are frequently mentioned. In fact, Bucyana was lynched by the PSD youth militia in retaliation for the assassination of Gatabazi, who, according to well-informed sources, was murdered by the RPF, a perfect example of how murders imputed to Hutu extremists provoked a vengeance in kind by the

---

[12] Susan Thomson's anecdote about Aimable, "an ethnic Tutsi who presents with stereotypical Twa features – physically distinguishable by his smaller height and weight," offers another illustration of the risks, and in this case the benefits, involved in associating ethnic identities with phenotypes. "Having the appearance of a Twa saved my life (during the 1994 genocide)," he admitted. See her fine analysis of the new Rwanda in Susan Thomson, *Rwanda: From Genocide to Precarious Peace* (New Haven, 2018), p. 25.

targeted party, in this case the PSD. Reflecting on the side effects of the murders, Guichaoua writes: "The assassinations of Gatabazi and Bucyana provoked violent clashes among party militias, leading to thirty-seven casualties in Kigali. The clashes only stopped when the leadership of the various parties began to take stock of the political dividends the RPF was reaping from those clashes."[13] In the climate of fear and uncertainty created by *ibyitso*-sponsored murders it is easy to see why youth militias were given a free hand to act as protective shields against arbitrary violence. Their memberships ballooned, but did little to scale down the frequency of political assassinations.

As we now realize the chief of orchestrator of the *ibyitso*-sponsored killings was Karenzi Karake, described by Judi Rever as "one of Kagame's most willing executioners."[14] In his capacity as head of the DMI at the time he had a virtually free hand in the recruitment of the *infiltrés*, the planning of the assassinations, the distribution of weapons and the disinformation following the murders. André Guichaoua calculates that 45 political assassinations were committed between July 1991 and September 1992 by the RPF, and was thus able to "destabilize political parties and demonize the *mouvance présidentielle*, as it was inevitably held responsible."[15] Indeed, nothing could have done more to instill fear and mutual suspicions of complicity among party officials than Karake's fiendishly elaborated divide-and-rule strategy.[16]

The violence that swept across the Mutara region, in the northeast, in the days following the invasion, was an altogether different calamity. Host to thousands of Hutu refugees from Burundi, many of the involved in rice cultivation, and also to many Hima pastoralists, this is a region of lush grasslands and rice paddies. Having worked on a rural development project associated with the *Office de Valorisation Agro-Pastoral du Mutara* (OVAPAM) in the 1970s, I recall my amazement upon discovering the diversity of ethnicities and occupational activities found in this magnificent borderland area, contiguous to Uganda. What reduced the Mutara to a devastated war zone is the more or less systematic cleansing of civilian populations by invading armies, first by the FAR in the days immediately following the October 1 invasion, leading to the killing of an untold number of Hima

---

[13] André Guichaoua, *From War to Genocide: Criminal Politics in Rwanda, 1990–1994*, copyrights by the Board of Regents of the University of Wisconsin System, reprinted by courtesy of the University of Wisconsin, Madison 2015, p. 112.

[14] Rever, *In Praise of Blood*, p. 328.

[15] See Guichaoua's interview with Stephen Smith in *Le Monde*, May 7, 2004.

[16] The arrest in the UK and subsequent release of Kareke at the request of the Westminster Magistrates Court is a commentary on the extent to which Western judicial procedures have contributed to impunity. As Guichaoua reports,

> the British court was persuaded by the arguments of Cherie Blair, spouse of the former UK prime minister who led General Karake's defense team and carefully decided it was not competent to examine the crimes alleged against the General. Emmanuel Karenzi Karake was immediately released and returned to Rwanda where he received a hero's welcome.

> (Guichaoua, *From War to Genocide*, p. 349)

people, including a vast number of Hima pastoralists, and subsequently by the RPF, when thousands of Hutu refugees from Burundi resettled in the rice-growing areas of the Mutara were wiped out. As the RPF moved southward, occupying increasingly large tracts of land, tens of thousands of rural Hutu families formed an uninterrupted flow of refugees, which, in the weeks preceding the genocide, numbered approximately a million. It was among this critical mass of uprooted families that the *interahamwe* recruited many of its most fervent supporters. The MRND's deepest roots were in the north to begin with, owing to Habyarimana's Kiga origins; the massive inflow of refugees fleeing the advance of the RPF only served to intensify its extremist dispositions at the same time that it reaffirmed its regional identity.

At this stage it became imperative that the *interahamwe* be more effectively integrated into the central organization of the MRND. This could only be done by relegating to the side lines Mathieu Ngirumpatse, the head of the party secretariat known for his strong antipathy towards the northerners, and elevating the Akazu-connected Nzirorera to the top echelons of the party. Other moves followed: a tighter control of the party finances made it possible to attract new recruits and ensure regular military training of the militias by units of the FAR. Three years later, writes Guichaoua, with the full knowledge of the MRND leaders, "their offspring had turned into a monster."[17] Ndadaye's death helps explain the monstrous mutation.

Ndadaye's assassination and the "Pawa" split

However serious the divisions caused by the multi-party competition, even more daunting were the fractures provoked by the news of Ndadaye's assassination in Burundi.

The significance of the event is succinctly captured by the late Alison Des Forges in her classic contribution: "The movement known as Hutu Power (pronounced Pawa in Kinyarwanda), the coalition that would make the genocide possible, was built upon the corpse of Ndadaye."[18] Almost overnight, the surge of Hutu radicalism played havoc in the balanced configurations of the political landscape. Sympathy for Ndadaye and anti-Tutsi feelings combined to generate parallel "Hutu Power" factions across a wide spectrum. One after the other – PSD, MDR, even PL, the sole genuinely ethnically integrated party – suffered splits, with Hutu Power breakaways making every effort to set the tone for a more radical stance. The Hutu-controlled media had a field day portraying Kagame as the invisible hand behind Ndadaye's murder. The same theme was echoed in party meetings, most stridently by the vitriol-spewing MDR leader Froduald Karamira, who explicitly accused Kagame of plotting Ndadaye's death. Again to quote from Alison

[17] Guichaoua, *From War to Genocide*, p. 142.
[18] Alison Des Forges, *Leave None to Tell the Story: Genocide in Rwanda* (New York, 1999), p. 137.

Des Forges, "With the consolidation of Hutu Power, party allegiances faded before he opposing poles of Hutu and Tutsi."

What few glimmers of hope followed the Arusha process and the installation of a broadly-based provisional government quickly vanished. The Arusha accords of August 4, 1993 went through great lengths to hammer out an agreement on a number of critical issues: the recognition of the rule of law, the establishment of transitional institutions pending general elections, the repatriation of refugees, the resettlement of IDPs, and the integration of the two armies into a unified military. Of crucial significance was the provision that general elections would be held two years after putting in place a transitional National Assembly.[19] Among the institutions discussed at the negotiating table, none was more promising – on paper if nowhere else – than the Broadly-Based Transitional Government (BBTG). Ominously, it was on February 21, on the eve of the inauguration of the BBTG, that Félicien Gatabazi, minister of public works and executive secretary of the PSD, was assassinated.[20] An even more serious reason to worry was Kagame's stubborn opposition to relinquishing control over the security situation to the UN. Despite the insistence of the UN Special Representative Jacques-Roger Booh-Booh, and Force Commander Romeo Dallaire that they be allowed to fulfill their mandate, Kagame was obdurate. An angry exchange followed. As he reported to Colin Waugh, "finally I told them to go to hell, it's not going to happen. Either we don't go and that's the end of the story, or if we have to go we go with our own force." According to Colin Waugh, "he described it as a make or break issue. And later on, the UN leaders agreed. So now the issue became how many (RPA troops) would go… We started with a brigade and later brought it down… Finally, it became 600 men."[21]

And so it was that, as 1993 drew to a close, some 600 heavily armed RPA soldiers moved into the Kigali parliament building, the *Conseil National de Développement* (CND). The refugee warriors had never been closer to the gates. After years of fighting, they found themselves within striking distance of their target.

---

[19] As Kagame undoubtedly realized, there was little chance that the RF would win the elections, which is one reason among others why he saw recourse to force as the best option. For an excellent commentary on the Arusha peace deal, described by its critics as "the great illusion," see the statement issued by a score of civil society organizations in 2001, *Y Aura-t-il une fin au drame Rwandais? Un Groupement d'Associations Dénonce*, mimeo. Buzet, April 4, 2001.

[20] Other presumed victims of the FPR around the same time included Martin Bucyana, president of the CDR, Fidele Rwambuka, MRND deputy, and Emmanuel Gapysi, member of the political bureau of the MDR.

[21] Waugh, *Paul Kagame and Rwanda*, p. 62. Copyright 2004, Colin M. Waugh by permission of McFarland & Co, Jefferson, NC 28640.

5 Mass murders in Rwanda
Unhealable wounds

The story of the Rwandan genocide cannot be reduced to one of good vs. evil. It is far more complicated, and more nuanced, than that. However, Western politicians such as Tony Blair, Bill and Hilary Clinton, former British development secretary Claire Short have consistently glossed over these complications to portray a one-sided and largely inaccurate picture of what happened in Rwanda.

Timothy B. Reid (former UN Human Rights Investigator), "It's time for a reckoning for Kagame and his Western Cheerleaders," *Mail and Guardian*, April 23, 2019

Once the fabric of society has been rent so comprehensively it is virtually impossible to piece it together again. Once a crime is unpunished its effects fester; fear takes root; divisions harden. Herein lay the essence and the accuracy of the Serbian calculation.

– Roger Cohen, *Hearts Grown Cruel*, p. 169

So, also, the calculation of the Rwanda *génocidaires* on both sides of the ethnic fault line. The numbers boggle the mind. Over half a million, some claim twice as many, were exterminated in a span of one hundred days. This is how Susan Thomson sums up the scale of the carnage: "In a nation of an estimated seven million people, at least half a million Tutsi were killed in a hundred days. Approximately one in eight Rwandans, and nearly three in four ethnic Tutsi perished between April and July 1994." She is careful to underscore that the losses were by no means mono-ethnic: "Thousands of Hutu also lost their lives, chiefly those who opposed the genocidal campaign or refused to join in the killings."[1] But regardless of the actual number of Hutu killed, in proportion to their share of the population the losses suffered by the Tutsi minority were vastly superior. Statistics, at any rate, are notoriously inadequate to convey the horror of individual tragedies.

---

[1] Susan Thomson, *Rwanda: From Genocide to Precarious Peace* (New Haven, 2018), p. 24.

Such dramas are etched in my mind with two names. Lando Ndasingwa, a leading personality of the *Parti Libéral* (PL), is one of them. I learned of his death on April 9 while on a USAID mission in Guinea's capital Conakry, from a newspaper article found in the hotel where I stayed. The shock I experienced I cannot put into words. All I know is that I remained grief-stricken for the rest of the day, unable to find my bearings. For Lando – the brother of Louise Mushikiwabo, who served as Kagame's minister of foreign affairs before being appointed to the presidency of the International Francophone Organization (IFO) – was the closest friend I had in Rwanda. His knowledge of the history and politics of the country was unmatched, he knew every personality of any significance, and every bit of gossip surrounding their public or private lives. His help proved invaluable, and his friendship irreplaceable. We had met years before, when his Canadian wife worked as a secretary at the US Embassy in Kigali. Armed with a degree in linguistics from a Canadian university he ended up with various teaching positions and ultimately got deeply involved in the politics of the Liberal Party, which at the time was the only party likely to attract substantial support from both Hutu and Tutsi. As the party vice-president, he stood as a promising new leader. Gregarious, outgoing, with a wonderful sense of humor, and an ever-present smile, he also had an unshakable commitment to a cause: the rebirth of a Rwanda free of ethnic prejudice. Scribbled on the yellow cover of the Liberal Party program is a dedication that best be quoted in the original French: "Ces quelques pages traduisent une vision. Un rêve debout de bâtir un Rwanda égalitaire transcendant les complexes séculaires Hutu–Tutsi pour donner les mêmes chances à un Munyarwanda fier, en sa qualité de ressource humaine, d'être l'unique et vraie richesse du Rwanda. Connaissant ton affection pour ce pays et l'amitié fraternelle que tu me portes, je suis sur que tu suivras de près notre aventure politique."[2] His "political adventure" ended all too soon. On April 8 he and his wife and their two young children were sent to their graves.

The other name etched in my memory is that of Immaculata. Of a more brilliant and delicately graceful young lady I cannot think. We met twice in Kigali, and each time I came away with the impression of having met a *mwamikazi* (queen) of sorts in the pantheon of republican Rwanda. Her young child was her most precious possession. The last time we met was at the Hotel Mille Collines in Kigali, where, by chance, we ran into her would-be benefactor, a Hutu notable by the name of Noel Mbonabaryi. I had met him before on several occasions, aware of his considerable political clout both as a native of Bushiru, a region at the heart the presidential turf, and a high-ranking functionary in the ministry of public works.

---

[2] "These few lines express a vision, a dream awake to build an egalitarian Rwanda, transcending the age-old Hutu-Tutsi complexes, in order to give the same life chances to all Rwandans, proud of themselves as Rwanda's unique and only real source of wealth. Knowing your affection for this country, and our fraternal friendship, I am sure you will keep a close watch on our political adventure."

Suddenly an angry Immaculata, like a bolt out of the blue, reminded him (in French) of the sexual favors he demanded of her and his failure to deliver her reward – the job she had been expecting in return. Taken aback by the sudden outburst I watched in silence as her abuser walked out, unfazed. This was the last time I saw her.[3] I later learned from a friend of hers, that she too had been killed. To imagine her and her child falling under the blows of a *massue*, or the blade of a machete, is painful even to imagine. Even more sobering is the sheer number of those who met the same fate.

Why? Why did hundreds of thousands of innocents have to pay for crimes they did not commit?

Non-starters

Much ink has been spilled to elucidate the answers. Before venturing some tentative explanations, let me set aside three of the least plausible, each associated with an analyst of considerable renown.

The first is Jared Diamond's Malthusian collapse theory set forth in his discussion of "Malthus in Africa: The Rwanda Genocide," one of several arresting chapters in his 2005 best-seller.[4] Few would deny that Rwanda's population density is one of the highest in the continent, that the rising population pressure on the land is a source of serious social tension, and that over time violent conflicts are bound to occur.

But if Malthus may well be summoned to shed light on future violence, it is of little assistance to explain the timing of the genocide, the manner in which it was carried out, or the underlying causes of the killings. I received a letter from the author before he completed the manuscript inviting me to share with him my views about the roots of the genocide. I was happy to comply. While making clear the difficulty of arriving at a definitive judgment, I took pains to underscore the role of singular individuals and ethnicities. To grasp the roots of the genocide, I said, it is essential to put it in the perspective of the long civil war, and consider the role played by militias (*interahamwe*), parties (MRND, CRD) and army men (Bagosora) in precipitating the bloodbath. The point I tried to impress upon the author seemed straightforward: to reduce the genocide as the outcome of a Malthusian dilemma is a non-starter. As I found out when I received a copy of the book my counsels went unheeded. But the author's self-exculpation is

---

[3] Years later I came upon the following passage about Mbonabaryi's "sexual appetite" in Valens Kajeguhakwa's memoir:

> An eminent member of the Bagesera clan, the clan of Mrs. Habyarimana, and thus brother in law of the president... he was well known for his vast sexual appetite at an age when others could keep them under control... In order to obtain their compulsory work permit, young ladies, predominantly Tutsi, were obligated to see him in person and strike a bargain to get the precious document. Many preferred to remain jobless rather than to pay the price.(Kageguhakwa, *Rwanda: De la terre de paix á la terre de sang*, op. cit., pp. 230–231)

[4] Jared Diamond, *Collapse: How Societies Choose to Fail or Succeed* (New York, 2005).

worth noting: "One should not misconstrue a role of population pressure among the Rwanda genocide's causes to mean that population pressure automatically leads to genocide anywhere around the world... Instead I conclude that population pressure was one of the important factors behind the genocide."[5] What the other factors are and how they fit into the overall picture is for the reader to find out.

Hardly more convincing is the notion of genocide as the by-product of a racist ideology. That many of the pro-regime newspapers and broadcasts issued by Radio Mille Collines reeked of racist tropes is undeniable; that they were the prime mover behind the killings is doubtful. Whether described as a re-enactment of the Holocaust, or as the expression of a "tropical Nazism," to use Jean-Pierre Chrétien's pithy formula, the parallel simply does not hold. I have explained why in an article published some years ago[6] in which I argued that, although there is a sense in which the analogy might seem compelling, the chain of events leading to the Rwanda carnage has to be seen through a different lens. Put succinctly, at no time in their history did Jews invade their killers' territory or reach out to a neighboring state to push their way in, or commit revenge killings comparable to those attributed to the RPF. None of this moved the French historian to think again. In fact, his "tropical Nazism" trope is further amplified in his co-authored discussion of "racism and genocide" in Rwanda.[7] In it the author draws some surprising parallels: the wandering Jew meets his alter ego in the invading Tutsi; the legendary Oriental charm of the *Belle Juive* has its pendant in the subversive attractiveness of Tutsi women; echoes of the Nazi press (*Der Stürmer*) and French anti-Semitic media (*Gringoire, Je suis partout*) can be found in the pro-Hutu newspaper *Kangura*. Whether any such outlandish analogs can help shine a light on the Rwanda bloodbath is best left to the reader's appreciation.

Yet another misperception might be characterized as "savagery unbound," a trait best exemplified by Philip Gourevitch's widely acclaimed best-seller.[8] Once detached from their historical context it is all too tempting to view the killings as the expression of uninhibited tribal savagery, an ingrained perversity so breathtakingly inhuman as to defy explanation. Could it be that genocidal violence is somehow wired into the killers' genetic code?

To accuse the author of a voyeuristic bias is besides the point. His purpose, made explicit by the book's subtitle, is to introduce the reader to "stories" about the genocide, not to explain it. Nonetheless, I find it hard to disagree with the strictures penned by Felix Holmgren, Sweden's ambassador at large in Kigali: "There is no fault to be found in Gourevitch's reproduction

[5] Diamond, *Collapse*, p. 327.

[6] "Rwanda and the Holocaust Reconsidered," in Lemarchand ed., *The Dynamics of Violence in Central Africa*, pp. 109–128.

[7] Jean-Pierre Chrétien and Marcel Kabanda, *Rwanda: Racisme et Génocide* (Paris, 2016).

[8] Philip Gourevitch, *We Wish to Inform You That Tomorrow We Will Be Killed with Our Families: Stories from Rwanda* (New York, 1998).

of distressing eyewitness accounts... But his rudimentary analysis takes us no further than the most schematic notion of how to stage a genocide: evil leaders and sheep-like subjects... He treats important facts as mere details. For example, the genocide happened in parallel with a bloody civil war, which over the preceding three years had put a large part of the population in flight. It was triggered by the murder of the Rwanda president Juvenal Habyarimana, which unleashed panic in an already confused political situation; the genocide took place against the background of an ongoing power struggle between several elite groups, and the first to be killed by extremists following the murder of the president were not Tutsi but Hutu members of parliament, among them the Prime Minister."[9] Such indeed are the missing parameters that need to be factored in.

The same sort of criticism applies to Jean Hatzfeld's best-selling books. He too offers some gut-wrenching stories, in the form of lengthy interviews with perpetrators and relatives of their victims. Although the elegant phrasings attributed to the interviewees are patently his own, his narratives bring us straight into the realm of the unspeakable; echoes of the Holocaust resonate through the lived experiences of the survivors; his stories, like Gourevitch's, are a testament to the sufferings inflicted on hundreds of thousands. All of which is, of course, to be expected when you consider the nature of the subject. But nowhere is the reader given as much as a clue as to why it happened. By leaving the historical context out of the picture the reader is left wondering whether the horror is not inscribed in the perpetrators' DNA. All we need is to remind ourselves of "the key" handed to him by one of the génocidaires: "Before casting his first gaze on the world around him, the newly born (Hutu) is swaddled in hatred of the Tutsi."[10] What more striking example of how racist theories, by design or by accident, can be twisted into an explanatory model?

Fresh insights

Important new research has been done since the publication of Gourevitch's "stories"; what follows is a brief summary of the new breakthroughs brought to light over the last few years, which together suggest a very different angle from which to look at the genocide.

Contrary to what many had assumed, the genocide was not the product of a long-planned, carefully engineered project; it happened in a matter of days immediately after the shooting down of the aircraft that killed the presidents of Rwanda and Burundi, on April 6, 1994. The decisions made in the following days were largely improvised, in the midst of considerable confusion and intramural infighting among intimates. To argue, as Alex de

---

[9] Felix Holmgren, "How Philip Gourevitch Wrote the Victors' History Book," www.euro-zine.com/articles/2010-01-15-holmgren-en.html.

[10] In an interview with Colette Braeckmnan, *Le Soir*, April 5, 2004, p. 10. Among his several widely acclaimed works on Rwanda, see, especially, *Dans le Nu de la Vie* (Paris, 2000).

Waal does in a 1997 article, that the genocide was the logical outcome of three and a half years of careful preparation, during which "a coterie of extremists around the president and his wife developed the tools of genocide" is simply not the case.[11]

Nor is there any basis for the notion of a massive participation in the killings, wildly estimated by some pro-Kagame commentators as close to 100 percent of the Hutu male population.[12] The point has been argued persuasively by Scott Straus in his important reconsideration of the dynamics of the carnage: "My interviews with perpetrators show that most Rwandans did not participate in the genocide because they hated Tutsi as despicable 'others,' because they adhered to an ethnic nationalist vision of society, or because racist propaganda had instilled racism in then." Furthermore, contrary to claims of a massive participation of the Hutu population in the killings he shows that the figure of 150,00–210,000 is closer to the mark. "My estimate of the number of perpetrators," he writes, "equals 7–8 percent of the active adult Hutu population, and 14–17 percent of the active adult male Hutu population." Such estimates, horrific as they are, are a far cry from the official figures cited. While some were more violent than others, he goes on to note that "ethnic hatred and distance, as well as exposure to some of the most virulent propaganda do explain which perpetrators were the most violent."[13]

Among such hard-line *génocidaires* was a predominance of northerners, of Hutu elements originating from the Kiga sub-group. That Kiga extremists played a major role in in orchestrating the killings is well established. Not only because the deceased president was himself of Kiga origins, or because the *akazu* was a nest of influential Kiga power-holders, or because the Kiga are historically and culturally distinct, but more likely because of their residual animus toward Hutu from the south-central region, often seen by northerners as too closely associated with the Tutsi by the ties of physical proximity and mixed marriages and thus posing an obstacle to the effective organization of the killings. This is made poignantly evident in Guichaoua's analysis of how groups of exterminating entrepreneurs, under the guidance of the sinister Pauline Nyiramasuhuko, were sent out from the north to mobilize the population against the two-week long courageous resistance of the Tutsi prefect of Butare, until he too was killed for preventing the killings.[14] Another point emphasized by Guichaoua is the control of industrial enterprises exercised by Kiga elements, which gave them access to means of communication (cars and trucks) and financial resources to facilitate involvement in the carnage. This is not to imply that the Hutu of the south-central region were immune to genocidal instincts; but these may

---

[11] Alex de Waal, "Group Identity, Rationality and the State," *Critical Review*, vol. 11, no. 2 (Spring 1997), p. 287.

[12] See Benjamin Sehene, *Le piège ethnique* (Paris, 1999), p. 120.

[13] Scott Straus, *The Order of Genocide: Race, Power and War in Rwanda* (Ithaca and London, 2006), pp. 118, 134–135.

[14] André Guichaoua, *Rwanda 1994: Les politiques du génocide à Butare* (Paris, 2005).

not have been awakened so swiftly and so violently in the absence of a Kiga stimulus.

Once this is said, only by considering the historical context of mass murder can one begin to make sense of its dynamics.

The revolution undone

Two critical interrelated phenomena lie in the background of the genocide: the outbreak of a vicious civil war, and the challenge it posed to what the Hutu revolution had accomplished – often referred to as *les acquis de la révolution*, i.e. the achievements of the revolution. The stakes were huge.

No matter how brutal the role of the tutelle as the historic midwife of the revolution, the tangible gains brought to the Hutu peasants were not insignificant. Access to land, freedom from corvée labor, the abolition of obligations inherent in clientage ties, the casting aside of chiefly overrule were gains of enormous significance. Just as significant was the nascent sense of belonging to a new community, based on republican values, not the least of which was equality. Although practice rarely followed promise, the emergence of a new collective identity, identified with the nation reborn, is undeniable. As Tutsi-sponsored counter-revolutionary threats persisted, from within and from without, Hutu ethnicity became ever more salient, though never to the point of eradicating intra-Hutu splits.

How the birth of a new revolutionary order may create the preconditions of mass murder has been ably explored by Melson in his comparison of the Armenian genocide and the Holocaust. His conclusion is worth noting: "Some revolutions may lead to genocide because all revolutions attempt to redefine and recast the political community, and in the process, they exclude certain communal groups and classes. It is this exclusion that becomes the necessary condition for genocide." He reflects on how in this volatile context domestic foes and international enemies join hands to undermine the achievements of the revolution: "those who earlier have been labeled as enemies of the revolution are part of an insidious plot with the regime's international foes ready to undo the revolution or even to destroy the state and the political community itself."[15] In such circumstances, reconciliation is not an option.

This is where parallel emerges with other genocides, but the case of Rwanda also has its own peculiarities. Anxieties at the prospect of a return of the monarchy went hand in hand with the anticipation of a fearsome punishment. How the two combined to produce a kind of collective psychosis leading to popular outbursts of violence is dramatically illustrated by the wanton killings of thousands of Tutsi civilians that followed the December 1963 refugee-led raid into southern Rwanda: fear, more than anything else, was the motive force that drove dozens of Hutu burgomasters and their followers to turn against their Tutsi neighbors.

[15] Robert Melson, *Revolution and Genocide: On the Origins of the Armenian Genocide and the Holocaust* (Chicago, 1992), pp. 280, and 18–19.

Fear, to repeat, was the critical factor which, three decades later, drove thousands of Hutu citizens into a killing spree. The October 1990 invasion sent waves of panic among many Hutu and Tutsi; mutual suspicions grew rapidly within and between each group; with the January 1991 RPF raid on Ruhengeri security concerns reached a new high, yet the enemy seemed elusive. As the RPF invaders relentlessly pushed their way southward official statements ceased to reassure. With the *ibyitso* infiltrations becoming more widespread, and assassinations more frequent, a sense of panic took hold of the population. The conflict was not just between Hutu and Tutsi but between Hutu and Hutu, northerners (Kiga) against southerners (Nduga), moderates against extremists, commune against commune. As threat perceptions grew more intense, and vulnerability more real, mutual distrust became omnipresent. Uncertainty about who killed whom, and why, fed a sort of collective paranoia.

Contributing in no small way to this atmosphere the infamous news network, Radio Mille Collines, never missed an opportunity to spread disinformation through deliberate falsehoods and malicious distortion of the facts.

It was in this climate of extreme tension that was fired the missile that brought down Habyarimana's plane, killing the presidents of Rwanda and Burundi and their accompanying officials. Putting one and two together meant that in less than six months three Hutu presidents – Ndadaye, Ntaramira, Habyarimana – had been killed by Tutsi assassins.

The crash that lit the tinder

That the crash was the precipitant that touched off the genocide is a point on which everybody agrees. There is disagreement on just about everything else.

To this day radically different opinions oppose those who point the finger at Hutu extremists, anxious to eliminate a moderate president, and those who see the RPF as the real culprit. So as to avoid possible misunderstandings let me say at the outset that I am firmly convinced, after looking at the evidence, that the man who ordered the shooting down of Habyarimana's plane was Kagame himself. I have stated my views on a number of occasions, though not always with impunity;[16] here I want to review the

---

[16] In my contribution to the volume of essays edited by Samuel Totten and William Parsons, *Century of Genocide: Critical Essays and Eyewitness Accounts* (New York, 2009) I wrote: "Despite continuing speculation by some analysts of an *akazu*-sponsored plot intended to eliminate the moderates, there is growing evidence to suggest that Kagame was indeed the central actor behind the crash" (p. 490). Although the editors asked me to leave out that statement I refused, in turn prompting them to add the following incredibly sloppy disclaimer in parenthesis (Editors' note: There, in fact, continues to be speculation that various actors might have planned and carried out the downing of the plane. Among those under suspicion are: the akazv [sic], the French government and the Rwandan Patrivtie [sic] Front.) After contributing chapters on Rwanda and Burundi to three earlier editions of the book I was informed by the editors that I would no longer be among their list of contributors so as to give readers the benefit of alternative points of view. In the book's fourth edition appears a chapter on Rwanda by the notoriously tendentious Gerald Caplan that sets things right, implicitly putting me in the category of deniers: "various genocide deniers have insisted the RPF leadership was responsible, though without persuasive evidence for this counter-intuitive charge" (p. 457).

evidence, look at the dissenting views and then turn to the highly ambivalent role played by France during the ensuing bloodbath.

What is the evidence pointing to the responsibility of the RPF?

"There is no smoking gun" is the mantra one hears again and again when
it comes to assigning blame; but the circumstantial evidence is overwhelming. Part of it is inscribed in the terms of the August 4, 1993, Arusha peace
accord, which, in addition to providing the basis of the Broadly-Based
Transitional Government (BBTG), stipulates that general elections would
be held 22 months after the inauguration of the BBTG. One only needs to
look at the proportion of Hutu to Tutsi, and the deepening chasm between
them, to realize that the chances of an RPF victory at the polls were virtually nil. What better opportunity to avoid this nightmare scenario than to
shift attention to another, opening the way for a seizure of power by force?

Equally beyond doubt, thanks to Filip Reyntjens's painstaking research,[17]
is that the Russian-made SAM-16 missiles fired at Habyarimana's plane,
recovered by the FAR, were in the possession of the Ugandan army *before*
they were handed over to the RPF. They bore the same serial number series
as the unexploded missile fired at one of FAR aircraft on May 18, 1991.
Curiously, none of this was ever mentioned in the official counter-actual
evidence produced by the Kagame government.

Nor were the testimonies offered by RPA defectors considered. The weight
of evidence available from former high-ranking officials is crushing. Theogene Rudasingwa, Kagame's former chief of staff and first Rwandan ambassador to the US, doesn't mince his words: "The truth must now be told.
Paul Kagame, then overall commander of the Rwanda Patriotic Army...
was personally responsible for the shooting down of the plane. In July 1994
Paul Kagame himself, with characteristic callousness and much glee, told
me he was responsible for shooting down the plane... Paul Kagame has
to be immediately brought to account for this crime and its consequences."[18] Echoes of this can be found in interviews with Kayumba Nyamwasa,
former chief of army staff, much of which would probably have been confirmed by Patrick Karegeya had he lived long enough to testify.

A wealth of further evidence can be gathered from the testimonies of RPF
defectors. One of the most telling is from the late Colonel Abdul Ruzibiza,
who had a ringside seat, so to speak, as a member of the highly trained
Network Commando sent out to oversee the tactical preparations for the
job. Interviewed in 2005 over a two-day exchange with André Guichaoua
and Claudine Vidal in Oslo, where he had found asylum, he offers the most
detailed account available of the meetings preceding the fateful date, who
were the participants, when and how the SAM-16 missiles were smuggled
into the CND, and who fired them (the first by Corporal Eric Hakizimana,
the second by Lieutenant Frank Nziza). The story is told by Ruzibiza himself

---

[17] Filip Reyntjens, *Trois jours qui ont fait basculer l'histoire* (Paris, 1995).
[18] Theogene Rudasingwa, *Healing a Nation: A Testimony* (Charleston, 2013), p. 415.

in the book-length testimony excellently edited by Guichaoua and Vidal.[19] How, after such overwhelming evidence anyone could still entertain doubts about Kagame's responsibility is puzzling. That the book was never translated into English is not the only reason. A more persuasive argument is that true believers are rarely swayed by the logic of seemingly irrefutable proof.

Nor was the enthusiasm of the pro-Kagame rooting section in France and elsewhere dampened by the investigations conducted by the highly respected French magistrate, Jean-Louis Bruguière, and his Spanish colleague Judge Andreu Merrelles.[20] Though both reiterated earlier accusations targeting Kagame as the chief villain, their brief failed to convince a number of sympathetic observers, including, of course, the villain himself who now decided to go on the offensive.

The Mutsinzi investigation was Kagame's response to Bruguière's. Headed by an "independent commission" whose members all belonged to the ruling RPF, the aim was to investigate "the causes, circumstances and responsibilities" involved in the attack against the presidential plane. As many would have predicted, the report went through great lengths to demonstrate that the plane was brought down by Hutu extremists in an attempt to neutralize the moderates in the government, including Habyarimana himself. All facts pointing to Kagame's responsibility were conveniently ignored, along with the presence in the plane of a sample of highly influential hard-liners, hardly the incarnation of the moderates intended to be killed in the crash.[21] Though deeply flawed by a number of factual errors, inaccuracies and improbable assertions, the Mutsinzi report found a receptive echo among a number of journalists, historians and genocide scholars in France and elsewhere.

Unsurprisingly, the report received rave reviews from Philip Gourevitch. In his *New Yorker* article on the Mutsinzi report he admitted "not having had time to absorb the report and its multiple annexes in their entirety," but to having "read around in it to offer some initial thoughts." Here are some of them: "The assassination was a coup d'Etat. At the time of his death Habyarimana was on the point of implementing the Arusha Accords, a power-sharing peace agreement with the Rwanda Patriotic Front... but the Hutu Power genocidaires wanted to consolidate their power through their campaign of extermination. Habyarimana, then, appears to have been killed as a traitor to the Hutu Power cause." Many would beg to differ. What makes the report "most remarkable," we are told, is the "thoroughness and seriousness of the underlying investigation." Compared to this unswerving *J'accuse*, the Bruguière report is dismissively described as a "pack of lies," so

[19] Lieutenant Abdul Joshua Ruzibiza, *Rwanda: L'histoire secrète* (Paris, 2005). The book, unfortunately, has yet to be made available to English-speaking readers.

[20] For further details, see Filip Reynjens, *Political Governance in Post-Genocide Rwanda* (Cambridge, 2013), p. 147 ff.

[21] Namely Maj. Gen. Deogratias Nsabimana, chief of staff of the FAR, Juvénal Renzaho, advisor to the president, Col. Elie Sagatwa, personal secretary and brother-in-law of the resident, Emmanuel Akingeneye, the president's personal physician, Maj. Thaddée Bagaragaza, aide de camp.

much so that "even the French press treated it as a joke."[22] There is no use challenging convictions so deeply anchored in ideological preconceptions. The more important point to note is that public reactions to the report only served to deepen the fault line between pro- or anti-Kagame sentiments.

The polarization of public opinion about the Mutsinzi report finds an echo in another, equally contentious document, the Mucyo report. Although the method is the same – a National Independent Commission was appointed, headed by a former minister of justice, Jean de Dieu Mucyo – the terms of reference are different, i.e. to collect evidence to show the implication of the French State in the 1994 genocide. Its report, issued in 1998, rejected wholesale Bruguière's conclusions, shifting the onus of guilt entirely to the other side: responsibility fell squarely on the French authorities at the highest level, including President Mitterrand and 13 senior officials, all accused of complicity in the preparation and execution of the genocide. Though promptly dismissed by French authorities as "unacceptable," the report nonetheless raises a number of questions that need to be addressed.

France's role re-examined

What role, if any, did the French play in the unfolding of the bloodbath? At what level were critical decisions made? How did they affect the life or death of individual citizens?

The debate, reduced to its essentials, is between those who would exonerate the French government of all wrongdoing, while recognizing that mistakes were made, and those who would not hesitate to denounce France's deliberate and substantial political, military and financial assistance to the Habyarimana government. On the strength of the evidence I have seen – and there is still much to be disclosed – I am inclined to agree with the latter, but with some caveats. Contrary to what some have claimed, here is no evidence that French soldiers actively participated in the killing of Tutsi civilians. While the Turquoise operation could have done more to save Tutsi lives, it did save a substantial number, though how many will never be known. And while President Mitterrand must ultimately bear the blame for some of the most grievous errors made by his government, there is no reason to hold him personally accountable for some of the more disastrous decisions made by the French embassy or the French military assistance mission on the ground.

France's military thrust begins with the RPF invasion of October 1, 1990. Under the code-named Opération Noroit two companies were sent to Rwanda – officially to protect he lives of French citizens, but in fact to provide a much needed prop to the ill-trained, poorly led 7,000-trong FAR. Military assistance on a larger scale followed the withdrawal of the short-lived Belgian military intervention and Mobutu's rag-tag army, which

[22] Philip Gourevitch, "The Mutsinzi Report on the Rwanda Genocide," *The New Yorker*, January 8, 2010.

proved a far greater danger to the civilian populations they were expected to protect than to the RPF.

The next step came in the weeks following the October 4/5 masquerade, when the Rwanda government staged a fake attack on the capital: in response, the number of French troops on the ground reached some 600, later rising to 1,100. As the conflict intensified, France's military cooperation – officially known as *Détachement d'assistance militaire* (DAMI) – began to assume important operational responsibilities, including manning artillery batteries, the interrogation of prisoners and training of army and gendarmerie (police) units.

France's military presence raised serious hurdles for the RPF in its campaign in the north, a fact openly acknowledged by Ruzibiza in his explanation of why it failed to capture Byumba in June 1992: "our decision to withdraw from Byumba came after violent combats led and supervised by French advisers (who) brought in 105 mm Howitzers, 122 mm Howitzers, and many helicopters... The information we receive indicated that French military advisers instructed the FAR on how to anticipate the enemy's next move and how to best position their artillery pieces... France has been a big obstacle for the FPR... Many of our men were killed by French shells."[23] If we are to believe Ruzibiza it is difficult to accept French claims of a politically neutral stance, while at the same time hinting at suspicions of Anglo-Saxon perfidy mediated through the Uganda-assisted RPF.

By a fateful irony, the decisive role played by the DAMI in stopping the RPA in its tracks during the large-scale attack of February 2, 1993, led to a reshuffling of the diplomatic cards that played directly into Kagame's hands. His immediate priorities during the ensuing cease-fire negotiations was the withdrawal of French troops and the establishment of a demilitarized safe zone. He obtained satisfaction on both counts. The safe zone was promptly penetrated by RPF spies, and the repatriation of the bulk of the French contingent by December 1993, besides weakening Habyarimana's position, meant a more or less free hand to bring in large quantities of weapons from Uganda and plan the RPA's next move for the capture of Kigali. Tough intended to make up for the French withdrawal, the UN Military Mission in Rwanda (UNAMIR), created on June 22, 1993, proved, to put it kindly, unequal to the task.

France reacted to the news of the genocide with a sense of shock and disbelief. Long before the US, and in contrast to Clinton officials' incredible dilly-dallying over the appropriateness of referring to the cold-blooded murder of tens of thousands as genocide, the French government did not hesitate to use the g-word, but its support for its client state remained undiminished. While UNAMIR was downsized by almost 90 per cent to 270 men, Belgium pulled out of the mission altogether and the US responded to a UN request for vehicles by insisting on payment first. It was to France's credit, acting in conformity with a UN resolution, to have taken the initiative

---

[23] Ruzibiza, *Rwanda: L'histoire secrète*, pp. 166–167.

to lay the groundwork for a new 3,500-strong military intervention aimed at protecting the lives of civilians. Code-named *Opération Turquoise* its stated objective was to be strictly humanitarian, it should not exceed more than two months on the ground (June 22–August 21), and should not act as an interposition force between the parties to the conflict. How the mission came to be interpreted and carried out is where controversies begin to emerge.

Turquoise was France's second military intervention since the beginning of the genocide. The first, code-named *Amaryllis*, involving 359 paratroopers, was intended to protect and evacuate French citizens. But this did not prevent the rescue and evacuation of a number of disreputable high-ranking Rwandans closely associated with the defeated regime, including Habyarimana's wife, Agathe. In fact both missions came under considerable criticisms, and for very good reasons. How anyone could have turned a deaf ear to the imploring pleas of scores of Tutsi employees at the French Embassy and Cultural Center, while every effort was made to save the lives of Habyarimana's closest advisers along with his wife, is morally inexcusable. French hypocrisy was on full display in the days immediately following the killings, when Ambassador Jean-Michel Marlaud refused to authorize the evacuation of the children of the assassinated MDR Prime Minister Agathe Uwilingiyimana, and Francois-Xavier Nsansuwera, Rwanda's public prosecutor, known for his impeccable credentials, which caused him to be consistently in the cross-hairs of the militias.[24] Only after long and painful wrangling with French officials in Paris and Kigali were they able to board a plane out of Rwanda.

As for Turquoise, the record is more ambivalent though by no means beyond reproach. The argument that nothing was done to prevent the passage of Hutu *génocidaires* to the Congo, or that French troops went so far as to facilitate heir crossing, is unconvincing. Anyone familiar with the terrain knows that the border, extremely porous, can be crossed with relative ease by simply walking around the checkpoints. A more serious criticism concerns the performance the French military in saving Tutsi lives. Given the modesty of the results one can better understand the anger of the local head of *Médecins Sans Frontières* (MSF), Hervé Bradol, as he heard French officials voicing their pride in the humanitarian work accomplished by Turquoise: "When I hear over the radio the Minister of Cooperation Bernard Debré speak of arms deliveries (to Rwanda) after the beginning of the genocide, while I am on the ground attending to the needs of the wounded,

---

[24] This episode is described in detail by André Guichaoua in the French version of his book, *Rwanda: De la Guerre au Génocide* (Paris, 2010), p. 355 ff. He deserves considerable credit for his sustained and courageous efforts to help evacuate Uwlingiyimana's children, along with Nsansuwera and his wife, despite the obstacles raised by the French Embassy.

I am not feeling a sense of pride."[25] The shameful arms transactions handled by Théoneste Bagosora, the willing executioner par excellence, evaluated at 80 tons, all of which were delivered *after the killings began*, and at a price tag of some $1.3 million,[26] make Bradol's lament all the more convincing.

As some may remember the initial objective of Turquoise was to capture Kigali, as a last-ditch effort to roll back the RPA and possibly reinstall what was left of the Habyarimana government. The reason it failed is that the PRA was ahead of the curve, moving into Kigali on July 4, exactly two weeks after Turquoise got under way. Shifting gears proved problematic. A mission initially conceived as a (thinly disguised) military thrust was now repurposed as a humanitarian endeavor. Just how and why this incredible snafu happened remains unclear.

Disagreements among French decision-makers is no excuse for such bungled-up job, but they help explain why so much remains unsaid, and why to this day France's share of responsibility in the genocide remains a highly sensitive question.

Whether the appointment of a special commission in charge of investigating the archival materials (much of which has remained beyond the reach of scholars) is likely to shed light on the many unresolved issues surrounding France's role is hard to say. But the controversy unleashed by the absence of reputable Rwanda scholars on the commission raises questions about its capacity deliver the missing evidence.

Meanwhile debates persist on a range of major issues, not the least of which hinges on Mitterrand's reference to a "double genocide." While there are few dissenting voices about the genocide of Tutsi, whether the g-word also applies to the mass murder of Hutu by the triumphant RPF remains highly controversial.

The other mass murder

As I look back at the endless debates over how best to pin down the causes of the Tutsi genocide, I doubt that anything constructive can emerge from another attempt at bringing to light another horrifying carnage. Nonetheless, the evidence pointing to deliberate, premeditated, systematic mass murder of Hutu civilians in the wake of the Tutsi genocide is overwhelming.

That every genocide is different is a banality on which most would agree. In what ways, and with what consequences, is where opinions diverge. One of the most contentious propositions raised by my work on Rwanda concerns the use of the phrase "retributive genocide," a characterization I

---

[25] Cited in Patrick de Saint-Exupéry, *L'Inavouable: La France au Rwanda* (Paris, 2004), p. 227. For some horrifying eyewitness testimonies by MSF medical teams, see Francoise Bouchet-Saulnier and Frédéric Laffont, *Maudits soient les yeux fermés* (Paris, 1995), pp. 72–73.

[26] de Saint-Exupéry, *L'Inavouable*, pp. 201–203.

borrowed from Helen Fein's seminal inquest.[27] The implication is that not all genocides are ideologically motivated; some occur in response to threats, real or imagined. The cases of Rwanda and Burundi are obvious examples. Behind the 1972 genocide of Hutu in Burundi lay the intense fear experienced by many Tutsi that, after the killing of their kinsmen in Rwanda in 1959–1962, they would be next in line. Again, there is no way one can explain the apocalypse of 1994 in Rwanda without considering the mortal threats posed to the Hutu as a group by the Tutsi-led invasion.

Each time I tried to summon historical facts in support of my argument in front of an African audience the response was mixed. The criticism I encountered most often when discussing the case of Rwanda was that my argument was at bottom a justification for the genocide.[28] I am not sure there is a very clear distinction in Kinyarwanda or Kirundi between justify and explain. On this I stand to be educated. Objections to the use of the phrase are by no means limited to Africans. The point I want to underscore though is familiar to genocide scholars: not only is the quest for an agreed-upon definition of genocide highly problematic, but so is the search for a consensus on the motives or prime movers behind mass killings.

Should we speak then of mass killings instead of genocide, of war crimes instead of mass killings, of atrocity crimes instead of war crimes? When is one phrase more appropriate than the other? There are no clear answers.

But there is compelling evidence to show that the crimes committed by the RPF against Hutu civilians are of a scale comparable those attributed to Habyarimana's *génocidaires*. For this we are indebted, among others, to the findings of Luc Reydams and Roland Tissot, both recognized experts on the demographics of the genocide, in their important article about "Rwanda's male deficit after the violent 1990s." After a close scrutiny of census figures and demographic data from a variety of sources, they reach the conclusion that as many as 110,000 Hutu males were killed by the FPR in the months following the 1994 genocide of Tutsi, thus accounting for the "male deficit"

---

[27] Helen Fein, "Genocide: A Sociological Perspective," *Current Sociology*, esp. the section on Retributive Genocides and Plural Society Theory, vol. 38, no. 1 (Spring 1990), pp. 86–91.

[28] Least expected was the rap on the knuckles I got from a former Rwandan student of mine, a Tutsi, at the University of California at Berkeley, Jean-Pierre Karegeye, then attending the Jesuit School of Theology at Berkeley, who, I might add, fully deserved the high marks I gave him in my course on Comparative Genocide. I was looking forward to attend the panel on Rwanda that he organized at the 2003 International Association of African Studies in Baltimore. But instead of a friendly exchange I found myself sternly reprimanded and then turned into public ridicule, amid guffaws and sarcasms, for coming up with the idea of a "genocide by retaliation." Denied the opportunity to fully respond, I would like to think that his quirky change of attitude is more a reflection of my own limitations as a teacher than a product of his Jesuitic background.

inscribed in census figures,[29] a figure which leaves out an undetermined number of children and women. Looking at the total number of Tutsi victims between April 6 and July 19, 1994, Omar S. McDoom estimates that between 491,000 and 522,000 were killed (contrary to the over a million deaths claimed in official Rwandan documents). Tempting as it may be to subtract that figure from the official number of genocide victims to figure out the number of Hutu deaths, the size of the Hutu losses during and after the genocide is more complicated. Combining different time frames and kill zones within and outside Rwanda invites considerable caution. As Omar McDoom suggests, drawing his insights from Scott Straus, the time periods to be considered are the following: (a) October 1990 to April 1994, the pre-genocide killings; (b) the genocide, April to July 1994; (c) the consolidation of power by the RPF, August 1994–1995; (d) the pursuit and killing of Hutu refugees in the DRC, 1996–1997; (e) the insurgency and counter-insurgency in Rwanda's northwest, 1997–1998; (f) authoritarian repression inside Rwanda, 2000 onwards.[30] Figuring out the totality of Hutu losses over such time lines will take time and will not go unchallenged. By way of a first approximation of the organized slaughter that has presided over Hutu losses one can do no better than turn to the painstaking research undertaken by Judi Rever, sometimes at great risk to herself, and now available in her hard-to-put-down blockbuster, *In Praise of Blood*.

It will come as no surprise to those of us familiar with the history of post-genocide Rwanda that the Kagame regime bears a huge responsibility for the horrifying human rights abuses committed against Hutu civilians. But so wide is the range and depth of human rights abuses, so varied are the motives and diverse the contexts that it numbs the mind. There is, of course, something distasteful about parsing atrocities. It suggests that some are more offensive than others; that extenuating circumstances obtain one case and not in another; that some deserve absolution and others retribution. But regardless of how you cut it (*si j'ose dire*) there are compelling reasons to distinguish among the types of criminality attributed to the Kagame regime.

From the raft of evidence available from defectors, human rights observers, scholarly inquisitors and journalists, emerge three distinctive types of

[29] See Roland Tissot, "Beyond the Numbers Game: Reassessing Human Losses in Rwanda in the 1990s," *Journal of Genocide Research*, vol. 22, no. 1 (March 2020), pp. 116–124; and Luc Reydams and Roland Tissot, "The Fog of Genocide: Rwanda's Male Deficit after the Violent 1990s," forthcoming. One of the authors adds a cautionary note in an email to this writer:

> if the RPF also killed let us say 100,000 women then the number of Hutu killed increases to 210,000. We hope to come up with a demographically sound estimate of the total of Hutu mortality, male and female, in our next paper.

See also Luc Reydams, "'More Than a Million': The Politics of Accounting for the Dead of the Rwanda Genocide," *Review of African Political Economy*, vol. 47, no. 163 (2020), forthcoming.

[30] Omar S. McDoom, "Contested Counting: Toward a Rigorous Estimate of the Death Toll in the Rwandan Genocide," *Journal of Genocide Research*, p. 91.

criminality, associated with manipulative killings, targeted assassinations, and systematic mass murder. The calculated killings of opposition figures aimed at playing one group off against another is illustrative of the first type. The "work" done through *ibyitso* penetration of opposition movements goes beyond the elimination of well-known individual personalities (such as Emmanuel Gapyisi and Martin Bucyana, among others); it also involves the collateral vengeance killings of dozens of people identified with one group or the other.

Targeted assassinations have sent to their graves scores of former political allies turned into enemies or merely expendable chips on the political chessboard. The names of Seth Sendashonga, Alexis Kanyarengwe, Theoneste Lizinde, and, more recently, Patrick Karegeya are among those which immediately come to mind. Many others could be added.

The third type is where accusations of genocide enter the realm of the possible.

The truly appalling scale of the killings ordered by Kagame is made evident in Abdul Joshua Ruzibiza's description of "the beginning of the genocide of the Hutu," in response to "the beginning of the genocide of the Tutsi." In Kabuye, near Byumba, 3,000 young men were massacred by Captain Gcinya's team in the month of April 1994; in Byumba's stadium, where the weapon of choice at first was the hoe, the job proved beyond the capacity of the killers and in the end 2,500 Hutu civilians were machine-gunned; in Kageyo, Meshero, Mukarange, Kisaro, in Kibali's primary school at least 6,000 victims were killed at different intervals; horrific massacres were also committed at the Nyacyonga camp, where many Hutu had taken refuge, in the Mutara region and even in Giti, one of the few communes where "the protection of Tutsi had been exemplary."[31]

The tit-for-tat dialectic presiding over the reciprocation of atrocities is just as plain in the horrendous killings of Tutsi civilians. In the prefecture of Gikongoro, where close to 50,000 had found refuge in the primary schools of Murambi and the churches of Kaduha and Cyanika, most were "executed with machetes in one night by groups of *interahamwe* aided by elements of the gendarmerie. The order came from (interim President) Theodore Sindukubwabo."[32] This is only one of the many genocidal episodes chronicled by Ruzibiza.

Where Judi Rever's narrative breaks important new ground is in her detailed depiction of the chain of command from Kagame's High Command to the DMI and lower echelons; in the comprehensive picture she draws of where the killings took place, when, how, under whose supervision; and in her use of confidential information. Nor does she hold her punches when criticizing the myopic vision of the Washington Consensus.

The picture she draws of the DMI reminds me somehow of a cross between the FBI and the Communist Party. Created in 1990, it bears traces

[31] Ruzibiza, *Rwanda*, pp. 260, 283.
[32] Ruzibiza, *Rwanda*, pp. 281–282.

of Kagame's rich background as Museveni's spy chief in the 1980s. Its inves-
tigatory functions are obvious from its name, but for its explicitly inquisito-
rial role we need to look at other sub-sections: counter-intelligence, criminal
investigation and prosecution, research, records and registry, external intelligence. Its wide-ranging penetration of subordinate units, ranging from the
republican guard, to training wing, gendarmerie and military encadrement
(*abadaka*), is reminiscent of nothing so much as of the blueprints I once
used with my students to chart the all-encompassing organization of Communist Parties, with the High Command as the rough equivalent of the
Political Bureau.

The uniqueness of the DMI lies in its efficiency as a killing machine.
Under the guidance of DMI-trained "technicians," the art of killing reached
a high degree of sophistication. In a confidential report to the ICTR we
learn that special courses became part of the Training Wing curriculum:
"the following courses were given: Course Chemical where they learned
how to poison water, to use the pharmaceutical products to kill; Course
of self-defense where they learned how to kill with a cord, with a plastic bag, oil injected into the ear with a syringe, techniques *akondoyi* and
agafuni; Course of combat in an urban environment where they learned
the use of bayonet, guns and grenades; Course of Field Engineering, where
they learned the installation of mines and mines clearance and the ruse of
remote controlled bombs." In effect, it refashioned the army into a tool of
mass murder. "Its agents have thoroughly infiltrated the regular army, with
representatives at every level of each battalion, from the company to the
platoon to the smallest section... The DMI became the main instrument
through which crimes were inflicted on Rwandans during the genocide, and
in the continuing source of control and violence against Rwandans and
Congolese. DMI staff killed, maimed and conducted sabotage throughout
Rwanda and the region from 1990 through the genocide, the counterinsurgency and the conflict in the Congo."[33]

The litany of abominations revealed by Rever makes for painful reading.
What happened in Byumba in the first weeks of April is only one of several
nightmarish episodes. "Getting Away with Mass Murder in the Byumba
Stadium" (the title of Chapter 5) must be seen as the most horrifying piece
of evidence of a genocidal intent. Where Ruzibiza offered the briefest evo-
cation of the killings, she shows how the victims were lured into a trap,
massively exterminated, hastily buried before being exhumed a few days
later and incinerated, so as to destroy all traces of the crime.

The victims were refugees from the Nyacyonga camp, most of them
forced out of their homes in the Mutara region by RPA attacks. The camp
at one point was estimated to shelter close to a million. Many were those
who probably joined the *interahamwe* but the vast majority were hapless
civilians, including thousands of women and children and elderly people.
Exterminating tens of thousands could not be improvised. It required a

[33] Rever, *In Praise of Blood*, p. 65.

plan, a method, and willing executioners. On all three counts, the DMI proved equal to the task. At the heart of the plan was a ruse: to persuade the refugees to move en masse to Byumba as a half-way station before returning to their homes; once in Byumba, following an exhausting trek, they would be ordered into the stadium to wait for nourishment and rest. No sooner were they assembled in the stadium than the trap closed in on them. A handful of high-ranking RPA commanders, including Kagame himself, James Kabarebe and Kayumba Nyamwasa, the head of the DMI, made a brief appearance. Rever's informants, Theo and Pina, both witnesses to the scene, "grew increasingly concerned that something was about to occur, but there were so many Hutu inside the stadium that they could not imagine what it would be." Orders were issued to first pick out the strongest men; after they were dealt with by grenades and automatic weapons would come the more time-consuming chore of the systematic killings of thousands of men, women, and children by executioners wielding the *agafuni* (the hoe). This is how Rever describes what happened: "Theo and his friend Pina stayed outside at their post all night listening in horror to the screams. 'It was agony. I will never forget it. It went on until six o'clock in the morning.' At dawn Theo saw some of the first trucks come to haul away the dead. Getting the corpses out of the stadium was an overwhelming task. The stadium was slick with blood and had to be cleaned from top to bottom."[34] No less overwhelming was the order that came from higher up a few days later, to unearth the corpses and take them to the Akagera park to have them incinerated.

Such deliberate, massive extermination of human beings makes it difficult to take seriously the notion that, yes, the RPA did commit some crimes, but the few that happened were unfortunate events, most of the time motivated by an instinctive urge to avenge the deaths of their own relatives.

In shedding light of these events Rever was fortunate to have access to confidential documents, notably the treasure trove of information available through the *General report on the special investigations concerning the crimes committed by the Rwanda Patriotic Army (RPA) during 1994*, submitted to International Criminal Tribunal for Rwanda (ICTR) in October 2003. But even more revealing are the countless interviews conducted in Belgium and France with a number of turncoats. Instead of the ICTR's cut-and-dry accounting, Rever puts a human face on the inhumanity of their crimes. Here is Deus Kagiraneza, furtive and mercurial, Abdallah Akishuli, looking vulnerable, boyish, unsettled, Simbi, a former child soldier in 1994: his hands are small and his skin soft, his voice and manner quiet and steady. All were witness to and indeed took an active part in the most chilling murders imaginable. But, unlike many others, they had a capacity for remorse

Why did it take so long for atrocities committed on such a scale to enter our consciousness?

---

[34] Rever, *In Praise of Blood*, pp. 73–74.

Conspiracies of silence

As one who worked and lived in Rwanda in the mid-1960s I am struck by the contrast between the collective image then projected by the Tutsi as a group and that which has since come into view. The distorting effect of the Cold War lens was nowhere more evident than in the reductionist illusion that made them a Communist-inspired threat to Western values and interests in Central Africa. If the notion of feudal counter-revolutionary cockroaches in league with international Communism sounds like a bit of a stretch all we need to remember is the sense of paranoia exhibited by Western embassies in Rwanda in the face of Tutsi involvement in the eastern Congo upheavals in 1964–1965 and the support they received from Communist China and Cuba via Tanzania and Burundi. A visiting State Department official I met in Kigali in 1965 made no bones of the imperative need to give every support we could to President Kayibanda's fledgling republican order, the only hope for democracy out of the ashes of ex-Belgian Africa.

Cold War issues are no longer shaping our cognitive map. Today the shoe is on the other foot. The image of the Tutsi as a victim of genocide eclipses everything else. With few exceptions, popular sympathies here and abroad go to the RPA for stopping the killings, and for Kagame for his exceptional military skills in his fight against the *génocidaires*. That he could have precipitated the carnage by shooting down Habyarimana's plane, and could have saved many more Tutsi lives had he not chosen to ignore their vulnerability for strategic reasons, are issues that have been consistently dismissed out of hand as a form of denial.

How can one account for such an extraordinary cover up?

It would be the height of hypocrisy to deny the horrors of the genocide committed against Tutsi civilians. Nor do I question the necessity of remembrance; it is imperative that such crimes be recognized, memorialized, and sanctioned. What I do not hesitate to call into the question is the analogy with the Holocaust, the role of the ICTR as a legitimate vehicle of international justice, and the (resistible) pressures exerted by US policymakers in obstructing the course of justice. On all three counts the truth has been ignored, denied or manipulated in order to exonerate the Kagame government of all wrongs.

The Holocaust analogy is perhaps the most normal reaction on the part of those observers whose relatives perished at the hands of the Nazis. Filip Gourevitch and Jean Hatzfeld are cases in point. To hold them to task for misperceiving or ignoring the realities of the other genocide would be unfair. But the fact remains that imputing to the Hutu *génocidaires* motives similar to those of the butchers of Auschwitz misses the point. It leaves out of the picture the paroxysmic fears that stemmed from the RPA's invasion and the mortal threats posed to the achievements of the Hutu revolution. When the parallel with the Holocaust is articulated with the persuasive literary style of a Gourevitch, it is easy to see why it should become conventional wisdom. If the Tutsi of Rwanda stand as the metonym for the Jews how can one conceivably point an accusing finger at the victimized group?

Media attention generates its own momentum. Another example of how, by selectively sifting out the evidence, the genocide of Tutsi emerges as the only case of mass murder is the avalanche of testimonies and commentaries spawned by the London-based NGO African Rights. Under the collaborative tandem of Rukiya Omaar and Alex de Waal, the magnitude of the crimes committed by the Hutu *génocidaires* eclipses and ultimately reduces to a blank space those committed by the RPF. This is made abundantly clear in their heavy brief, *Death, Despair and Defiance*, published in September 1994, but as new evidence has surfaced, there is reason to trust Judi Rever's observation that African Rights can best be described as a propaganda machine in the pay of the RPF.[35] As for de Waal's take on the genocide, it is with some skepticism that we must accept the view that in order "to understand Hutu extremism one needs to delve into the origins of Hutu identity," including presumably the fantasies of the Hamitic hypothesis.[36] Unlike his colleague and sister-in-arms, however, he has since left the organization and made amends for his previously misguided takes.[37]

To measure the impact of *Death, Despair and Defiance* there is no better source than Luc Reydams's outstanding investigation of the hidden face of African Rights. The close connection between Rukiya Omaar and RPF heavyweights is laid bare in considerable detail. So are the NGO's multiple sources of funding, including the EU's "financial contribution" to the tune of 464,135 euros as well as undisclosed amounts from the RPF. But perhaps the most arresting segment of his research concerns the determining influence of African Rights on the medias, and, even more significantly, on the ICTR's perceptions. "The Bible" is how the massive volume was referred to in the early years of the tribunal, according to Reydam: "The African Rights report was on every desk of the Office of the Special Prosecutor," a frequent visitor to the ICTR told him. "The book seemed of much more practical value than other reports."[38] If the tendentiousness of the report is by now acknowledged, few are willing to admit its enduring influence in shaping the vision of the ICTR as well as that of a fair number of influential policy makers in the UK and the US.

---

[35] Rukiya Omaar appears to have received $100,000 from the RPF for work that African Rights did in connection with the tenth anniversary of the genocide. Rever, *In Praise of Blood*, p. 130.

[36] Alex De Waal, "The Genocidal State," *The Times Literary Supplement*, July 1, 1994.

[37] See his "Writing Human Rights and Getting It Wrong," *Boston Review*, June 6, 2016.

[38] Luc Reydams, "NGO Justice: African Rights as Pseudo-Prosecutor of the Rwandan Genocide," *Human Rights Quarterly*, vol. 38, no. 3 (August 2016), p. 580.

The ICTR on trial

However much one may disagree about African Rights' ultimate impact, the ICTR's outrageous travesty of justice is well established, though not widely publicized. Among other things it has knowingly dissimulated the crushing body of evidence brought to its attention, refrained from the prosecution of RPA suspects, and caved in under US pressures.

The responsibility of the ICTR in lending legitimacy to the victor's justice paradigm is a tale as tawdry as any in the annals of international justice. It has been told with greater persuasiveness than I can summon by other scholars.[39] Here I only want to sketch out how a major piece of incriminating evidence has been withdrawn from public scrutiny in response to pressures from Washington. The document in question is the previously mentioned *General report on the Special investigations concerning the crimes committed by the Rwandan Patriotic Army (RPA) during 1994*. Submitted to ICTR Prosecutor Hassan Boubacar Jallow on October 1, 2003, the report is a summary presentation of the activities of a three-member Special Investigation Team appointed in February 1999 by Bernard Muna, deputy prosecutor, at the request of Louise Arbour, the ICTR prosecutor. The investigators focused their inquest on the crimes committed by the RPA in the communes of Giti, Byumba, Kabgaye, and Butare. They correctly anticipated the reluctance of their informants to be interviewed: "The major problem which we faced and will continue to face was the reticence even the mistrust of our interlocutors. Generally, they did not believe in the determination of the Prosecutor to engage in prosecutions against the RPF." Their fears turned out to be amply justified.

This was not the first time the crimes of the RPF had been brought to public attention. Alison Des Forges estimated the number of Hutu killed in 1994 at the hands of the RPF between 25–30,000. A UN official, Robert Gersony, mentioned 25–45,000 Hutu deaths between April and late July 1994. The testimonies gathered by the UN investigating team go considerably further in assessing the scale of the mass murders, in identifying the suspects and the circumstances of their crimes.

Consider the following macabre vignettes: At the commercial center of Musambira "one group of Intelligence Staff killed 350 persons by using plastic bags that they put on the head of the victim until suffocation. The group also used *agafuni*. Another method used by this group consisted in laying down the victims on their bellies their hand tied in the back, then put a cord with slipknot at the neck. While holding the bust against the ground using the foot, one member of the group pulls on the cord which strangled the victim (p. 11)... In the Rambura commune The 59th battalion

---

[39] Those from whose work I have wantonly pilfered include Rever, *In Praise of Blood*, esp. Chapter 11; Cruvellier, *Court of Remorse*; Victor Peskin, "Victor's Justice Revisited," in Scott Straus and Lars Waldorf eds., *Remaking Rwanda: State Building and Human Rights after Mass Violence* (Madison, 2011).

set up a barrier by which the population returning from the Turquoise zone must pass through (sic). This population was screened at the barrier. The majority were killed only because they were Hutu. The soldiers in charge of this task were divided into six groups of eight men chosen exclusively from among Tutsi. They killed their victims with *agafuni*... The slowest teams killed between 20 and 30 persons per night, but the specialists of *agafuni* could kill 100 per night... The number of victims of this carnage was evaluated at between 2,000 and 3,000 according to the witness who used to be an RPA soldier and who participated in the attack... (p. 12). In September 1994 Australian soldiers with UNAMIR discovered fifty bodies covered with leaves in a wooded area in the commune of Save. When the soldiers returned two weeks later, they could not find the fifty bodies. The local population reported that the RPA in that area had executed one thousand and seven hundred and fifty (1,750) persons" (p. 14). "At the market of Gihara, there were about 300 people who had taken refuge. They were mixed Hutu and Tutsi. The Intelligence Officer of the 101st battalion gave the order to separate the Hutu from the Tutsi and kill the Hutu. 25 Tutsi who were not killed were put on the side. All other Hutu were killed. Among the 25 saved people Major Sam Bigabiro had wanted to have sex with a Tutsi woman from Bagogwe who was pregnant. She refused. He tried with another woman but she also refused. These 25 people were killed on the order of Major Sam Bigabiro and his head of escort, named Lt. Célestin, carried out the order" (p. 11).

This is only a small sample of the countless atrocities committed by the RPA that were never allowed to come under prosecutorial scrutiny. The responsibility lies in part with the last two prosecutors, Carla Del Ponte and Hassan Boubacar Jallow, neither of whom had the will to resist the pressures exerted by US defenders of the so-called Washington Consensus. Ironically, although Del Ponte deserves credit for initiating the legal procedure to investigate the crimes committed by the RPA, the way she went about it caused her undoing. Rever has no qualms calling her decision to inform Kagame of her move a colossal error of judgment, a mistake she further aggravated by holding a press conference to announce that she could have an indictment against the PRA within a year. This was enough to set in motion Kagame's counter-move. His sense of alarm found a receptive echo in Washington as well as in London, where he could count on the unstinting support of Tony Blair and his pro-Kagame cohorts.[40]

Knuckling under to pressures from within the UN Security Council, relayed in large part by the US Ambassador-at-large for war crime issues,

---

[40] According to a *Sunday Times* article of December 20, 2009, in Rwanda Blair's charity the Africa Governance Initiative, pays for a nine-strong team of staff to work permanently in Kigali, many in the president's office, where they are supporting local ministers and helping to stamp out corruption... he also plans to work with Rick Warren to use the faith network in Rwanda to distribute medicine and mosquito nets to fight malaria.

Pierre-Richard Prosper, in mid-2002 Carla del Ponte "took the unprecedented step to suspend the activities of the Special Investigation Unit (SIU),"
and then "to instruct members of the SIU to suspend contact with their
informants and witnesses."[41] Despite Del Ponte's tergiversations, and subsequent decision to rescind her suspension of the SIU's activities, the die was
cast. She traded her role as chief prosecutor for ICTR for the same title at
the International Criminal Tribunal for ex-Yugoslavia (ICTY). Her successor at the ICTR, Hassan Boubacar Jallow, predictably trimmed his sails to
the prevailing wind, though not without facing some adverse reactions. In
a letter of January 11, 2005, Filip Reyntjens referred to the "compelling
evidence (gathered by the SIU) on a number of massacres committed by the
RPF in 1994." "These crimes," he added, "fall squarely within the mandate
of the ICTR, they are well documented, testimonial and material proof is
available, and the identity of the RPF suspects is known. If they are left
unprosecuted the ICTR will have failed to eliminate one of the root causes
of genocide and other crimes – impunity." Kenneth Roth, the HRW director,
echoed the same concerns, but with similarly negative results: "We request
that you execute our mandate to prosecute persons responsible for serious
violations of international humanitarian law and that you act on credible
evidence of serious crimes committed by senior RPF commanders which
we believe your office has gathered. The reported killing of 30,000 people
by RPF soldiers as documented by the UN High Commission for Refugees
(UNHCR), is by any standard sufficiently serious to merit prosecution."[42]
This is as fair an assessment as can be made of an international institution
that has thoroughly discredited itself by turning a blind eye to irrefutable
evidence of criminal responsibility. What it leaves out is the complicit role
played by the US in obstructing the course of international justice.

In her book, *The Hunt: Me and My War Criminals* (New York, 2008),
Carla del Ponte takes a retrospective look at one of the ways in which
the US threw its weight behind the RPF: "The Rwanda authorities already
controlled each stage of our investigations. We knew that the intelligence
services of Rwanda received monitoring equipment from the US which
was used for phone calls, faxes and the internet. We suspected that the
authorities had also infiltrated our computer network and placed agents
among the Rwandan interpreters and other members of the team in Kigali
Laurent Walpen, former chief of investigations for the prosecution, also
knew that the US, for obvious reasons, did not want the investigators to be
equipped with the latest encryption Swiss telephones. In other words, the
Rwandans knew, in real time, what the investigators of the tribunal were
doing." As anyone familiar with Kagame's communications skills, including
his talent for masking the truth, will realize, this form of assistance proved
extremely valuable for penetrating the SIU, and for possibly ensuring the

[41] Rever, *In Praise of Blood*, p. 158.
[42] The quote from Reyntjens is from a copy of his letter to the author; Roth's statement is
quoted in Rever, *In Praise of Blood*, p. 172.

disappearance of its informers. But along with such "technical assistance," US diplomats also played a significant role in strengthening the (im)posture of the RPF. We already mentioned the name of Pierre-Richard Prosper, the US Ambassador at large for war crimes. Thierry Cruvellier draws a lively picture of the young lawyer of Haitian origin: At 36, when serving in the Office of the Prosecutor (OTP) in Kigali, "he had a working knowledge of French which he used to his advantage in the officially bi-lingual tribunal. Above all he was a successful product of US law schools, confident, polished and pragmatic. the embodiment of the American dream."[43] This said, if anyone deserves credit for influencing the work of the ICTR in a sense favorable to the RPF, he does: It was he who brokered the shameful deal between the US Embassy in Kigali and the Rwandan regime by which the OTP would agree to share information with the government of Rwanda concerning the special investigations against RPF perpetrators. Specifically, it was agreed, among other things, that "the OTP will not seek an indictment or otherwise bring a case before the OTP unless it is determined that the Government of Rwanda investigation or prosecution is not genuine... The OTP will share any related evidence, as appropriate, with the Government of Rwanda." As Rever sums it up, "In black and white the ICTR had become a surrogate of Washington... It had granted Kagame legal immunity from war crimes and terrorism."[44]

Twenty years after its creation, as the ICTR was winding up its investigations, its achievements seem distressingly modest, especially when set against the costs (tens of millions of dollars). It brought to justice and tried 75 individuals in 55 cases; 49 individuals were convicted; 14 were acquitted; 12 were awaiting the outcome of appeals. Not a single RPF case was brought for prosecution. Indeed, the highest cost of the ICTR must assessed in terms of the self-inflicted moral discredit attendant upon its appalling performance as a legal instrument. No other international tribunal – with the possible exception of the Nuremberg tribunal – has done more to give an appearance of respectability to the anomalies of the "victor's justice." If for no other reason all four of its former prosecutors stand to be condemned, at least morally.

Crime without punishment

In his crisply crafted portrayal of Kagame, "The global elite's favorite strongman," Jeffrey Gettelman writes that compared to other African heads of state "he seems like a godsend. Spartan, stoic, analytical and austere, he routinely stays up to 2 or 3 a.m. to thumb through back issues of the economist or study progress reports from red-dirt villages across his country, constantly searching for better, more efficient ways to stretch the billion dollars

---

[43] Cruvellier, *Court of Remorse*, p. 24.
[44] Rever, *In Praise of Blood*, p. 161. For the full text of the "deal" between Gerald Gahima, general prosecutor for the Supreme Court, and Prosper's office, see ibid.

his government gets each year from donor nations that hold him up as a shining example of what aid money can do in Africa... The Clinton Global Initiative honored him with a Global Citizen award, and Bill Clinton said that Kagame 'freed the heart and mind of his people.'"[45]

Could it be the same person who sent tens of thousands to their graves, who gave the approving nod to mass murderers, who turned a deaf ear to his victims' pleas for clemency?

The answer comes clear and loud from the extraordinary 57-page document released in August 2010 under the anodyne title of Rwanda Briefing.[46] What makes it exceptionally noteworthy is that its authors, all Tutsi, were among the most powerful aides to Kagame before their decision to flee the country and set up a new opposition party, the Rwanda National Congress (RNC). General Kayumba Nyamwasa was army chief of staff and later ambassador to India; Gerald Gahima was prosecutor general and vice-president of the Supreme Court; his brother, Theogene Rudasingwa served as secretary general of the RPF, ambassador to the US and chief of staff of the president; the late Patrick Karageya was chief of external security services before his assassination by courtesy of Kagame in his hotel room in Pretoria. Nyamwasa barely escaped the same fate after being shot at and wounded by another of Kagame's killers. The remaining two survivors are prudently keeping a low profile, hoping to avoid the assassin's bullet.

Besides offering an illuminating picture of the "challenges facing Rwanda in the aftermath of the genocide," the most revealing passages of the document draws a portrait of Kagame that seems closer to a Cosa Nostra kingpin than to Gettelman's iconic global elite hero. The authors make their case by exploding one myth after another. "*Kagame as an exemplary strategic thinker and visionary leader*" (myth no. 1) is better seen as "having made mistakes of phenomenal proportions which led to dire consequence for the people of Rwanda"; "*Kagame as incorruptible, austere man of absolute integrity*" (myth no. 2) is in fact "responsible for financial impropriety and theft of public resources on a grand scale... his lifestyle is not just scandalous, it is criminal... he treats the national treasury as his own personal bank account"; "*Kagame as a reforming, unifying leader*" (myth no. 3) is a notion that sits uneasily with his actual policies in the wake of the genocide, "occasioning intense polarization along the lines of ethnicity... Kagame has become a polarizing figure whose continued leadership is only certain to lead to perpetuate conflict and to lead to new violence, even of genocidal proportions in years to come."

Their argument, however well-intended, would have been more convincing had the "four renegades" – to use the phrase of the rejoinder issued by the government – not been themselves actively involved in the construction

---

[45] Jeffrey Gettelman, "The Global Elite's Favorite Strongman," *The New York Times*, September 4, 2013.

[46] Kayumba Nyamwasa, Theogene Rudasingwa, Patrick Karegeya, and Gerald Gahima, *Rwanda Briefing*, August 2010 (Typescript).

of the state they now hoped to dismantle. The point is made clear in Susan Thomson's commentary: "Gahima and Rudasingwa helped eliminate the political opposition; Nyamwasa participated in the carnage during the 1997–1998 counterinsurgency in the northwest; Karegeya was involved in the disappearance or assassination of RPF critics at home and abroad."[47] Little wonder if so far the RNC has failed spectacularly to get off the ground.

Other voices convey a distinctly more frightening image of the globalist strongman. The story told by Claire Uwamutara, a Tutsi survivor, of how her husband and son were assassinated on Kagame's orders, reveals his cold-blooded cruelty. In an interview from Malawi where she sought asylum,[48] she described her ordeal:

> During the genocide I went into hiding at Saint Paul parish until mid-June when I was evacuated by RPF soldiers. Ndahiro Danny, a lieutenant, was in charge of the Bravo unit. All Tutsi survivors were taken to Rebero hill. During that time I served as a nurse, to give assistance to the wounded. After the war I married Ndahiro Danny. I left Rwanda on July 1, 2009 after the assassination of my husband Colonel Ndahiro Danny and my son Ndahiro Magnifique (nine years old). The assassination was carried out at 4 am at our home in the village of Kibagabaga in Miroko, district of Kigali.

She explains how after the genocide

> Kagame set up a group of soldiers whose mission was to kill and eliminate all suspects (indésirables), principally Hutu. This group of killers, known as Gacurabwenge was under the command of Katabarwa Fred. My husband was appointed to serve as advisor... During their first meetings the item at the top of their agenda was how to assassinate Twagiramungu Faustin, Pasteur Bizimungu along with other high-ranking Hutu in the government. My husband refused to have anything to do with this plan. He was later arrested on the pretext that he was passing government secrets to Twagiramungu. He spent two months in the Kabingi prison in Kimihurura.

She recalls attending one of the group's meetings at a hotel on June 4, attended by Kagame and Tito Rutaremara:

> I had been invited because I was a nurse at the hospital and would be given instruction regarding the killings. Also, because my husband was an officer in the RPA. First on the agenda was how to go about the killing of people coming out of jail, business people, Hutu intellectuals

[47] Thomson, *Rwanda*, p. 226.
[48] *Témoignage oculaire de Mme Uwamutara Claire sur l'assassinat de son mari et de son fils le 1 juillet 2009 à Kigali* (Author's files).

and many others seen as suspects. All of them were to be killed along with members of their families by any means possible... In the course of this meeting my husband raised questions about the reasons for killing these people and the consequences at the international level since the war had come to an end. He urged the participants to think twice about what they were about to do. After that meeting my husband was arrested.

After a short time in jail he was appointed to the Unity and Reconciliation Commission.

He soon again fell foul of the authorities when he refused to change his mind on the killings. "My husband was again arrested in December 2007 and taken to the G2 jail. This is an underground prison, which seals the fate of several innocent lives. A few days after he was arrested Lt. Uwayezu Fidele, Sgt. Habiyaremye Oswald of the DMI, accompanied by four military policemen, came to see me just as I was coming home from the hospital. They showed me a warrant of arrest. They took me to the same prison as my husband. They tortured me with a hot liquid that they poured under my toe nails. They wanted me to make a false testimony about my husband's ties with the Hutu, especially those living abroad and what sort of rewards we were expecting from them. They kept torturing me, and ended up breaking my arm... I spent two years in jail, in Mulindi, until May 2009. My husband stayed in this prison until March 2009, when he was taken to the Kamembe Training Center for rehabilitation exercises. He had become handicapped because of the tortures he endured. I saw him again on June 29, 2009 when he suddenly showed up in our home around 11:00 pm. He told me a military Jeep had just dropped him off. Two days later, on July 1, they came to assassinate him, early in the morning at 4:00 am as I said earlier. Panic-stricken, we fled to our neighbor and waited until we heard the Jeep driving out through the gate. Coming into the house all we found was a piece of my husband's ear. The corpses of my son and husband had been taken away. Gripped by fear we decided to flee the country by crossing into Uganda."

As the interview drew to a close Claire recalled some of the more horrifying moments she witnessed, some of which strain credulity: "When I was transferred to the Mironko hospital I realized this was to test me even further: to assassinate women and their babies at the time of childbirth; for Hutu survivors of road accidents the order was to cut off their arms and legs regardless of the gravity of their wounds. I never could agree to these instructions and soon was sent to Muhima prison known as 1930, where I saw prisoners in a terrible condition after being tortured. The dearth of appropriate medication was intentional... The Tutsi were unhappy about the assistance I was trying to bring to the Hutu prisoners, so much so that a woman named Trifoni and the Tutsi survivors association (Ibuka) summoned me and asked for explanations. I told them I was here to look after patients, not to kill them... After being released from jail I was sent to the

Kicukiro health center. Again, I was given instructions to reduce the number of Hutu newly born and find ways of complicating their mothers' recovery... The order was that out of 100 cases of maternity 30 mothers and 20 babies had to die."

Regardless of how much credibility can be given to parts of this narrative, the picture it suggests – one of deliberate, systematic elimination of Hutu lives – is in keeping with the traits of brutality revealed by critics of Kagame, from Judi Rever to Filip Reyntjens, from Abdul Ruzibiza to David Himbara, one of his former senior advisors now living in exile, and many others. None of this has gone unnoticed by Western donors and policymakers. One Western diplomat cited by Gettelman sums up the cynical quid pro quo behind US support of Kagame: "He has become a rare symbol of progress on a continent that has an abundance of failed states and a record of paralyzing corruption... You put your money in and you get results... Yes, Kagame was utterly ruthless, but there was a mutual interest in supporting him... We needed a success story and he was it."[49]

Rwanda's economic miracle needs to be set against the far more problematic landscape drawn by Marc Sommers in his appropriately titled inquest into the absence of economic social opportunities faced by up and coming generations:[50] "Stuck" is indeed the term that can best capture the dilemma confronting urban youth as they try to make their mark in life. Based on extensive field work and interviews with scores of respondents, Sommers's findings bring into relief the "desperate, extreme poverty, and social isolation" facing a large number of youths in Kigali: their sense of hopelessness and entrapment, he writes, best conveyed by the term *rubiyikuro wihebye* (hopeless youth), "makes them vulnerable to manipulation and exploitation." While acknowledging "the fact that so many youth feel trapped in a life of looming failure is hardly a recipe for stable peace,"[51] he also takes pains to underscore the absence of violent responses among those most vulnerable to extreme poverty. The ever-present threat of sanctions would seem the obvious explanation, yet in the absence of reliable comparative data on ethnic identities among urban youth – the one variable most conspicuously lacking in this otherwise admirable investigation – one can only speculate about the factors that might impede or stimulate violence and its underlying motives.

While there is no gainsaying the remarkable economic progress accomplished by Rwanda over the last 25 years, the past still resonates. The Kigali Genocide Memorial is a poignant reminder of the 1994 carnage. But since references to ethnic identities are constitutionally prohibited, there is no point in raising questions about the mass murder of Hutu. That said, from everything I have heard or read about, the new Rwanda is unlike anything I can remember from its previous First or Second Republic incarnations.

[49] Gettelman, "The Global Elite's Favorite Strongman."
[50] Marc Sommers, *Stuck: Rwandan Youth and the Struggle for Adulthood* (Athensa, 2012).
[51] Sommers, *Stuck*, pp. 197–198.

To return to Barnes's metaphor, what tourists are invited to discover is a 21st-century Lotus-land.

A *New York Times* travel section projects an image of Kigali that beckons with "myriad East African charms," including a booming restaurant scene (you can enjoy pork filet mignon sautéed with tagliatelle and mustard cream), interesting art galleries, bookshops and giftshops where you can buy "batik-printed cotton fabrics and dazzling souvenirs." Rwanda, it seems, has emerged from its somber past as the Shangri La of East Africa.

As I write these lines, I learned that the ballet company Dance Africa is about to celebrate the country's rebirth with a brilliant choreographic performance at the Brooklyn Academy of Music, "Rwanda Reborn: the Remix." This will be the occasion for the *Inganzo Ngari*, a traditional Rwandan company, to make its United States debut. Exactly what mix of fantasy and reality enters in to the Remix remains unclear. I can only applaud such efforts to help the people of Rwanda to reinvent themselves. If the case of post-war Germany is any index, coming to terms with the past is the only viable path to reconciliation – as long as the past is not recast to fit a lopsided political agenda.

This is where questions arise. Is it enough to erase ethnic memories by the stroke of a pen to ensure the primacy of an all-encompassing national consciousness? Can "We Banyarwanda" submerge "We Hutu" or "We Tutsi"?

There are reasons to be optimistic, not the least being the economic miracle brought into existence by massive infusions of financial assistance by the international community. Thanks to this collective act of contrition the country claims a growth rate of some 7 percent, one of the highest in the continent. Even though prosperity is by no means evenly distributed, the vast majority of the population is unquestionably better off today than at any time during the first and second republics. To this must be added an efficient and easily affordable public health system and educational facilities unrestricted by ethnic quotas. Equally worth noticing, about 40 per cent of the population were born after the genocide. This does not mean that they are unaware of the trauma experienced by friends and relatives. Nonetheless, growing up in an environment relatively free of ethnic violence made a very significant difference.

The negative side of the ledger is not to be dismissed. No matter how impressive Kagame's performance in creating new sources of wealth – and bringing an end to corruption – one wonders how long the existing rate of demographic growth can be sustained without causing serious ethnic tensions. Compared to the 2.5 million population registered in 1960, when I first came to Rwanda, the present figure of 13 million raises obvious questions about the sustainability of population pressure on the land: the prospect of a country the size of Rwanda – the size of Maryland – inhabited by, say, 26 million in another half a century is difficult to imagine. Again, the influx of refugees from neighboring states, notably from Burundi, most of them Tutsi, is another complicating factor. That refugee flows can indeed upend a state and create chaos is not news to Kagame; that it could happen again is not beyond the realm of the possible. With tensions rising along the Rwanda–Uganda border, anti-Rwandan distrust still present in the Congolese DNA, and the false twins exchanging mutual accusations of meddling in each other's internal affairs, the picture that emerges is not one of enduring stability.

The paradox is that the false twins have never been more deserving of the usual metaphor. Both are ethnically dominated dictatorships; both are under the unfettered control of a dominant ruling party; in each case, army men hold key positions in the state hierarchies and operate in close cooperation with intelligence nets. To carry the paradox to its ultimate conclusion: if Rwanda claims a flourishing economy while its neighbor to the south wallows in extreme poverty, this is no small part due to the enormous economic subsidies it continues to enjoy from the West. Distasteful as it may sound to many, here is a sense in which genocide yields exceptionally handsome dividends.

Despite, or because of, such convergence the possibility of a resurgence of ethnic conflict cannot be ruled out, whether by design or by accident. Perhaps the only thing that seems reasonably clear is that ethnic memories will not disappear into thin air. Efforts to legislate them out of existence are bound to fail. Just as illusory is the pretense of power-sharing where everything points to a growing concentration of power in the rulers' hands. Only by admitting that both communities have suffered horrific genocides at each other's hands, and in roughly equal numbers, can one hope to bridge the gap of unstated crimes; only then will it be possible in each state to commune in an effort to forgive. Only then will the wounds begin to heal. The false twins still have a long way to go to erase the falsity of their claimed identities.

6 Concluding thoughts
Lessons learned (and unlearned)

The six years I spent in Africa working for the United States Agency for International Development (USAID) – four in Abidjan (1992–1996) and two in Accra (1997–1998) – were among the most interesting and productive of my professional life. Besides meeting and working with friendly and competent colleagues, I was able to travel in parts of West and Central Africa I knew little about, where I owed it to myself (and to my employer) to reach out to local communities in an effort to look at conflict zones from the ground up. The years I spent working for USAID were a wonderful learning experience.

But one thing I quickly realized after joining the USAID brotherhood is the difficulty of putting into practice the "Logical Framework" gospel, especially when dealing with mass crimes. Officially described as "a methodology mainly used for designing, monitoring and evaluating international development projects," in this one-size-fits-all model the socio-cultural context is largely irrelevant; so are the historical constraints and political crises that stand in the way. All that is required is a firm grasp of the structure and intervention logic inherent in the model, i.e. the project strategy, the intermediate results, the outputs and activities, along with the indicators applying to each box, including the sources of verification, the objectively verifiable indicators, and so forth; assumptions and risks come last, almost as an afterthought.

To learn that it has been "widely used by multilateral organizations, such as AECID, GIZ, SIDA, NORAD, DFID, SDC, UNDP, EC" (the alphabet soup acronyms extend even further) is anything but reassuring. The track record of some of these organizations is not exactly unblemished. I have yet to be convinced that the model has significantly helped the implementation of any of the USAID projects. Part of the problem, aside from paying too little attention to contextual specificities, is that the model is surrounded by a halo of optimism which denies the possibility of failure. The goals are "doable" as long as we get our logic right, the boxes correctly filled out, and the variables properly lined up.

Just as problematic is the appropriateness of the logical framework for capturing the fluidity of conflict across boundaries. This dimension, though by no means unique to the Great Lakes region, has been the overarching theme of this book: how bloodshed spills across borders, propelled by refugee flows, intensified by tit-for-tat retribution, encouraged by ethnic entrepreneurs, with outside interveners, however well-meaning, at a loss to figure out how to stop the hemorrhage.

The porousness of the Congo's boundaries invites contagion in both senses. It manifests itself most recently and dramatically in the rapid spread of the Ebola virus from North Kivu to Ituri, from Ituri to Uganda and Tanzania. The struggle to stop the Ebola epidemic underscores some familiar traits of the Congo situation: the weakness of the state, and the inaccessibility of conflict zones, the high levels of corruption, the absence of medical outreach capacities, all of which have accelerated the spread of ethno-regional tension. If we add to the list the distrust inspired by Western "experts," often aggravated by their internal discords, not to mention the anxieties fed by imaginary threats among displaced populations, tinged with paranoia and recourse to traditional remedies and fetishes, we can better appreciate the limitations of the logical framework.

Difficult as it is to calibrate the types of intervention most likely to yield the expected results, the challenge is even more daunting when policy recommendations are either ignored or run foul of choices and preferences framed at higher levels, Embassy or State Department; disagreements between them – as happened in Burundi in 1996, when a bitter wrangle erupted between Ambassador Krueger and Special Envoy Howard Wolpe – can make the implementation of the logical framework even more complicated. Unsurprisingly, of the 15 country reports I wrote at the request of US embassies on issues of governance and democracy, few generated anything approaching a constructive response.

Just as problematic are situations where State Department reports pay little or no attention to facts, more concerned as they are with how they fit into a pre-existing policy framework, or indeed the absence of a policy. Rwanda is, of course, the example par excellence. Under Habyarimana, the US government decided not to act, thus giving the green light to the Hutu *génocidaires*, and when Kagame came to power his halo of near sanctity gave him a free hand to engage in mass crimes. To say that the US government never had a coherent policy towards Rwanda – and likewise towards Burundi – is tragically clear, as are the consequences, the perpetuation of ethnic violence and the practice of systematic political exclusion.

This said, the question remains as to whether other methodologies could have succeeded where the Logical Framework has failed. Rather than venturing any further into this slippery terrain, let me turn to some of the lessons I learned while making every effort to skirt around the trap of the one-size-fits-all model.

- One is the importance of language as a point of entry into the realm of politics: just as the language of politics helps us understand the texture of political life, including its volatility and complexity, the politics of language illuminates the part played by political discourse to mitigate the clangor of disharmonies or, on the other hand, to taunt, demean or debase the Other.

- There is indeed an important connection between the use (or misuse) of language and the salience of ethnicity, and both are in turn critical elements in the analysis of inequality. This is where another lesson comes into focus: to try to institutionalize multiparty democracy without taking into account the hurdles raised by inequality, both as a fact of political life and a cultural given, is a nonstarter.

- A third lesson refers to the enduring impact of seismic events on the political trajectory of entire communities. Such traumatic ruptures, all too often ignored for what they really are, sow the seeds of unsolvable conflicts; they tear apart the fabric of society; they generate immense sufferings and lasting resentments. This is most cruelly evident where refugee populations become widely politicized, as has been the case throughout the region.

- A closer look at the plight of refugee populations suggests one final lesson: while posing serious challenges to humanitarian interventions, threatening to engulf huge areas with the germs of further conflicts, the ever-shifting loyalties of refugee communities confront humanitarian initiatives with intractable issues, most of them defying immediate solutions.

- We conclude with a few random thoughts on the politics of ethnic memories, followed by an attempt to sketch out some historic legacies and how they are likely to impinge on the region's future convulsions.

The language of politics

Of all the limitations I have faced in the course of my field work the most serious has been my lack of aptitude – as well as lack of opportunities – for learning Kinyarwanda and Kirundi. Language, said Ernest Renan, is the only way to really understand a people's culture. The truth of this axiom I learned at my expense.

No one has explored the singular significance of the language of politics more convincingly than Aidan Russell: "The language of politics is as changeable as notions of ethnicity or concepts of nationhood, and terms of reference, fashions of expression and tone are no more insulated from history than the things that are done with them. But the language of politics represents the stuff that politics are made of. It helps see why ethnic identity, ideas of nationhood, concepts of authority and citizenship or claims of grievance can gain relevance or lose it, how people come to unite around them or ignore them even when some are shouting about their deadly urgency... The language of politics in action lets us see how politics works and what makes it matter."[1]

Semantic fields are never static, any more than the meanings attached to words. "*Ukuri ni kumwe*" ("there is only one truth"), says the Kirundi

[1] Aidan Russell, *Politics and Violence in Burundi*, p. 11.

proverb, but, as Russell convincingly shows, political discourse in Burundi is anything but univocal. The multiplicity of takes on events is matched by a variety of interpretations and ultimately of intended truths. Contributing to this linguistic peculiarity is a curious quirk: the positive connotation attached to one's talent for concealing the truth (as long as one can get away with it). The term *ubwenge* in Kinyarwanda (or *ubgenge* in Kirundi) captures this trait common to both cultures: a sort of street-smart knack to tell lies and get away with it.[2]

The language of politics is a language of ambiguity. A specific example comes to mind: in pre-colonial Burundi the term Hutu had a social connotation quite different from its present usage. It meant "social son" or "*fils social*," to use Father F. Rodegem's phrasing,[3] Which meant that a Tutsi client of someone higher up, Hutu or Tutsi, could qualify as Hutu, while a Hutu who earned the favors of his wealthy Tutsi patron could – through a process known as *Kwihutura* – become a Tutsi. Such nuances and neither here-nor-there distinctions are virtually unknown in contemporary Burundi, and if today the term Hutu and Tutsi bear the stigma of the racial construction imposed by the colonial state, it is significant that there is no word for ethnicity in either language. While in time the word "*ubwoko*" became largely synonymous with ethnic divisions, its original meaning refers to any kind of division, ranging from family, clan, race, locality, regions, and so forth. Only when ethnic oppositions became the most obvious and violent source of division did *ubwoko* become clearly associated with Hutu and Tutsi.

What few phrases I was able to manage reveal only a glimpse of the immense richness of Kinyarwanda and Kirundi on subjects central to their culture – such as the countless ways of describing the famous lyre-horned cattle, the traditional symbol and source of prestige and power, and therefore closely associated with Tutsi identities. Just as surprising is absence of terms which, in Western cultures, are inseparable from democratic norms. It is worth noting that in neither language is there a word to translate "equality" and "liberty." Which is not to deny the capacity of individuals to grasp the meaning of such concepts, yet it does suggest ways in which language can shape behavior.

---

[2] Writing in 1958, in a Belgian review, Stanislas Bushayija, a member of the Catholic clergy of Tutsi origins, distinguishes between the European form of intelligence (*ubwenge bwo mu gitabo*) and Tutsi intelligence:

> Si le Mututsi reconnait à l'Européen ses compétences dans le domaine technique – electricité, physique, mathématique, etc. – s'il lui reconnait l'intelligence du livre, il déplore son absence de finesse d'esprit. Savoir travestir la verité, donner le change sans éveiller le moindre soupcon est une science qui fait défaut à l'Europeen et que le Mututsi est fier de posséder: le génie de l'intrigue, l'art du mensonge sont à ses yeux des arts dans lesquels il s'enorgueillit d'etre fort habile: c'est là le propre du Mututsi, et par contagion et par réflexe de défense, de tout Munyarwanda.

> Stanislas Bushayija, "Aux origines du problème Bahutu au Rwanda," *Revue Nouvelle*, no. 12 (December 1958), pp. 594–597

[3] In a letter to the author.

The politics of language

That language can be instrumentalized to serve a political agenda is clear from the contrasting examples of Rwanda and Burundi.

Kagame's decision to eliminate the terms Hutu and Tutsi from the lexicon of modern politics stems from a calculated move to eradicate what he claims was the root cause of genocide: the perversely twisted ethnic categories inherited from the colonial state (never mind that the terms were in usage, albeit with a very different connotation, long before the advent of colonial rule). Language manipulation is not risk-free. Quite aside from the sanctions incurred by those brave enough to ignore legal and constitutional provisions,[4] one wonders whether ethnic identities, inseparable from the traumas experienced by each community, can be wiped off the memorial slate. There is no simple way out of what might be called an enforced amnesia, *une amnésie commandée*, to borrow Paul Ricoeur's phrase. Some might argue in support of ethnic amnesia on pragmatic grounds. But the dangers arising from the suppression of ethnic identities cannot be dismissed out of hand. To forgive and forget is more easily said than done when dealing with the massive human rights violations inflicted on an entire ethnic community.

If Rwanda is an extreme case, Burundi shows another example of linguistic manipulation, not by imposed amnesia but through expressions designed to discredit and divide opponents. The aim is to inspire moral contempt. Consider how Anne-Claire Courtois describes "the particular discourse" associated with President Nkurunziza's dictatorial rule: "Any kind of opposition is considered as a betrayal and the opponents are even called *bajeri* (wild dogs), to be eliminated. To establish a political dialogue in these conditions seems impossible. The ruling party confines itself in a rhetoric of truth which justifies repression and violence against any one seen as an opponent."[5] The rhetoric of truth is indeed central to an understanding of Nkurunziza's strategy: *nyakurisation* (from *nyakuri*, truth) is the process by which opposition parties are split into allies and enemies. Only the former qualifies as trustworthy, that is as *abagumyabanga* ("those who heed the leader's line unswervingly"), in contrast with the *ahamenabanga* ("those who cannot follow a straight line"). Truths and untruths come through in various ways and nuances, but official verities are the sole guide to salvation.

Once the chips are down, and for all their particularities, Rwanda and Burundi are both dictatorships. Both are dominated by specific ethnic communities, and both have made a mockery of electoral processes. And while

---

[4] Article 13 of the constitution enshrines the penalties arising from "revisionism, denial and trivialization" of the genocide, and Article 33 is aimed at sanctioning "the propagation of ethnic, regional, racial discrimination or any other form of division." The language of the law does not specifically penalize mention of ethnicity, but most would agree that ethnic references are made at one's own risk.

[5] Anne-Claire Courtois, "Le Burundi en crise: pirates contre vrais combatants," *Fondation sur la Recherche Stratégique*, Note no. 11/17.

carefully selected opponents are allowed to contest elections for propaganda purposes, Burundi is reluctantly the more tolerant of oppositional voices. There is no denying their shared aversion for free and fair elections, yet one is under the sway of a Tutsi dictator, the other under the rule of a tiny group of power-holders claiming to represent the Hutu majority. Inequality is the hallmark of both states, but only in Rwanda, arguably, are some more conspicuously equal than others.

Inequality and democracy

While serving as a regional consultant on governance and democracy with USAID I often came close to talking myself out of my job. Breaking a lance in support of electoral democracy while being reminded almost day after day of the pitfalls of majority rule, and the precariousness of minority rights, is not an easy task to handle. To expect pluralist democracy to flourish in environments so conspicuously inhospitable to anything remotely approaching our conception of participatory democracy boggles the mind.

That some societies may internalize the concept of inequality in ways that make them culturally and normatively incompatible to the values of democracy – a fact patently clear in both pre-colonial and post-genocide Rwanda,[6] though substantially less so in Burundi – is one of the important lessons I have learned.[7] Aside from the intractable issues raised by the numerical discrepancies between Hutu and Tutsi – bringing into sharp relief the dilemma of the tyranny of the majority vs. the rights of minorities – institutionalizing democracy is a rare achievement where individuals are rank-ordered according to socio-ethnic origins, and where recognition of political equality as a desirable norm is the exception rather than the rule.[8] How can one convey the merits of electoral democracy in a setting where Hutu and Tutsi account respectively for about 85 and 15 per cent of the electorate, and where electoral contests are more often than not synonymous with ethnic referenda? The argument often heard among Tutsi observers that they are condemned to remain a minority cannot be dismissed, any more than the claims of the Hutu that their electoral gains have been consistently stymied by the Tutsi-led military.

[6] And nicely captured in the title of Jaques J. Maquet's work, *The Premise of Inequality in Rwanda: A Study of Political Relations in a Central African Kingdom* (Oxford, 1961).
[7] I scarcely need to add that even in the absence of a culturally rooted "premise of inequality" vast discrepancies of wealth are no less of a hurdle to electoral democracy, as shown by the Case of the DRC, where the gap between the super-rich and the rural poor has been cited time and again as proof of the staggering levels of corruption among the ruling elites and the main obstacle in the way of minimally free and fair elections. See, for example, the wealth of examples cited by Theodore Trefon in *Congo Masquerade: The Political Culture of Aid Inefficiency and Reform Failure* (New York, 2011).
[8] The most notable exception occurred in Burundi during 1993 multi-party elections: before the results were vetoed by the army coup that led to Ndadaye's assassination, the 1993 elections were widely applauded by the international community as remarkably free and fair.

The first multi-party elections held in Burundi in May 1965 saw the Hutu winners robbed of their victory when King Mwambutsa turned to one of his courtiers to serve a prime minister, and in so doing set an unfortunate precedent. Coup-making and ethnic violence are the twin motifs that have accompanied the country's experiments in multi-party democracy. As will be recalled, the most disastrous example of the military's veto of an electoral verdict occurred in 1993 after the election of Melchior Ndadaye to the presidency and the control of parliament by the Hutu-dominated Frodebu. The assassination of the president elects by the Tutsi-dominated army and the ensuing civil war left a permanent mark on Burundi society.

The history of Rwanda tells much the same tale of woe, but with notable variations. The communal elections of 1961, followed by the 1963 legislative elections, confirmed the dominance of the Hutu – and their inability to bridge the gap between north and south – but did little to effectively bring Tutsi elements into the government much less to negotiate a solution to the civil war triggered by the RPF. invasion.

The next phase in the country's experience in electoral democracy focuses attention on Kagame's predictable landslide victories in 2003, 2010 and 2017 with scores that would have made Stalin envious. The fate met by Victoire Ingabire, head of the predominantly Hutu *Forces Démocratiques*-igikingi (FDU-igikingi), for challenging Kagame's one-party rule speaks volumes for the limits set on free speech. In a public statement at a genocide memorial site, she underscored the shared sufferings endured by Tutsi and Hutu, but the reference to the latter was seen as a provocation.[9] Accused of spreading "genocide ideology" she was promptly arrested and later subjected to a trial that turned out to be a parody of justice.

Unlike Burundi, where pro-forma opposition parties are the tribute paid by corrupt politicians to electoral virtue, Kagame does not even try to conceal the arbitrariness of his rule.

The mantra one often hears among democracy activists is that democracy doesn't happen overnight; it needs to be encouraged, nurtured, tested, irrespective of the many false starts and impasses. The argument makes sense, except that the false starts often result in real bloodbaths. In societies where ethnic asymmetries are so painfully evident, and the premise of inequality all-pervasive, one wonders whether the "one man one vote" formula is a viable route to democracy. A more useful path would focus on the rights of minorities, and the power-sharing arrangements most likely to protect such rights. Although the experience of Burundi on that score is far from conclusive,[10] it has spared the country the worst excesses of its neighbor to the north, and this at a time when it could easily have followed suit.

---

[9] For excerpts from Ingabire's statement, see Reyntjens, *Political Governance*, p. 48.

[10] See Stef Vandeginste, "Briefing: Burundi's Electoral Crisis – Back to Power-Sharing Politics as Usual?," *African Affairs*, August 2015, pp. 1–13.

Seismic events and why they matter

One such event was the shooting down of President Habyarimana's plane; another was the murder of President Melchior Ndadaye. The first I described as the crash that lit the tinder; the second was the murder that re-ignited the Hutu–Tutsi conflict in Burundi (strikingly similar, in its tectonic after-effects, to George Floyd's martyrdom in Minneapolis). Neither received the sustained attention they deserved in explaining the consequences. Nor are they the only ones that come to mind.

The dates are like so many reminders of human tragedies of a magnitude that numbs the mind: 1959, 1994 in Rwanda, 1972, 1993, 1996 in Burundi, 1996, 1997, 1998 in the Congo. Each stand as turning points in their tormented trajectories. We are talking about millions of human lives lost, tens of thousands pushed out of their homelands, homeless, not knowing where their next meal is coming from. How many died of hunger, disease and exhaustion is impossible to tell. What is undeniable is the devastating and enduring impact of such catastrophes on millions of human lives.

Assessing the political effects of such tragedies is not easy. In part, because they were not always perceived as major calamities, and even if they were, their critical role as precipitants of violence was not always grasped.

How many, at the time if the 1972 killings of Hutu in Burundi, were able to see in these events the vengeful retribution of 1959 in Rwanda? How many, at the time of the 1994–1998 civil war in Burundi understood the tragic side-effects of Ndadaye's assassination?

Adding to this difficulty are the sharp disagreements among donors, scholars, and human rights activists about who should be held responsible and why, a debate that tends to obscure the magnitude of the ensuing human tragedy. A textbook example is, of course, the continuing controversy over the crash of Habyarimana's plane on April 6, 1994, the triggering factor that precipitated the Rwanda bloodbath. There is the "Hutu did it" argument, which underscores the responsibility of radical Hutu elements turning against their all-too-moderate president, the better to engage in their dastardly plot to exterminate all Tutsi in sight; and there is the "Kagame did it" narrative, which lays the onus of guilt squarely on the shoulders of the Rwandan rebel leader. This is not the place to review the pros and cons, except to reiterate my own position that here is a crushing body of circumstantial evidence to demonstrate the direct personal involvement of Kagame. Very different consequences follow from such diametrically opposed interpretations: besides revealing the chasm between pro- and anti-Kagame supporters, the result has been to convey a one-sided picture of a very complicated turn of events, to shift the weight of public opinion in the UK and the US in support of the so-called Washington Consensus, to encourage the International Criminal Tribunal to seriously shirk its responsibilities, and to lessen the chances of a major recasting of the narrative about the roots of the genocide. All of which is unlikely to promote ethnic reconciliation. A seismic event has been reduced to an almost banal divergence of opinion about who was responsible for bringing down Habyarimana's plane. The significance of the crash as a trigger, the credibility of the evidence surrounding the event, and its impact on the genocide narrative, are likely to remain on the back burner for some time.

Attempts to find solutions are not made any easier by the preconceptions and prejudices of Western policymakers and international civil servants as they try to grapple with the subtleties of crisis management. Indifference, inertia or buck-passing at a time when resolute action was most urgently needed offers a clue to their inability to engage constructively with such crises. Naming names is, of course, too facile, possibly unfair. Nonetheless, among the top bureaucrats in charge of shaping US policies in Central Africa, some rank unusually high on a roster of incompetence. Herman Cohen – who served as director of the Central African Affairs desk in the Africa Bureau of the State Department in 1972 and later assistant secretary for African Affairs under President Bush (1989–1992) – is one example among others. One would have expected him to know at least the date of independence of Rwanda and Burundi (1962, not 1960), and to come up with a more credible assessment of the number of Hutu victims in Burundi in1972 (75,000 vastly underestimates the scale of the bloodshed). Michael Hoyt, the DCM in Bujumbura in 1972, known for his honest reporting of the killings, was told by Cohen to make his cables to the State Department "less colorful," which later prompted Hoyt to wonder, "I might well have asked him 'what is the color of blood?'"[11] As for the momentous events of 1959 in Rwanda, one would have hoped for a somewhat more elaborate explanation: "In Rwanda, with the help of certain Belgian political parties, the Hutu staged a revolution and grabbed power."[12] Yes, just like that! It comes as no surprise that what little he has to say about the circumstances of the shooting down of Habyarimana's plane should dutifully reflect the official Washington Consensus line: "A small group of politicians, military officers and Hutu racists formulated and implemented the genocide. They decided to play the extreme version of the ethnic card to retain their power and wealth."[13] In short, what triggered the bloodbath was a move by Hutu racists to retain their power and wealth. However incongruous, echoes of Alice in Wonderland resonate through much of Cohen's *apologia pro vita sua*.

Refugees: the plight of the unwanted

Of an estimated 65 million refugees world-wide, hundreds of thousands are victims of conflicts raging in the Great Lakes region. In his previous

[11] Michael Hoyt, *The Burundi Cables: The American Embassy and the 1972 Genocide* (Unpublished manuscript, 2002).
[12] Herman Cohen, *Intervening in Africa: Superpower Peacemaking in a Troubled Continent* (New York, 2000), p. 166.
[13] Cohen, *Intervening in Africa*, p. 177.

incarnation as UN High Commissioner for Refugees, UN Secretary General Antonio Guterres recounts how, in December 2007, while visiting IDP camps in the North Kivu province, he listened to account after account of people who had "lost control of their lives (and) talked about their suffering at the hands of armed men who roam the countryside murdering, maiming, raping and robbing with impunity." At the time a total of 800,000 displaced people lived in what he described as "squalid camps."[14]

A one-time Vietnamese refugee and Pulitzer Prize-winning author, Viet Thanh Nguyen, elaborates on the true nature of refugee camps: he depicts them as "belonging to the same inhuman family as the internment camp, the concentration camp, the death camp." The camp, he adds, "is the place where we keep those who we do not want to see as fully being human."[15] As such, he explains, many are unwanted: "These displaced persons are mostly unwanted where they fled from; unwanted where they are, in refugee camps; and unwanted where they want to go."[16]

Such indeed is the fate of refugees everywhere. But what makes the refugees from the Great Lakes special case is the depth of hostility most of them face. Unwantedness translates into unalloyed enmity in the places they fled from and those they fled to. Examples are found among Hutu and Tutsi. The story they tell is of refugees turning into insurgents, insurgents into incumbents, and incumbents into avengers.

The zigzagging trajectory of the Tutsi who joined the RPF is instructive in this regard. As refugees from the 1959 Hutu revolution, those who sought asylum in Uganda founded the Rwanda Refugee Welfare Foundation (RRWA), later to become the Rwandan Alliance for National Unity (RANU), ultimately to be known as the Rwanda Patriotic Front (RPF); in their transition from refugees to insurgents, they attracted to themselves the widely shared anti-Tutsi hatred that led to the 1994 carnage; and as triumphant conquerors they evolved into avengers, soon to mutate into *génocidaires*, causing over a million Hutu refugees to move to the Congo, where untold numbers were massacred.

The route trodden by Hutu refugees is no less tortuous. Their Burundi odyssey begins in 1972, when, after the genocidal killing of over 200,000, hundreds of thousands found asylum in Rwanda and the Congo. Many of the most enthusiastic participants in the 1994 extermination of Tutsi were Hutu refugees from Burundi living in Rwanda, more often than not in inhumane conditions. But with the turning of the tide in July 1994, in the wake of the FPR seizure of power, more than a million Hutu, mostly civilians, accompanied by a toxic mix of ex-FAR, *interahamwe* and MRND militants, found asylum in eastern Congo, which would soon turn into a

[14] Antonio Gutteres, "Millions Uprooted: Saving Refugees and the Displaced," *Foreign Affairs*, vol. 87, no. 5 (September–October 2008), p. 94.
[15] Viet Thanh Nguyen ed., *The Displaced: Refugee Writers on Refugee Lives* (New York, 2018), p. 18.
[16] Nguyen ed., *The Displaced*, p. 17.

mass grave. The slaughter of Hutu refugees in the Congo, remains to this day one of the biggest stains on the conscience of the RPF.

Where is the moral touchstone when both sides share the responsibility for countless atrocities?

Merely to raise this question gives us a clue as to why humanitarian activists are sometimes headed into an impasse. Where purveyors of charity are liable to be seen as supporters of genocide – even though their intentions are evidently otherwise – many will be tempted to call into question the motives of humanitarian intervention. In situations where the recipients of humanitarian aid are generally associated with human rights violations – as was clearly the case when a large number of hard-core Hutu *génocidaires* joined the outflow of civilian refugees to North Kivu in 1994 – the case for humanitarianism is hard to sustain. In such circumstances the unintended consequence is to prolong conflict, complicate the quest for solutions, and invite criticism.

In Goma (North Kivu) at the height of the refugee crisis as many as 120 French and international humanitarian organizations were involved in aiding.[17] There is no question about the life-saving impact some of them have had; nor in there any doubt that their mixed record has generated a vigorous debate about their capacity to remain neutral. However noble their code of behavior – "aid is given regardless of race, creed or nationality on the basis of need alone," "aid will not be used to further a particular political or religious standpoint" – their performance turned out to be so patently at variance with these principles that many of them, including *Médecins sans Frontières* (MSF), withdrew their assistance from the camps. The executive director of MSF Joelle Tanguy, did not mince her words: "In Bukavu the situation has deteriorated to such an extent that it is now ethically impossible for us to continue abetting the perpetrators of the Rwanda genocide... The members of the former Rwandan authorities, military and militia exert total control over the civilians in the camps in Bukavu, keep them hostages and manipulate humanitarian aid."[18] Failure to distinguish between perpetrators and victims, oppressors and oppressed, hostages and hostage-takers, makes them complicit in in the human sufferings they ostensibly claimed to assuage.

The claims of ethnic memories

On the strength of the evidence reviewed here, there are few grounds for optimism. Multiple and contestable truths, manipulated polls, persisting inequalities, unrecognized collective traumas, unwanted refugees doubling as *génocidaires*, all of the above are among the hurdles that stand in the way of a sustainable regional stability. But there is another face to the coin,

---

[17] For a discussion of their positive impact, see Roland Noel's moving account, *Les blessures incurables du Rwanda*, Preface by Jean-Christophe Rufin (Paris, 2015), p. 50.
[18] Cited in Waugh, *Paul Kagame and Rwanda*, p. 105.

provocatively brought to light by David Rieff in his compelling essay on the politics of memory, *Against Remembrance* (Melbourne, 2011).

Rather than mindlessly heeding the *devoir de mémoire* mantra, why not forget about the past once and for all, forget the horrors committed by one group or another, and simply move on? Why insist for the sake of a never-never land of reconciliation that justice be done, when all the evidence shows that the dice are loaded in support of impunity? What are the grounds for defending the cause of justice when peace is better served by accepting injustice? "Peace is always urgent" argues Rieff; "without peace the killing goes on and on. Those who say that there can be no peace without justice are simply deluding themselves."[19]

In other words, on closer inspection Kagame's agenda is not nearly as objectionable as one may think. By penalizing semantic references to genocide ideology, and by implication condemning the duty to remember, Kagame is taking a leaf from Rieff's questioning of historical memory as a practical path to peace. "Historical memory is rarely as hospitable to peace and reconciliation as it is to grudge-keeping, dueling martyrologies, and enduring enmity. This is why a strong case can be made that what ensures the health of societies and individuals alike is not their capacity for remembering but their capacity for *eventually* forgetting."[20] If so, the measures taken to rule out references to ethnicity are a step toward peace, just as in Burundi the reigning code of impunity is a guarantee of social stability. The key is not the duty to remember but the obligation to forget.

Although I have serious reservations about his argument, Rieff's plea needs to be taken seriously. Some of the examples he cites in support of his thesis are persuasive. Revealingly, however, none are taken from Rwanda's history. The reason, I suspect, has to do with the singularity of the Rwanda atrocities. In at least one respect they stand as an exception in the roster of mass murders punctuating the last century: From the Armenian bloodbath to the Shoah, from the Cambodian carnage to the killings in Bosnia, perpetrators met with little or no resistance from the victimized community or bystanders; no retaliation ensued. Only in Rwanda was the initially one-sided extermination of Tutsi civilians immediately followed by anti-Hutu genocidal vengeance.[21] The two-sidedness of the bloodshed is seldom admitted. Rather than the sheer scale of violence, horrific as it is, the more important point to bear in mind is the lopsidedness of post-genocide accusations; although there is irrefutable evidence that violence has been

[19] David Rieff, *Against Remembrance* (Melbourne, 2011), p. 72.
[20] Rieff, *Against Remembrance*, pp. 68–69. The author takes pains to underscore that he is not arguing that "this forgetting should take place in the immediate aftermath of a great crime or when its perpetrators are still at large" (p. 69) but doesn't say how much of an interval makes forgetting appropriate.
[21] The closest parallel is that of Czechoslovakia in 1945, when a Czech-sponsored anti-German backlash against the German-speaking communities of Bohemia and Moravia (the so-called Sudeten Germans) resulted in countless victims and the forceful expulsion of some 4 million Sudeten Germans from their homeland.

committed by representatives of the two communities, it is attributed in the media, and not just in Rwanda, overwhelmingly to Hutu perpetrators.

Asymmetry in the apportionment of guilt is at the heart of the issue over which Kagame and I crossed paths (before crossing swords).

Our differences were brought to my attention by Kagame himself when, against all odds, he proceeded to take me to task for misrepresenting the impact of the genocide on collective memories. The occasion for this unexpected backlash was a chapter I had contributed to an edited volume on the theme of post-conflict reconstruction in Rwanda.[22] In it I expressed considerable misgivings about the wisdom of eradicating ethnic labels as a formula for preventing future conflict. To the question of whether the exclusion of ethnic memory can bring the people of Rwanda closer to building the mutual trust necessary for a peaceful co-existence, I argued that "reconciliation, assuming it can ever be achieved, requires the past to be confronted, not obliterated." Poaching on the insights of Stanley Cohen and Paul Ricoeur I went on to show how collective memories can be pressed into shape by being repressed, as when memory is thwarted, manipulated or abusively enforced (*la mémoire empêchée, la mémoire manipulée, la mémoire abusivement commandée*)."[23] A more sensible way of promoting peaceful co-existence, I concluded, would be to have recourse to what Ricoeur calls "le *travail de mémoire*," a concept that invites us to search for radically different narratives for re-interpreting the past. It suggests a sharing of traumatic experiences inscribed in the past, and this in the interest of moving beyond the repetitive, formulaic, and ultimately sterile rehashing of the horrors e ach group inflicted on the other.

Instead of coming to grips with the argument Kagame dismisses as unacceptable this type of "emerging revisionism": "Objective history," he writes, "illustrates the degeneracy of this emerging revisionism." Especially objectionable, I was told, is the allegation that "there is an equivalence between the genocide crimes and the isolated crimes committed by rogue FPR members."[24] The gospel according to Kagame is straightforward: only the Hutu have committed a genocide, to argue otherwise is tantamount to heresy.

A more sustained exploration of this theme would take us too far afield. Let us instead return to David Rieff's argument as it applies to Burundi. Given that impunity is most often cited as a major impediment to the country's quest for reconciliation, what is one to make of the statement that "those who say that there can be no peace without justice are simply deluding themselves"? Are we to remain silent in the face of countless extensively documented human rights violations for the sake of peace, or because of

[22] "The Politics of Memory in Post-Genocide Rwanda," in Phil Clark and Zachary D. Kaufman eds., *After Genocide: Transitional Justice, Post-Conflict Reconstruction and reconciliation in Rwanda and Beyond* (London, 1988), pp. 65–77; for Kagame's Preface, see pp. xiv–xxvi. Though written in his name I have reason to suspect that the author is Louise Mushikawabo, then serving as his minister of foreign affairs.
[23] "The Politics of Memory in Post-Genocide Rwanda," p. 69.
[24] "The Politics of Memory in Post-Genocide Rwanda," p. xxiii.

"the moral defensibility of an ethic of forgetting"? Are we, then, in effect reaching for the moral high ground by forgetting the crimes committed against Ndadaye and his supporters, by forgetting the atrocities committed by Hutu and Tutsi in 1993, and on and on from one horrific episode to another?

There are reasons to be doubtful. For one thing, impunity is by no means a guarantee of peace any more than forgiveness is rewarded by kindly oblivion. The stains on Nkurunziza's human rights record are enough to prompt the strongest reservations about the virtues of "forgive and forget" as a path to social harmony. If anything, recourse to an even-handed retributive justice would better serve the cause of peace between Hutu and Tutsi than refusal to mete out a just punishment. The problem lies elsewhere. Since horrific crimes have been committed by extremists on both sides of the ethnic fault line, and sanctions would apply to those proven guilty irrespective of ethnic identity, the result has been something resembling a conspiracy of silence based on a tacit understanding that no one will be punished, at least not through judicial processes, no matter how serious the offense. While this may seem like a vindication of Rieff's thesis, impunity in these circumstances is less a guarantee of peace than a deferred settling of accounts. For if the power-sharing arrangement worked out at Arusha did spare the country another bloodbath in the years following Nkurunziza's election to the presidency, since then the trend has been toward an increasingly repressive, dangerously militarized regime, where the instruments of control are firmly in the hands of high-ranking army men. Whether continued injustice, enforced by bayonets, can ensure peace is doubtful.

A tangle of conflicted legacies

"History has no libretto," Isaiah Berlin used to say. Nor is there a road map to help us chart the future of the Great Lakes. All we can do is sketch out some of the ways in which history, past and present, has mortgaged the region's unending quest for peace.

It takes a strong-willed leader and no small amount of political and military skills to stop a genocide, emerge triumphant from a civil war, stitch together a new government coalition, bring to justice wrongdoers, redefine the country's ethnic map, organize country-wide elections, restore economic output to exceptionally high levels, and re-establish the international legitimacy of a post-genocide regime.

But if we look at Kagame's legacy through the wider lens of the regional context what comes into focus is not so much a Nietszchean superman as a deeply polarizing figure.

The ravages that have swept across huge swathes of eastern Congo will not be soon forgotten. The picture drawn by Dr. Denis Mukwege, a Congolese gynecologist who shared the 2018 Nobel Peace prize with Nadia Murad, gives us pause: "hundreds of thousands of women have been raped, more than four million people have been displaced and six million people have been killed[25] at the hands of militias, bandits, government soldiers and foreign armies." Even though a relatively small fraction of lives lost are battlefield casualties, the collateral damage – crops, homes, property and infrastructures destroyed, families torn asunder, economic resources and mineral wealth plundered – is still widely felt. Further contributing to social and economic disarray are the lethal fantasies born out of despair as much as from mythologies about race and ethnicity.

That some of the worst depredations suffered by the Congo happened to be the work of Rwandan proxies did little to lessen popular resentment of Kagame. Uganda also attracted its share of enmity, and for the same reasons. Between 1999 and 2003, writes Helen Epstein, "Museveni's military stoked ethnic conflict deliberately by supporting at one time or another 10 different militant groups in Ituri, and then standing by as they massacred each other along with civilians they suspected of collaborating with their opponents."[26] Much the same horrific scenario might well apply to the military prowess attributed to a Nkunda or a Ntaganda.

By 1999 Museveni and Kagame were at each other's throats, and again in 2000 and 2001, as they fought tooth and nail over the gold and diamond deposits of the Kisangani area. Here also, the collateral damage, did not go unnoticed: over a thousand civilians died in the crossfire. Only by a miracle of British diplomacy was a full-fledged war avoided between the former co-conspirators.

Burundi, as always, is a special case in this polarized landscape. Since President Nkurunziza's decision to run for a third term in 2015, in violation of the constitution, the country has been tottering on the edge: first an abortive coup (instigated by Godefroid Niyombare, a Hutu in charge of the intelligence apparatus) followed by a brutal repression causing the flight of hundreds of thousands of refugees to neighboring states. Of these some 40,000 were of Tutsi origins who sought protection in Rwanda. The stage was set for a flurry of mutual accusations, Bujumbura blaming Kigali for giving political and military assistance to Tutsi refugees, and Kigali denying any such move while heaping scorn on its neighbor. This exchange of niceties is nothing new, except that today's context is different. As Burundi sinks ever deeper in a morass of economic penury, social tension and military repression, Rwanda looks increasingly as the more attractive model. It serves a magnet for thousands of Burundians in search of a more promising tomorrow. Both states are aware of the fragility of the status quo, but neither can prevent a signal from being misread. That they happen to stand for distinctive ethnic constituencies, contrasting claims to legitimacy, and different sets of supporters in the international arena only adds to the reigning uncertainty.

[25] See Benjamin Mueller, "Laureates Urge Red Line on Mass Rape," *The New York Times*, December 11, 2018.

[26] Helen C. Epstein, *Another Fine Mess: America, Uganda and the War on Terror* (New York, 2017), p. 128.

As I try to put the last pieces of the puzzle together I must resist the temptation of another leap into the past. Suffice to note that the 1972 mass murder of Hutu in Burundi would not have happened without the mobilizing presence in the country of thousands of Tutsi refugees from the 1959 upheaval in Rwanda; that the long smoldering fuse that sparked the 1990 FPR invasion, and ultimately paved the way to the 1994 genocide, is also found in the regional fallout from the 1959 revolution; that a significant number of perpetrators were none other than Hutu refugees from Burundi who fled to Rwanda after Ndadaye's assassination in 1993. For historians critical of what some might refer to as "presentism" this *tour d'horizon* only offers a partial insight into the underlying forces at work during colonial and pre-colonial times. I shall leave it to more talented minds to delve into the violent confrontations they experienced long before the advent of colonial rule, and persisted, in one form or another, long thereafter.

Memento Mori

A more appropriate closure to these reflections is to pay a posthumous homage to the many victims of an unprecedented regional scourge – Congolese, Rwandans, Burundians, Hutu Tutsi and Twa – that few will forget even if many are ready to forgive. The hours I spent in their company – hoping to bear witness to their agonies, listening to voices from beyond the grave, trying to separate right from wrong in a maze of intersecting mayhem where the dividing line between them is forever shifting – are part of my *devoir de mémoire*. Their haplessness, their gestures of despair, their anguished voices, these too, are part of the memorial legacy I have inherited from their martyrdom. May this small book be a modest tribute to their memory.

References

Autesserre, Severine. *The Trouble with the Congo: Local Violence and the Failure of International Peacebuilding.* Cambridge: Cambridge University Press, 2010.

Chrétien, Jean-Pierre, and Marcel Kabanda. *Rwanda: Racisme et Génocide: L'Idéologie hamitique.* Paris: Belin, 2016.

Des Forges, Alison. *Leave None to Tell the Story: Genocide in Rwanda.* New York and Paris: Human Rights Watch and Fédération Internationale des Droits de l'Homme, 1999.

Des Forges, Alison. *Defeat is the Only Bad News. Rwanda Under Musinga 1896-1931.*Madison: University of Wisconsin Press, 2011. Edited by David Newbury. Foreword by Roger V. Des Forges.

Destexhe, Alain. *Rwanda: Essai sur le génocide.* Bruxelles: Editions Complexe, 1994.

Devlin, Larry. *Chief of Station, Congo: A Memoir of 1960–67.* New York: Public Affairs, 2007.

Doom, Ruddy, and Jan F. J. Gorus, eds. *Politics of Identity and Economics of Conflict in the Great Lakes Region.* Bruxelles: VUB University Press, 2000.

Epstein, Helen C.. *Another Fine Mess: America, Uganda, and the War on Terror.* New York: Columbia Global Reports, 2017.

Faye, Gael. *Small Country.* London: Hogarth, 2018.

Gleijeses, Piero. *Conflicting Missions: Havana, Washington and Africa, 1959–1976.* Chapel Hill: University of North Carolina Press, 2002.

Guichaoua, André. *From War to Genocide: Criminal Politics in Rwanda 1990–1994.* Madison: University of Wisconsin Press, 2015. Translated by Don E. Webster. Foreword by Scott Straus.

Harroy, Jean-Paul. *Rwanda: De la Féodalité a la Démocratie, 1955–1962.* Bruxelles: Hayez, 1984.

Harroy, Jean-Paul. *Burundi 1955–1962: Souvenirs d'un combattant d'une guerre perdue.* Bruxelles: Hayez, 1987.

Hoare, Mike. *Congo Mercenary.* London: Robert Hale, 1967.

Hochschild, Adam. *King Leopold's Ghost.* New York: Houghton Mifflin Co., 1998.

Kinzer, Stephen. *A Thousand Hills: Rwanda's Rebirth and the Man Who Dreamed It.* New York: Wiley and Sons, 2008.

Kaburahe, Antoine. *Hutsi: In the Name of US All.* Bujumbura: Editions Iwacu, 2019.

Kitchen, Helen, ed. *Footnotes to the Congo Story.* New York: Walker and Co., 1967.

Lanotte, Olivier. *Congo Guerres Sans Frontières: De Joseph-Désiré Mobutu à Joseph Kabila.* Brussels: Editions Complexe, 2003.

Lemarchand, René. *Rwanda and Burundi.* London: Pall Mall Press, 1970.

Lemarchand, René. *Burundi: Ethnic Conflict and Genocide.* New York and Cambridge: Woodrow Wilson Center Press and Cambridge University Press, 1994.

Lemarchand, René. *The Dynamics of Violence in Central Africa.* Philadelphia: The University of Pennsylvania Press, 2009.

Logiest, Guy. *Mission au Rwanda: Un Blanc Dans la Bagarre Tutsi-Hutu.* Bruxelles: Didier Hatier, 1988.

Longman, Timothy. *Memory and Justice in Post-Genocide Rwanda.* Cambridge: Cambridge University Press, 2017.

Mamdani, Mahamood. *When Victims become Killers: Colonialism, Nativism, and the Genocide in Rwanda.* Princeton: Princeton University Press, 2002.

Mbonimpa, Pierre-Claver. *Rester Debout: Entretiens avec Antoine Kaburahe.* Bujumbura: Editions Iwacu, 2017.

Mukasonga, Scholastique. *L'Iguifou: Nouvelles Rwandaises.* Paris: Gallimard, 2010.

Mukasonga, Scholastique. *Cockroaches.* Brooklyn: Archipelago Books, 2016. Translated by Jordan Stump.

Newbury, Catharine. *The Cohesion of Oppression: Clientship and Ethnicity in Rwanda, 1860–1960.* New York: Columbia University Press, 1988.

Newbury, David. *The Land beyond the Mists: Essays on Identity and Authority in Precolonial Congo and Rwanda.* Athens: Ohio University Press, 2009. Preface by Jan Vansina.

Power, Samantha. *A Problem from Hell: America and the Age of Genocide.* New York: Basic Books, 2002.

Prunier, Gérard. *The Rwanda Crisis: History of a Genocide.* New York: Columbia University Press, 1995.

Prunier, Gérard. *Africa's World War: Congo, the Rwandan Genocide and the Making of a Continental Catastrophe.* New York: Oxford University Press, 2009.

Rever, Judi. *In Praise of Blood: The Crimes of the Rwandan Patriotic Front.* New York: Random House, 2011.

Reyntjens, Filip. *Le Génocide des Tutsi au Rwanda.* Paris: Que Sais-Je? 2017.

Reyntjens, Filip. *The Great African War: Congo and Regional Politics, 1996–2006.* Cambridge: Cambridge University Press, 2009.

Reyntjens, Filip. *Political Governance in Post-Genocide Rwanda.* Cambridge: Cambridge University Press, 2013.

Rieff, David. *Against Remembrance.* Melbourne: Melbourne University Press, 2011.

Roessler, Philip, and Harry Verheoven. *Why Comrades Go to War.* New York: Oxford University Press, 2020.

Rudasingwa, Theogene. *Healing a Nation: A Testimony.* North Charleston: Independent Publishing, 2013.

Russell, Aidan. *Politics and Violence in Burundi: The Language of Truth in an Emerging State.* Cambridge: Cambridge University Press, 2019.

Ruzibiza, Abdul Joshua. *Rwanda: L'histoire secrète.* Paris: Editions du Panama, 2005. Preface by Claudine Vidal. Postface by André Guichaoua.

Sebarenzi, Joseph, with Laura Ann Mullane. *A Journey of Transformation: God Sleeps in Rwanda.* New York: Atria Books, 2009.

Sémelin, Jacques, Andrieu Claire, and Gensburger Sarah, eds. *Resisting Genocide: The Multiple Forms of Rescue.* Oxford and New York: Oxford University Press, 2013. Translated by Emma Bentley and Cynthia Schoch.

Sommer, Marc. *Stuck. Rwandan Youth and the Struggle for Adulthood*. Athens: University of Georgia Press, 2012.

Stearns, Jason. *Dancing in the Glory of Monsters: The Collapse of the Congo and the Great War of Africa*. New York: Public Affairs, 2011.

Straus, Scott. *The Order of Genocide: Race, Power and War in Rwanda*. Ithaca: Cornell University Press, 2006.

Straus, Scott, and Lars Waldorf, eds. *Remaking Rwanda: State Building and Human Rights after Mass Violence*. Madison: University of Wisconsin Press, 2011.

Thomson, Susan. *Rwanda: From Genocide to Precarious Peace*. New Haven: Yale University Press, 2018.

Trefon, Theodore. *Congo Masquerade: The Political Culture of Aid Inefficiency and Reform Failure*. New York: Zed Books, African Arguments, 2011.

Turner, Thomas. *Congo Wars: Conflict, Myth and Reality*. New York: Zed Books, 2017.

Van Acker, Tomas. *From Bullets to Ballots and Back? Arenas, Actors and Repertoires of Power in Post-War Burundi*. Ghent: CRG Ghent University, 2018.

Van Reybrouck, David. *Congo: The Epic Story of a People*. New York: HarperCollins, 2014.

Vansina, Jan. *Antecedents to Modern Rwanda: The Nyiginya Kingdom*. Madison: University of Wisconsin Press, 2004.

Waugh, Colin. *Paul Kagame and Rwanda: Power, Genocide and the Rwandan Patriotic Front*. Jefferson and London: McFarland Company, 2004.

Willame, Jean-Claude. *Banyarwanda et Banyamulenge: Violences ethniques et question de l'identitaire au Kivu*. Paris: L'Harmattan, 1997.

Wrong, Michela. *In the Footsteps of Mr. Kurtz: Living on the Brink of Disaster in Mobutu's Congo*. New York: HarperCollins, 2001.

Young, Crawford. *Politics in the Congo*. Princeton: Princeton University Press, 1965.

Young, Crawford. *The Politics of Cultural Pluralism*. Madison: University of Wisconsin Press, 1976.

Index

African Rights 115

Alliance des Forces Démocratiques pour la Libération du Congo (AFDL), 21; and crimes against humanity 22–23, 25

Arbour, Louise 116

Armée Nationale Congolaise (ANC) 9

Armée Populaire de Libération (APL) 11

Bagosora, Theoneste, role in Tutsi genocide 108

Banyamulenge xvi; early settlements in eastern Congo as the "people of Mulenge" 16; refugees as "fifty niners" 20; rising influence in Mobutu's Congo 17; Banyamulenge rebellion 19–23

Bihumugani, Leopold (aka Biha), Burundi prime minster 56

Bikomagu, Jean, army chief of staff and Melchior Ndadaye's assassination 65

Bimazubute, Glilles, vice-president of the National Assembly, assassinated 64

Bisengimana, Barthélémy Rwema, Tutsi refugee from Rwanda and Mobutu's *chef de cabinet* 17

Bishop Fulton Sheen on pro-communist students at Lovanium University 7

Black Lives Matter movement 77

Blumenthal, Erwin, on corruption in Mobutu's Congo 15

Bradol, Hervé, and Médecins sans frontières (MSF) 107

Broadly Based Transitional Government (BBTG) 94, 103

Bruguière, Jean-Louis 104

Buchman, Jean 8

Bucyana, Martin, CDR president 91

Bugesera massacre (Rwanda) 90

Bula Matari and state centralization 4; as patronage operation 15

Bunyoni, Alain Guillaume (Burundi), Minister of Public Security 71

Burundi, traditional society compared to Rwanda 51–52; civil war (1993–2000) causes an estimated 300,000 deaths 70; dynastic rivalries 54; eclipsed by media coverage of genocide of Tutsi in Rwanda 51–52; ethnic cleaning of Hutu students by *Sans échec et sans défaite* militia 65–66; genocidal response by Tutsi-dominated army 65; growing influence of orphans of 1972 carnage 74; Hutu revolt of 1972 56–58; 1972 killings of Hutu 48; the messianic-evangelist dimension of Burundi politics 72; the Ndayishimiye enigma 75; role of princely elites (*ganwa*) 52; role of Tutsi refugees from Rwanda 53

Burundi Human Rights Initiative 77

Central Intelligence Agency (CIA) and Mobutu's rise to power 5; in funding of academic research 8; in quelling Simba rebellion 9; role in Lumumba's overthrow 5

Chrétien, Jean-Pierre 61, 62, 98

Ciza, Augustin, FAR Lieutenant Colonel, later served as deputy president of Rwanda Supreme Court under Kagame, until "disappeared" 87

Clay, Jason 81

Clinton, Bill on Kagame 120

Coalition pour la Défense de la République (CDR) 88

Cohen, Stanley 138

College of Commissioners 4

Congo Desk as part of Rwanda's
External Security Operations 28
Congo, known as Republic of the
Congo after independence, renamed
Zaire in 1965 and Democratic
Republic of the Congo (DRC) in
1987 xvi; the Congo kill zone 23–24;
and Cuba's failed intervention
11–12; Katanga rebellions 14–15;
post-independence plunge into
violence 1–2; Second Congo War
(1998–2003) and new international
actors 20; US interests and role of
CIA 5–7
Congrès National pour la Défense du
Peuple (CNDP) 30
Conrad, Joseph 2
Conley, Robert (*New York Times*), on
Hutu atrocities 47
Conseil national des patriotes 75
Conseil National pour la Défense de la
Démocratie-Forces pour la Défense
de la Démocratie (CNDD-FDD),
Hutu-dominated authoritarian ruling
party in Burundi 70
Courtois, Anne-Claire, on the language
of Burundi politics 72–73
Cox, Richard 44
Classe, Léon, Msgr on risks of
withdrawing support from Tutsi
35, 36
Cruvellier, Thierry 86, 116

Dallaire, Romeo 91
De Coster, Thierry 50
Del Ponte, Carla, ICTR chief
prosecutor 86, 117, 118
Democratic Republic of the Congo
(DRC) *see* Congo
Des Forges, Alison 93–94, 116
Devlin, Larry and CIA 5; and Project
Wizard 6
Diamond, Jared 97
Directorate of Military Intelligence
(DMI) 87, 111–113
Doucy, Arthur, director of *Institut de
Sociologie Solvay* 8
Dulles Allen, CIA top boss 5
Dupaquier, Jean-Francois 62

Esmeralda, Princess 2

Faye, Gael 75
Fein, Helen, on "retributive genocide"
109

Force Publique 1
Floyd, George and Black Lives Matter
2, 77
Forces Armées de la République
Démocratique du Congo (FARDC)
30
Forces Armées Rwandaises (FAR) 84
Forces Démocratiques pour la
Libération du Rwanda (FDLR) 29
Forces Nationales de Libération 30
France's role in Rwanda 105–108;
military assistance to Habyarimana
105
Freedman, Jim 28
Fruchart, Vincent 67

Gahima, Gerald, ex-president of
Supreme Court under Kagame, now
in exile 120
Gapyisi, Emmanuel, MDR politician 91
Gatabazi, Félicien, executive secretary
of PSD 91, 92, 94
Gatumba killings 30
Génocidaires 21, 99, 100, 107
Genocides, of Hutu and Tutsi 95;
anxieties over return of monarchy
101; causes of 98; crash of
presidential plane as triggering factor
104; definitions 109; explaining vs.
justifying 109; fear as a motive 13;
mass murder of Hutu civilians by
FPR 109; misinterpretations of 99;
responsibility of FPR 104; Rwanda
genocide and threats to revolutionary
achievements 101
Gersony, Robert 116
Gettelman, Jeffrey 119, 120, 123
Gillon, Luc Msgr. Rector of Lovanium
University 7
Gitarama coup 49
Gitera, Joseph, founder of pro-Hutu
party Aprosoma 40
Gourevitch, Philip 98; on Mutsinzi
report 104, 105
Greenland, Jeremy 59, 61
Guevara, Che 10; revolutionary
setbacks 12–14
Guichaoua, André 92, 103

Habyarimana, Juvénal, Rwanda
President 19, 49; conversation with
author 89; crash of plane as cause of
genocide 102; murder of 99; and
Mutsinzi report 104
Hamitic hypothesis (Rwanda) 36

Harroy, Jean-Paul, Governor of Rwanda and Burundi 40, 47

Hatzfeld, Jean 99, 114

Havila Institute, Havila Annals, and self-described prince Bwejeri 37n4

Himbara, David 123

Hoare, Mike, aka Mad Mike, head of Congo mercenaries 10

Hochschild, Adam 2

Holmgren, Felix 98

Hoyt, Michael, US consul in Kisangani 11, 56, 60; later DCM in Bujumbura, on killings of Hutu in 1972 134

Human Rights Watch (HRW) 30

Hutu revolution (Rwanda) xvi; Bahutu Manifesto as early expression of political consciousness 38, 39; Hutu refugees in DRC as target of crimes against humanity 22; Hutu "social revolution" and jacquerie phenomenon 39; Logiest appointed as special military resident 41; Tutsi counter manifesto 39; and violence in Burundi 34

Hutu subject to corvée labor in Rwanda and rising political consciousness 80

Hutu-Tutsi conflict 35

Imbonerakure (Burundi), Hutu-dominated youth militia 70, 77

Institut de Sociologie Solvay 8

Institut pour la Recherche Scientifique en Afrique Centrale (IRSAC) xiii

Institut Supérieur de Développement Rural (ISDR) 32

Interahamwe (Rwanda), MNRD party militia 19, 88, 90, 90, 93, 97

International Criminal Court (ICC) 31

International Criminal Tribunal for Rwanda (ICTR) 113; role in cover up of Kagame's crimes 114–115

International Rescue Committee (IRC) 32

Jeunesses Nationalistes Rwagasore (JNR), later known as Jeunesses Révolutionnaires Rwagasore (JRR), a Burundi-based nationalist youth militia, played a key role in rounding up Hutu civilians during the 1972 killings 55, 58, 58, 63

Jewsiewicki, Bogumil and *Mami-Wata: La Peinture Urbaine auCongo* 1

Joris, Lieve 21

Kabarebe, James, Kagame's chief of staff 26; and intervention in DRC 26

Kabasele, Joseph 1

Kabila, Laurent 12, 14; turns against Kagame 25

Kaburahe, Antoine 74

Kagame, Alexis, and rise of Tutsi consciousness 37

Kagame, Paul 21; conspiracies of silence on his crimes 114; early career as intelligence officer 117; joins Museveni's National Resistance Army (NRA) in fight against Obote 82; and myth-making 120; his public image vs. reality 124; recipient of Global Citizen Award from Bill Clinton 120; responsibility for crash of Habyarimana's plane 103, 114; responsibility for mass murder of Hutu civilians 108–113; seen as a symbol of progress 123; stint at US Command and General Staff College at Fort Leavenworth 82; use of torture 122

Kanyarengwe, Alexis 86

Karamira, Frodouald 49, 93

Karegeya, Patrick 103, 111, 120

Karibwami, Pontien, president of Burundi National Assembly, assassinated 64

Katanga Tigers and Shaba I and Shaba II rebellions 14–15

Kayibanda, Grégoire, first president of Rwanda, as editor of newspaper *Kimanyateka* 38; co-opted as prime Minister 44; launches Mouvement Social Muhutu (MSM) and ultimately the Parti du Mouvement de l'Emancipation Hutu (Parmehutu) 40

Kiga, Hutu sub-group (Rwanda) 88; role in genocide of Tutsi 100, 102

Kigeme declaration (Rwanda) 86

Kimenyi, Alexander, editor of pro-Tutsi newspaper *Impuruza* 79; on death of Rwigema 82

King Leopold II and the Leopoldian Free State 2

Kiraranganya, Boniface on 1972 atrocities in Burundi 58, 60

Kissinger, Henry 52; on US interests in Burundi 52

Krueger, Robert, former US Ambassador to Burund 68–69

Lausche, Frank, Senator from Ohio 7
League of Nations Mandate 34
Legum, Colin 11
Leloup, Bernard 20
Lessons learned 126–141; the claims of
    ethnic memories 136–139; conflicted
    legacies 139–141; the continuing
    impact of refugee flows 135–136;
    importance of language as a point of
    entry 127–128; inequality vs.
    democracy 131–132; seismic events
    as turning points 133–134; USAID's
    "logical framework" as a flawed
    template 126–127
Leyka, Barnabas 7
Liberal Party (PL) 89, 90, 96
Lizinde Theoneste 84
Logiest, Guy (Colonel), Special
    military resident in Rwanda from
    1959–1962 41; and Gitarama coup
    49; and lends military support to
    Hutu candidates 43; on regime
    change 45, 47; replaces Tutsi chiefs
    by Hutu 41
Lovanium University 7
Lumumba, Patrice, and symbolic
    representations 2; and Eisenhower
    administration 6
Lusaka peace process 29

Mai-Mai militias and political
    fragmentation in DRC 28
Makarere College 80
Malthus 97
Mamdani, Mahmood 82
Manifeste des Bahutu (Rwanda)
    see Bahutu Manifesto
Martres, Georges, French Ambassador
    to Rwanda 83
Maus, Albert, Belgian settler supporter
    of Burundi-based pro-Hutu Parti du
    Peuple 55
Mbonyamutwa, Dominique 40
Mbumba, Nathanael 14
McDoom, Omar 110
Melson, Robert 101
Ménard, Francois 37
Micombero, Michel (Capt.), Tutsi/
    Hima, seizes power after flight of
    mwam iMwambutsa to Switzerland
    and execution of Hutu leaders in
    Burundi 56; mwamiship assumed
    by Mwanbutsa's younger son
    Charles Ndizeye, under dynastic
    name of Ntare, deposed on

November 28 1965, paving way for
    proclamation of first republic 56;
    interview with author 62
Minority Rights Group (MRG) report
    (*Selective Genocide in Burundi*) 60
Mirerekano, Paul, Burundi Hutu leader
    assassinated 55
Mitterrand, Francois 84; accused of
    complicity in genocide 8, 105; on
    "double genocide" 108
Mobutu, Sese Seko 2, 3
Mouvement Démocratique Répulicain
    (MDR) 90
Mouvement Populaire de la Révolution
    (MPR) 17
Mouvement Révolutionnaire National
    pour le Développement (MRND) 87;
    and multiparty competition 90
Mucyo, Jean de Dieu, Kagame's former
    minister of justice and author of
    report on implication of the French
    state in genocide 105
Mukasonga, Scholastique 46
Murego, Donat, and Hutu Power 49
Murigande, Charles, letter of protest to
    Mitterand over French assistance to
    FAR 83
Museveni, Yoweri 21, 49
Mushikiwabo, Louise 24, 96
Musinga, *mwami* (king), in Rwanda 36
Mutebutsi, Jules (Colonel) 30
Mutsinzi report 104
Mworoha, Emile, former general
    secretary of JRR during 1972 killings
    62, 63

National Security Council (NSC) and
    CIA 6
National Union for the Total
    Independence of Angola 25
Ndadaye, Melchior, Bururundi's first
    popularly elected Hutu president,
    elected president in 1993 19, 48; his
    assassination and birth of "Pawa"
    split 93–94; his assassination as a
    game changer 64–66; leader of Front
    Démocratique du Burundi (Frodebu)
    64; personality and political ideas 64,
    65
Ndahindurwa, Jean-Baptiste, half-
    brother of *mwami* Rudahigwa and
    claimant to the mwamiship of
    Rwanda 40
Ndahiro, Benny 121
Ndasingwa, Landoald 83, 89, 96

Ndayishimiye, Evariste, elected president of Burundi following Nkurunziza's death in 2020, formerly secretary general of CNDD-FDD 71, 75, 76; human rights abuses 77

Ndaywel e Nziem 2

Ndazaro, Lazare, Rader leader 47

Newbury, David, on refugee flaws 17n30; and Bisengimana's landholdings 17n30

Ngendandumwe, Pierre, Burundi's first Hutu prime minister assassinated by Tutsi refugee 55

Ngendahayo, Jean-Marie 65

Nixon, Richard, on 1972 killings of Hutu in Burundi 51

Niyongabo, Prime (Burundi), Head of police 71

Nkunda, Laurent 23; and killings in DRC 25

Nkurunziza, Pierre, Hutu elected president of Burundi's third republic in 2005, 66; his ambivalent legacy 69–72; human rights record 139

Nsabimana, Deogratias, Habyarimana's army chief of staff 104

Nsansuwera, Francois-Xavier, Rwanda public prosecutor under Habyarimana 107

Ntaganda, Bosco 29

Ntakarutimana, Etienne (Burundi), Head of Security services 71

Nyamwasa, Kayumba (General), ex-army chief of staff under Kagame, now in exile 120

Nyamwite, Alain 66

Nyiramasuhuko, Pauline 100

Nzirorera, Joseph, secretary general of MRND 87

Nziza, Frank (Lieutenant) 103

Office de Valorisation Agro-Pastoraldu Mutara (OVAPAM) 92

Omaar, Rukiya 115

Operation Turquoise 105, 107

Pagès, Father, author of *Le Rwanda, un royaume Hamite au centre de l'Afrique* 36, 41

Parti Démocrate Chrétien (PDC), Batare-led party in Burundi 54

Perraudin, Msgr, bishop of Kabgaye 38

Popular Movement for the Liberation of Angola (MPLA) 14

Poppe, Guy 53, 54

Power, Samantha 52

Prosper, Pierre-Richard, US Ambassador at large for war crimes 118

Radio Mille Collines 98

Rassemblement Congolais pour la Démocratie (RCD) 25

Rassemblement Démocratique Rwandais (Rader) 47

Republic of the Congo *see* Congo

Rever, Judi on mass murder of Hutu by FPR 110–111; on the Byumba carnage 111; chain of command in organizing and implementing techniques of killings 110; on ICTR 116–119; role of DMI 111–113

Reydams, Luc 109, 115

Reyntjens, Filip 103, 118, 123

Ricoeur, Paul 138

Rieff, David 137, 138

Roessler, Philip 22

Rosser, Andrew 67

Roth, Kenneth, HRW director 118

Rudasingwa, Theogene, Kagame's former chief of staff and first ambassador to US 103, 120

Rufyikiri, Gervais, Nkurunziza's former vice-president 74

Rusatira, Leonidas, FAR Colonel, author's correspondence with 84–85

Russell, Aidan, on multiplicity of truths conveyed in Kirundi 63; on moral dimension of language 60, 72

Rutaremara, Tito 121

Rutsindintwarane, Joseph, Unar leader 47

Ruzibiza, Abdul (Colonel) 103, 104, 111, 123

Rwabugiri, *mwami* (king) and corvée labor in Rwanda 36

Rwagasana, Michel, Unar leader 47

Rwagasore, Louis, eldest son of Burundi *mwami Mwambutsa* 54; assassinated 55; Belgian officials seen as responsible for his death 55; symbol of nationalist aspirations 55

Rwanda Alliance for National Unity (RANU) 80

Rwanda, Belgian colonial policies 32–33; and Christian Democracy 37; Mwima coup 40; role of Catholic Church 38; Tutsi reactions 38

Rwanda Patriotic Army (RPA) 23

Rwanda Patriotic Front (RPF) 5; invasion of Rwanda as cause of Hutu radicalism 82–83; and killing of Hutu opponents 86; raid on Ruhengeri 84; RPF members as lineal descendants of Unar 80–81; spearhead of the 1990 Tutsi refugee invasion 79; and targeted assassinations of Hutu politicians 111; and techniques of extermination 115
Rwanda Refugee Welfare Association 80
Rwasibo, Joseph 43
Rwigyema, Fred 82
Ryckmans, Pierre, Governor of Burundi, and later of Congo on Tutsi as superior race 37

Sagatwa, Elie, Habyarimana's son in law 88
Sans échec et sans défaite, extremist Tutsi-dominated militia 65, 66
Savimbi, Jonas 26
Scott, James 16
Sears, Mason, head of UN Trusteeship mission to Rwanda 43
Sebarenzi, Joseph, on death of Ciza 87
Seruguba, Laurent (Rwanda), Habyarimana's deputy chief of staff 88
Service National de Renseignements (SNR), Burundi intelligence service 72, 74
Shawcross, William 23
Shibura, Albert 48, 57, 62
Simbananiye, Arthémon, Burundi Tutsi orchestrator of Hutu bloodbath in 1972 before becoming a Born Again Christian 57, 59, 73
Sommers, Marc 123
Soumialot, Gaston, head of APL 11
Spaak, Paul-Henri, Belgian Minister of Foreign Affairs 45, 48
Stearns, Jason, on UN Mapping report 24
Straus, Scott 100

The Tablet, Catholic newsletter 7
Tanguy, Joelle 136
Thomson, Susan 95
Tissot, Roland 109
Trusteeship Territory of Ruanda-Urundi xiii; Rwanda as trusteeship Territory 33

Truth and Reconciliation Commission (TRC) 73
Tshombe, Moise 12
Tutsi in Rwanda 35; in Congo excluded from National Sovereign Conference 16; denied citizenship by Mobutu 18; cultural roots in Abyssinia 36; their inherent superiority 35

Umoja Wety (Our Unity) 30, 31
Union des Patriotes Congolais (UPC) 31
Union Nationale Rwandaise (Unar) 4, 40
United Nations Mapping Report on abuses committed against Hutu civilians 23–24; Rwanda's denial of report 21
United Nations Mission in Rwamda (UNAMIR) 106
Union pour leprogrès national (Uprona), and rise of nationalism in Burundi 54
Uwamutara, Claire 121
Uwilingiyimana, Agathe, Rwanda prime minister under Habiarimana, assassinated 107
Uwimana, Aloys, Rwandan ambassador to US under Habyarimana 79

Van Acker, Tomas 71
Van den Burgt, Johannes, missionary and linguist on Tutsi Semitic features 37
Van Reybrouck, David 15, 23, 30
Vansina, Jan 3, 36
Verhoeven, Harry 22
Vidal, Claudine 103

Waal, Alex de 100, 115
Walpen, Laurent 118
Watt, Nigel 74
Waugh, Colin 44
Waugh Evelyn, *Black Mischief* 7
Weissman, Stephen on CIA involvement in Congo 6, 7
World Council of Churches 46
Wrong, Michela 3, 28n51

Yellin, James 69
Young, Crawford 4

Zaire *see* Congo